Can the European Court of Human Rights Shape European Public Order?

In this book, Kanstantsin Dzehtsiarou argues that, from the legal perspective, the formula 'European public order' is excessively vague and does not have an identifiable meaning; therefore, it should not be used by the European Court of Human Rights (ECtHR) in its reasoning. However, European public order can also be understood as an analytical concept which does not require a clearly defined content. In this sense, the ECtHR can impact European public order but cannot strategically shape it. The Court's impact is a by-product of individual cases which create a feedback loop with the contracting states. European public order is influenced as a result of interaction between the Court and the contracting parties. This book uses a wide range of sources and evidence to substantiate its core arguments: from a comprehensive analysis of the Court's case law to research interviews with the judges of the ECtHR.

Kanstantsin Dzehtsiarou is a professor in human rights law at the University of Liverpool. His research interests include interpretation of the European Convention on Human Rights, reform of the European Court, administration of international justice, and comparative constitutional law. Kanstantsin is an editor-in-chief of the *European Convention on Human Rights Law Review*.

Cambridge Studies in European Law and Policy

The focus of this series is European law broadly understood. It aims to publish original monographs in all fields of European law, from work focusing on the institutions of the EU and the Council of Europe to books examining substantive fields of European law as well as examining the relationship between European law and domestic, regional and international legal orders. The series publishes works adopting a wide variety of methods: comparative, doctrinal, theoretical and inter-disciplinary approaches to European law are equally welcome, as are works looking at the historical and political facets of the development of European law and policy. The main criterion is excellence i.e. the publication of innovative work, which will help to shape the legal, political and scholarly debate on the future of European law.

Books in the Series

The Constitutional Boundaries of European Fiscal Federalism
Brady Gordon

Private Selves: Legal Personhood in European Privacy Protection
Susanna Lindroos-Hovinheimo

Fissures in EU Citizenship: The Deconstruction and Reconstruction of the Legal Evolution of EU Citizenship
Martin Steinfeld

The Boundaries of the EU Internal Market: Participation without Membership
Marja-Liisa Öberg

The Currency of Solidarity: Constitutional Transformation during the Euro Crisis
Vestert Borger

Empire of Law: Nazi Germany, Exile Scholars and the Battle for the Future of Europe
Kaius Tuori

In the Court We Trust: Cooperation, Coordination and Collaboration between the ECJ and Supreme Administrative Courts
Rob van Gestel and Jurgen de Poorter

Beyond Minimum Harmonisation: Gold-Plating and Green-Plating of European Environmental Law
Lorenzo Squintani

The Court of Justice of the European Union as an Institutional Actor: Judicial Lawmaking and Its Limits
Thomas Horsley

The Politics of Justice in European Private Law: Social Justice, Access Justice, Societal Justice
Hans-W Micklitz

The Transformation of EU Treaty Making: The Rise of Parliaments, Referendums and Courts Since 1950
Dermot Hodson and Imelda Maher

Redefining European Economic Integration
Dariusz Adamski

Human Rights in the Council of Europe and the European Union: Achievements, Trends and Challenges
Steven Greer, Janneke Gerards and Rosie Slowe

Core Socio-Economic Rights and the European Court of Human Rights
Ingrid Leijten

Green Trade and Fair Trade in and with the EU: Process-Based Measures within the EU Legal Order
Laurens Ankersmit

New Labour Laws in Old Member States: Trade Union Responses to European Enlargement
Rebecca Zahn

The Governance of EU Fundamental Rights
Mark Dawson

The International Responsibility of the European Union: From Competence to Normative Control
Andrés Delgado Casteleiro

Frontex and Non-Refoulement: The International Responsibility of the EU
Roberta Mungianu

Gendering European Working Time Regimes: The Working Time Directive and the Case of Poland
Ania Zbyszewska

EU Renewable Electricity Law and Policy: From National Targets to a Common Market
Tim Maxian Rusche

European Constitutionalism
Kaarlo Tuori

Brokering Europe: Euro-Lawyers and the Making of a Transnational Polity
Antoine Vauchez

Services Liberalization in the EU and the WTO: Concepts, Standards and Regulatory Approaches
Marcus Klamert

Referendums and the European Union: A Comparative Enquiry
Fernando Mendez, Mario Mendez and Vasiliki Triga

The Allocation of Regulatory Competence in the EU Emissions Trading Scheme
Jospehine van Zeben

The Eurozone Crisis: A Constitutional Analysis
Kaarlo Tuori and Klaus Tuori

International Trade Disputes and EU Liability
Anne Thies

The Limits of Legal Reasoning and the European Court of Justice
Gerard Conway

New Governance and the Transformation of European Law: Coordinating EU Social Law and Policy
Mark Dawson

The Lisbon Treaty: A Legal and Political Analysis
Jean-Claude Piris

The European Union's Fight Against Corruption: The Evolving Policy Towards Member States and Candidate Countries
Patrycja Szarek-Mason

The Ethos of Europe: Values, Law and Justice in the EU
Andrew Williams

State and Market in European Union Law: The Public and Private Spheres of the Internal Market before the EU Courts
Wolf Sauter and Harm Schepel

The European Civil Code: The Way Forward
Hugh Collins

Ethical Dimensions of the Foreign Policy of the European Union: A Legal Appraisal
Urfan Khaliq

Implementing EU Pollution Control: Law and Integration
Bettina Lange

European Broadcasting Law and Policy
Jackie Harrison and Lorna Woods

The Transformation of Citizenship in the European Union: Electoral Rights and the Restructuring of Political Space
Jo Shaw

The Constitution for Europe: A Legal Analysis
Jean-Claude Piris

The European Convention on Human Rights: Achievements, Problems and Prospects
Steven Greer

Social Rights and Market Freedom in the European Constitution: A Labour Law Perspective
Stefano Giubboni

EU Enlargement and the Constitutions of Central and Eastern Europe
Anneli Albi

Can the European Court of Human Rights Shape European Public Order?

Kanstantsin Dzehtsiarou
University of Liverpool

CAMBRIDGE
UNIVERSITY PRESS

CAMBRIDGE
UNIVERSITY PRESS

University Printing House, Cambridge CB2 8BS, United Kingdom

One Liberty Plaza, 20th Floor, New York, NY 10006, USA

477 Williamstown Road, Port Melbourne, VIC 3207, Australia

314–321, 3rd Floor, Plot 3, Splendor Forum, Jasola District Centre, New Delhi - 110025, India
103 Penang Road, #05-06/07, Visioncrest Commercial, Singapore 238467

Cambridge University Press is part of the University of Cambridge.

It furthers the University's mission by disseminating knowledge in the pursuit of education, learning, and research at the highest international levels of excellence.

www.cambridge.org
Information on this title: www.cambridge.org/9781108497367
DOI: 10.1017/9781108608794

First published 2022

A catalogue record for this publication is available from the British Library.

ISBN 978-1-108-49736-7 Hardback

For Anastasiia

Contents

Contents

Series Editors' Preface

It takes a degree of boldness to argue that a Court should cease using a well-established term within its case law. But this is exactly what Kanstantsin Dzehtsiarou does in his new monograph, *Can the European Court of Human Rights Shape European Public Order?*, which we warmly welcome to the series *Cambridge Studies in European Law and Policy*.

As a legal concept, Dzehtsiarou concludes in this book, 'European public order' is too vague and unclear to be usable as the basis for reasoning in the Court's case law. Only a highly abstract notion of *European* public order could be identified as an element on which the contracting parties to the ECHR could agree, and, at that level of abstraction, it could in practice never be clarified sufficiently to be a useful legal tool. In an alternative sense, Dzehtsiarou also suggests that European public order is an analytical concept, and here his attempts to understand this descriptive category with vague frontiers and a contestable concept lead him to consider whether or not the European Court of Human Rights can helpfully operate as a 'herald', which would see it bringing together ideas in a European consensus. This question leads him into an institutional analysis of the Court, which draws on a variety of legal and analytical perspectives, including the views of some of the judges of the Court itself.

Ultimately, Dzehtsiarou's approach is shaped by his adoption of a minimalist perspective on human rights within Europe and a belief that the Court of Human Rights should not be acting as a strategic actor, constructing some sort of bulwark against the apparently inevitable erosion that human rights norms seem to be facing in Europe at the present time. Like his injunction to the Court to stop using European public order as a tool of legal analysis, his preference for the organic emergence of human rights standards based on feedback loops involving the Court's interventions in individual cases and the engagement of the contracting parties with the ECHR as a set of norms is a bold and perhaps controversial claim. Yet it is arguable that creating the intellectual framework for such a debate about European public order is – in and of itself – some sort of provocative contribution to the seemingly endless discussion on how to define *ordre public* and how to assess whether it is a useful concept.

In sum, this analysis, dealing with some of the more neglected norms and institutions of European law, represents a very welcome addition to the series.

Jo Shaw
Laurence Gormley
Mark Dawson

Acknowledgements

In 2015 I submitted my first monograph to Cambridge University Press. In that book I examined the particularities of European consensus in the case law of the European Court of Human Rights (ECtHR or Court). Back then, I considered the acknowledgements to be the most important part of the book and therefore spent plenty of time drafting them. Shortly after the book was published, I realised through some empirical study among my friends, that almost nobody actually reads acknowledgements. For that reason, I will keep these comparatively short.

As soon as I had finished my book on consensus, I firmly decided that I would never write another book. That promise lasted for three months, after which time I started working on another project that seemed promising. I quickly learnt that it would be difficult to put everything that I wanted to say regarding that project in a journal article. The project focused on a question that had bothered me for some time, namely, whether the ECtHR is capable of shaping European public order. I felt it important to discuss the question with the ECtHR's judges and therefore spent a few weeks in September 2018 and September 2019 in Strasbourg, France, doing just that. I would like to express my gratitude to the Registry of the Court and to all those judges who found time to talk to me: Paulo Pinto de Albuquerque, Arnfinn Bardsen, Vincent A. De Gaetano, Dmitry Dedov, Yonko Grozev, Lətif Hüseynov, Ivana Jelić, Helen Keller, Egidijus Kūris, Julia Laffranque, Paul Lemmens, Roderick Liddell, Iulia Motoc, Angelika Nußberger, Péter Paczolay, Darian Pavli, Guido Raimondi, Linos-Alexandre Sicilianos, Robert Spano, Ksenija Turković and Ganna Yudkivska.

I presented the core ideas of this book in Edinburgh, Sheffield, London, Santiago and Liverpool and I am very grateful to all participants of the seminars and workshops who commented on the ideas that ended up (or not) in this monograph. I also benefited hugely from two research leaves from my other academic duties; I would never have been able to finish this book without them. I thank the School of Law and Justice of the University of Liverpool for making this possible. In particular I would like to thank Professors Debra Morris, Warren Barr, Padraig McAuliffe and Mike Gordon for supporting my applications. I would also like to thank Anna Vowles and other professional support staff of the University of Liverpool because they have always been kind to me.

Plenty of my friends helped me to shape my ideas, and read and commented on my drafts. Of course, any silly mistakes that are left in this book are my own, but my friends did their best to fix them. It would lengthen the acknowledgements considerably were I to mention all of them, so I will stick to my promise to keep them short and mention only a few: Filippo Fontanelli, Vassilis P. Tzevelekos, Tobias Lock, Colm O'Cinneide, Fiona de Londras, Donal K. Coffey, Ed Bates, Alan Greene and Rumyana van Ark. My thanks should also go to Amandine Garde for helping me to translate French quotes. I would also like to thank my research assistants Chryssa Mela, Maisie Law, Ewan Anthony and Eve Stott.

I would like to thank Kirill Koroteev for helping me to select the cover of this book. It is Wassily Kandinsky's painting 'Non-Objective', which can also be translated from Russian as 'Subjectless'. In this book I argue that the legal term 'European public order' does not have a clear content and this beautiful painting by Kandinsky illustrates this argument well. I also thank Maria Gigineyshvili for putting me in touch with 'Krasnodar Regional Art Museum named after F.A. Kovalenko', which has kindly allowed me to use this image.

I would like to thank my friends and family for supporting me and for their unconditional love. Perhaps the biggest thanks go to my partner Anastasiia.

The staff at Cambridge University Press were very helpful and supportive during the preparation of the book. I would especially like to thank Finola O'Sullivan and Marianne Nield for their help.

In August 2020, while I was writing the last chapters of this monograph, the presidential elections took place in my country of origin – Belarus – which is neither a member of the Council of Europe nor under the jurisdiction of the ECtHR. The elections were followed by peaceful protests against the government's fraudulent activity and lies. These protests were brutally dispersed: people were tortured and killed;

journalists were arrested; almost all human rights were systematically violated. This shows how fragile is the system of human rights protection and how important it is to ensure that the regional mechanism of human rights protection operates effectively.

Finally, the COVID-19 pandemic, which was in full swing in 2020, will likely have long-lasting consequences for how we perceive European public order. However, I hope that the protection of human rights will remain a priority irrespective of the political, economic or epidemiological climate in Europe.

Table of Cases

European Court of Human Rights

A

A., B. and C. *v.* Ireland [GC], no. 25579/05, ECHR 2010.
Advisory opinion concerning the recognition in domestic law of a legal parent-child relationship between a child born through a gestational surrogacy arrangement abroad and the intended mother [GC], request no. P16-2018-001, French Court of Cassation, 10 April 2019.
Advisory opinion concerning the use of the 'blanket reference' or 'legislation by reference' technique in the definition of an offence and the standards of comparison between the criminal law in force at the time of the commission of the offence and the amended criminal law [GC], request no. P16-2019-001, Armenian Constitutional Court, 29 May 2020.
Advisory opinion on certain legal questions concerning the lists of candidates submitted with a view to the election of judges to the European Court of Human Rights [GC], 12 February 2008.
Advisory opinion on certain legal questions concerning the lists of candidates submitted with a view to the election of judges to the European Court of Human Rights (no. 2) [GC], 22 January 2010.
Ahmed and Others *v.* the United Kingdom, 2 September 1998, Reports of Judgments and Decisions 1998-VI.
Airey *v.* Ireland, 9 October 1979, Series A no. 32.
Al-Dulimi and Montana Management Inc. *v.* Switzerland, no. 5809/08, 26 November 2013.
Al-Saadoon and Mufdhi *v.* the United Kingdom, no. 61498/08, ECHR 2010.

Al-Skeini and Others *v.* the United Kingdom [GC], no. 55721/07, ECHR 2011.
Aleksanyan *v.* Russia, no. 46468/06, 22 December 2008.
Alekseyev *v.* Russia, nos. 4916/07, 25924/08 and 14599/09, 21 October 2010.
Prosecutor Ališić and Others *v.* Bosnia and Herzegovina, Croatia, Serbia, Slovenia and the former Yugoslav Republic of Macedonia, no. 60642/08, 6 November 2012.
Aliyev *v.* Azerbaijan, nos. 68762/14 and 71200/14, 20 September 2018.
Amrollahi *v.* Denmark, no. 56811/00, 11 July 2002.
Anchugov and Gladkov *v.* Russia, nos. 11157/04 and 15162/05, 4 July 2013.
Angel Angelov *v.* Bulgaria, no. 51343/99, 15 February 2007.
Armenia *v.* Azerbaijan (42521/20).
Association de solidarité avec les témoins de Jéhovah and others *v.* Turkey, app 36915/10.
Austin and Others *v.* the United Kingdom [GC], nos. 39692/09, 40713/09 and 41008/09, ECHR 2012.
Austria *v.* Italy, no. 788/60, admissibility decision of 11 January 1961.
Avotiņš *v.* Latvia, no. 17502/07, 25 February 2014.
Azerbaijan *v.* Armenia (43517/20).

B

Baka *v.* Hungary [GC], no. 20261/12, 23 June 2016.
Banković and Others *v.* Belgium and Others (dec.) [GC], no. 52207/99, ECHR 2001-XII.
Bayev and Others *v.* Russia, nos. 67667/09 and 2 others, 20 June 2017.
Behrami *v.* France and Saramati *v.* France, Germany and Norway, 71412/01, (2007) 45 EHRR. SE10.
Beuze *v.* Belgium [GC], no. 71409/10, 9 November 2018.
Biao *v.* Denmark [GC], no. 38590/10, 24 May 2016.
Bosphorus Hava Yolları Turizm ve Ticaret Anonim Şirketi *v.* Ireland [GC], no. 45036/98, ECHR 2005-VI.
Bouyid *v.* Belgium [GC], no. 23380/09, ECHR 2015.
Buntov *v.* Russia, no. 27026/10, June 2012.
Burdov *v.* Russia (no. 2), no. 33509/04, ECHR 2009.
Burmych and Others *v.* Ukraine (striking out) [GC], nos. 46852/13 et al, 12 October 2017.

C

Campbell and Fell *v.* the United Kingdom, 28 June 1984, Series A no. 80.
Can *v.* Austria, 30 September 1985, Series A no. 96.
Catan and Others *v.* the Republic of Moldova and Russia [GC], nos. 43370/04, 8252/05 and 18454/06, ECHR 2012.
Centre for Legal Resources on behalf of Valentin Câmpeanu *v.* Romania [GC], no. 47848/08, ECHR 2014.
Centro Europa 7 S.r.l. and Di Stefano *v.* Italy [GC], no. 38433/09, ECHR 2012.
Chahal *v.* the United Kingdom, 15 November 1996, Reports of Judgments and Decisions 1996-V.
Chiragov and Others *v.* Armenia [GC], no. 13216/05, ECHR 2015.
Christian Democratic People's Party *v.* Moldova, no. 28793/02, ECHR 2006-II.
Christian Democratic People's Party *v.* Moldova (no. 2), no. 25196/04, 2 February 2010.
Christine Goodwin *v.* the United Kingdom [GC], no. 28957/95, ECHR 2002-VI.
Cruz Varas and Others *v.* Sweden, 20 March 1991, Series A no. 201.
Cumhuriyet Halk Partisi *v.* Turkey, no. 48818/17, 21 November 2017 (Decision of Inadmissibility).
Cyprus *v.* Turkey [GC], no. 25781/94, ECHR 2001-IV.

D

De Becker *v.* Belgium, 27 March 1962, Series A no. 4.
De Wilde, Ooms and Versyp *v.* Belgium, 18 June 1971, Series A no. 12.
Delfi AS *v.* Estonia [GC], no. 64569/09, ECHR 2015.
Deweer *v.* Belgium, 27 February 1980, Series A no. 35.
Dudgeon *v.* the United Kingdom, 22 October 1981, Series A no. 45.

E

Engel and Others *v.* the Netherlands, 8 June 1976, Series A no. 22.
Enhorn *v.* Sweden, no. 56529/00, ECHR 2005-I.
Eskinazi and Chelouche *v.* Turkey (dec.), no. 14600/05, ECHR 2005-XIII.
Evans *v.* the United Kingdom [GC], no. 6339/05, ECHR 2007-I.

F

Fabris *v.* France [GC], no. 16574/08, ECHR 2013.
Finger *v.* Bulgaria, no. 37346/05, 10 May 2011.
Frodl *v.* Austria, no. 20201/04, 8 April 2010.

G

G.I.E.M. S.R.L. and Others *v.* Italy [GC], nos. 1828/06 and 2 others, 28 June 2018.
Gäfgen *v.* Germany [GC], no. 22978/05, ECHR 2010.
Garib *v.* the Netherlands [GC], no. 43494/09, 6 November 2017.
Georgia *v.* Russia (II) (2012) 54 E.H.R.R. SE10.
Giniewski *v.* France, no. 64016/00, ECHR 2006-I.
Godelli *v.* Italy, no. 33783/09, 25 September 2012.
Gorzelik and Others *v.* Poland [GC], no. 44158/98, ECHR 2004-I.
Greece *v.* the United Kingdom, Application No 176/56, Decision of 26 September 1958.
Greens and M.T. *v.* the United Kingdom, nos. 60041/08 and 60054/08, ECHR 2010.
Güzelyurtlu and Others *v.* Cyprus and Turkey [GC], no. 36925/07, 29 January 2019.

H

Handyside *v.* the United Kingdom, 7 December 1976, Series A no. 24.
Hatami *v.* Sweden, 9 October 1998, Reports of Judgments and Decisions 1998-VII.
Hatton and Others *v.* the United Kingdom, no. 36022/97, 2 October 2001.
Hirst *v.* the United Kingdom (no. 2), no. 74025/01, 30 March 2004.
Hutchinson *v.* the United Kingdom [GC], no. 57592/08, 17 January 2017.

I

Ibrahim and Others *v.* the United Kingdom, nos. 50541/08 and 3 others, 16 December 2014.
Ilaşcu and Others *v.* Moldova and Russia [GC], no. 48787/99, ECHR 2004-VII.
Ilnseher *v.* Germany [GC], nos. 10211/12 and 27505/14, 4 December 2018.
Ireland *v.* the United Kingdom, 18 January 1978, Series A no. 25.

J

Jalloh *v.* Germany [GC], no. 54810/00, ECHR 2006-IX.
Jersild *v.* Denmark, 23 September 1994, Series A no. 298.

K

Khamtokhu and Aksenchik *v.* Russia [GC], nos. 60367/08 and 961/11, 24 January 2017.
Kondrulin *v.* Russia, no. 12987/15, 20 September 2016.
Korolev *v.* Russia (dec.), no. 25551/05, ECHR 2010.

L

Lawless *v.* Ireland (no. 1), 14 November 1960, Series A no. 1.
Leyla Şahin *v.* Turkey [GC], no. 44774/98, ECHR 2005-XI.
Loizidou *v.* Turkey (merits), 18 December 1996, Reports of Judgments and Decisions 1996-VI.
Loizidou *v.* Turkey (preliminary objections), 23 March 1995, Series A no. 310.
López Ostra *v.* Spain, 9 December 1994, Series A no. 303-C.

M

Mamatkulov and Askarov *v.* Turkey, Applications no. 46827/99 and 46951/99, Judgment of 4 February 2005.
Mann Singh *v.* France (ECHR, 13/11/2008/, no. 4479/07).
Mathieu-Mohin and Clerfayt *v.* Belgium, 2 March 1987, App No 9267/81, judgment of 2 March 1987.
Maumousseau and Washington *v.* France, no. 39388/05, 6 December 2007.
Michaud *v.* France, no. 12323/11, ECHR 2012.
Miragall Escolano and Others *v.* Spain, nos. 38366/97 and 9 others, ECHR 2000-I.
Mouvement raëlien suisse *v.* Switzerland [GC], no. 16354/06, ECHR 2012.
Mozer *v.* the Republic of Moldova and Russia [GC], no. 11138/10, 23 February 2016.
Muminov *v.* Russia, Application No 42502/06, Judgment of 4 November 2010.

N

N.D. and N.T. *v.* Spain [GC], nos. 8675/15 and 8697/15, 13 February 2020.
National Union of Rail, Maritime and Transport Workers *v.* the United Kingdom, no. 31045/10, ECHR 2014.
Navalnyy *v.* Russia [GC], nos. 29580/12 and 4 others, 15 November 2018.
Neulinger and Shuruk *v.* Switzerland [GC], no. 41615/07, ECHR 2010.
Nolan and K. *v.* Russia, no. 2512/04, 12 February 2009.

O

Öcalan *v.* Turkey, Application No 46221/99, Judgment of 12 May 2005.
Olaru and Others *v.* Moldova, nos. 476/07 and 3 others, 28 July 2009.
Oliari and Others *v.* Italy, nos. 18766/11 and 36030/11, 21 July 2015.
Othman (Abu Qatada) *v.* the United Kingdom, no. 8139/09, ECHR 2012.

P

P. and S. *v.* Poland, no. 57375/08, 30 October 2012.
Paez *v.* Sweden, 30 October 1997, Reports of Judgments and Decisions 1997-VII.
Paladi *v.* Moldova, Application No 39806/05, Judgment of 10 March 2009.
Parrillo *v.* Italy [GC], no. 46470/11, ECHR 2015.
Perinçek *v.* Switzerland [GC], no. 27510/08, ECHR 2015.
Petrovy *v.* Russia, no. 47429/09, 20 October 2020.
Pretty *v.* the United Kingdom, no. 2346/02, ECHR 2002-III.
Primov and Others *v.* Russia, no. 17391/06, 12 June 2014.

R

Rantsev *v.* Cyprus and Russia, no. 25965/04, ECHR 2010, para 197.
Refah Partisi (the Welfare Party) and Others *v.* Turkey, nos. 41340/98, 41342/98, 41343/98 and 41344/98, 31 July 2001.
Rinck *v.* France (dec.), no. 18774/09, 19 October 2010.
Roman Zakharov *v.* Russia [GC], no. 47143/06, ECHR 2015.
Rustavi 2 Broadcasting Company Ltd and Others *v.* Georgia, no. 16812/17, 18 July 2019.

S

S. and Marper *v.* the United Kingdom [GC], nos. 30562/04 and 30566/04, ECHR 2008.
S., V. and A. *v.* Denmark [GC], nos. 35553/12 and 2 others, 22 October 2018.
S.A.S. *v.* France [GC], no. 43835/11, ECHR 2014.
Saadi *v.* Italy [GC], no. 37201/06, ECHR 2008.
Sadak and Others *v.* Turkey (no. 1), nos. 29900/96, 29901/96, 29902/96 and 29903/96, ECHR 2001-VIII.
Sandu and Others *v.* the Republic of Moldova and Russia, nos. 21034/05 and 7 others, 17 July 2018.
Sargsyan *v.* Azerbaijan [GC], no. 40167/06, ECHR 2015.
Savriddin Dzhurayev *v.* Russia, no. 71386/10, ECHR 2013.

Scoppola *v.* Italy (no. 3) [GC], no. 126/05, 22 May 2012.
Sedletska *v.* Ukraine, no. 42634/18.
Sejdić and Finci *v.* Bosnia and Herzegovina [GC], nos. 27996/06 and 34836/06, ECHR 2009.
Simeonovi *v.* Bulgaria [GC], no. 21980/04, 12 May 2017.
Skoogström *v.* Sweden, 2 October 1984, Series A no. 83.
Soering *v.* the United Kingdom, 7 July 1989, Series A no. 161.
Söyler *v.* Turkey, no. 29411/07, 17 September 2013.
Svinarenko and Slyadnev *v.* Russia [GC], nos. 32541/08 and 43441/08, ECHR 2014.

T

Times Newspapers Ltd *v.* the United Kingdom (nos. 1 and 2), nos. 3002/03 and 23676/03, ECHR 2009.
Tysiąc *v.* Poland, no. 5410/03, ECHR 2007-I.

U

Ukraine *v.* Russia (I) (20958/14).
United Communist Party of Turkey and Others *v.* Turkey, 30 January 1998, Reports of Judgments and Decisions 1998-I.

V

Vallianatos and Others *v.* Greece [GC], nos. 29381/09 and 32684/09, ECHR 2013.
Vilho Eskelinen and Others *v.* Finland [GC], no. 63235/00, ECHR 2007-II.
Vinter and Others *v.* the United Kingdom [GC], nos. 66069/09 and 2 others, ECHR 2013.
Von Hannover *v.* Germany, no. 59320/00, ECHR 2004-VI.
Vona *v.* Hungary, no. 35943/10, ECHR 2013.

X

X *v.* Croatia, no. 11223/04, 17 July 2008.

Y

Yam *v.* the United Kingdom, no. 31295/11, 16 January 2020.
Young, James and Webster *v.* the United Kingdom, 13 August 1981, Series A no. 44.
Yumak and Sadak *v.* Turkey [GC], no. 10226/03, ECHR 2008.
Yuriy Nikolayevich Ivanov *v.* Ukraine, no. 40450/04, 15 October 2009.

Z

Ždanoka *v*. Latvia, no. 58278/00, 17 June 2004.

UN Human Rights Committee

Communication No. 1928/2010 (Shingara Mann Singh *v*. France) HRC, 26/09/2013, CCPR/C/108/D/1928/2010.

US Courts

Jacobellis *v*. Ohio, 378 U.S. 184 (1964).

Richardson *v*. Mellish, (1824) 130 Eng. Rep. 294, 303; 2 Bing 229, 251–52 (Burrough J.).

Swiss Courts

Federal Tribunal, Judgment 4A_490/2009 of 13 April 2010, *Atlético/ Benfica*.

Federal Tribunal, Judgment 4A_558/2011 27 March 2012, *Matuzalem*.

French Courts

Commune de Morsang-sur-Orge et Ville d'Aix-en-Provence, Council of State.

Abbreviations

ECHR	European Convention on Human Rights
ECtHR	European Court of Human Rights
EU	European Union
HUDOC	Human Rights Documents Database
NATO	North-Atlantic Treaty Organization
TRNC	Turkish Republic of Northern Cyprus
UK	United Kingdom
UN	United Nations
USA	United States of America

1 Introduction

1.1 The Core Questions

The European Court of Human Rights (ECtHR or the Court) makes a difference in Europe. It creates standards that are applicable in the forty-seven contracting parties to the European Convention on Human Rights (ECHR or Convention). The impact of the ECtHR has been extensively explored in academic literature.[1] The Court intervenes in the most fundamental, sensitive and controversial issues that the European nations debate;[2] it sets the standards for how European authorities should treat people under their jurisdiction; it creates and maintains the meaning of European human rights and develops the legal ideology of human rights protection. According to the Court, the Convention is a constitutional instrument of European public order.[3] Having said all this, there are limits to what the Court can do and how

[1] See, for example, Courtney Hillebrecht, 'The Power of Human Rights Tribunals: Compliance with the European Court of Human Rights and Domestic Policy Change' (2014) 20 *Eur J Int* 1100; Merris Amos, 'The Value of the European Court of Human Rights to the United Kingdom' (2017) 28 *EIJL* 763; Sameera Dalvi, 'Homosexuality and the European Court of Human Rights: Recent Judgments Against the United Kingdom and Their Impact on Other Signatories to the European Convention on Human Rights' (2004) 15 *U Fla JL & Pub Pol'y* 467; Helen Keller and Alec Stone Sweet (eds.), *A Europe of Rights: The Impact of the ECHR on National Legal Systems* (Oxford University Press 2008); Iulia Motoc and Ineta Ziemele (eds.), *The Impact of the ECHR on Democratic Change in Central and Eastern Europe: Judicial Perspectives* (Cambridge University Press 2016).

[2] Issues related to legality of abortions in *A, B and C* v. *Ireland* [GC], no. 25579/05, ECHR 2010; euthanasia in *Pretty* v. *the United Kingdom*, no. 2346/02, ECHR 2002-III; LGBTI rights in *Dudgeon* v. *the United Kingdom*, 22 October 1981, Series A no. 45; and *Bayev and Others* v. *Russia*, nos. 67667/09 and two others, 20 June 2017 and many others.

[3] *Loizidou* v. *Turkey* (preliminary objections), 23 March 1995, Series A no. 310, para. 75.

far it can intervene within European public order. The key questions that this book is posing are what exactly does European public order mean and how can it be shaped; and, more importantly, should an institution like the ECtHR aim to shape it?

Although legislators and courts have used the term 'public order' for a very long time, its meaning remains conveniently vague. It seems to refer to something fundamental, a set of principles so basic that they define a people, society, community or group of communities. These principles can perhaps trump any other rule or regulation. However, despite their fundamental importance, the precise content of these principles is unclear and can be disagreed over. The idea of this book is to explore whether the ECtHR can translate something very vague and imprecise into legal reality. One of the major challenges of this project is that one can intuitively (although sometimes wrongly) guess what European public order might mean but, as Chapter 3 shows, it cannot be properly defined. In this book, I will ask what European public order includes, who can shape it and how it can be done. I will examine whether the concept of European public order is at all helpful and whether it should be used by the ECtHR or rather be removed from the Court's vocabulary. I will also critically assess whether the ECtHR's ambition of being a herald of European public order is far-fetched or misplaced.

At the outset, I have to say that the answers to these questions often depend on the political standpoint of the particular observer. Many of them require value judgements on the role of human rights in social life and the degree of proper intervention of international human rights institutions in the national decision-making process. This book is based on a theory of minimalist effectiveness of the Court. By this, I understand that the best strategy of the Court is not to make revolutionary long-term strategic changes but to gradually adjust the standards in conformity with what is possible and acceptable at the national level. Therefore, this monograph suggests that a proper function of the ECtHR does not include strategically building European public order.

1.2 The Approach of the Monograph

1.2.1 The Rationale of the Monograph

This book is the first exhaustive analysis of the Court's role vis-à-vis European public order. Many commentators have examined issues that are closely connected to the notion of European public order. Some work has been done on questions of the proper functionality of the Court, its effectiveness and reach. A lot of academic papers have looked into more precise infrastructural issues such as the value of particular procedures or detailed discussion of certain judgments or groups of judgments. This monograph builds on these discussions but goes one step further. This monograph looks at the Court's ability to shape European public order from many angles. It approaches the interaction between the Court and European public order holistically, trying to consider what is possible, desirable and necessary for the Court to impact it.

Since 2006, when Steven Greer published his monograph,[4] it seems that there has been no comprehensive attempt to assess the role and vision of the ECtHR or to find its place vis-à-vis the contracting parties to the Convention in the form of a monograph. At the same time, since 2006, Europe has changed considerably: the backlash against the Court has intensified,[5] politically there has been a steady rise of illiberal democracies,[6] and some states now supply the ECtHR with a major number of applications alleging violations of the most fundamental rights. This monograph takes this context into account and tries to explain the recent developments of the ECtHR. It also attempts to build a normative argument as to why the ECtHR should not put forward an overly ambitious task of shaping European public order. This task might undermine the legitimacy and effectiveness of the Court.

This monograph suggests that the Court is likely to be more successful in achieving its aim if it develops its law incrementally through careful adjudication of individual complaints. The Court's impact on European public order happens as a logical consequence of its individual judgments. The Court should not use individual applications as an

[4] Steven Greer, *The European Convention on Human Rights: Achievements, Problems and Prospects* (Cambridge University Press 2006).

[5] See Mikael Rask Madsen, 'The Challenging Authority of the European Court of Human Rights: From Cold War Legal Diplomacy to the Brighton Declaration and Backlash' (2016) 79 *LCP* 141; Øyvind Stiansen and Erik Voeten, 'Backlash and Judicial Restraint: Evidence from the European Court of Human Rights' (2020) 64 *Int'l Stud Q* 770; Mikael Rask Madsen, Pola Cebulak and Micha Wiebusch, 'Backlash against International Courts: Explaining the Forms and Patterns of Resistance to International Courts' (2018) 14 *Int'l JLC* 197.

[6] See Wolfgang Benedek, 'Are the Tools of the Council of Europe Sufficient to Protect Human Rights, Democracy and the Rule of Law from Backsliding?' (2020)1 *Eur Conv Hum Rights L Rev*, 151; Ineta Ziemele, 'Liberal Values, Covid-19 and the Judiciary' (2020) 1 *Eur Conv Hum Rights L Rev* 159.

excuse to introduce revolutionary changes. This conclusion might be deemed useful in the context of other human rights tribunals with a weak system of implementation and quick rotation of judges.

Human rights can be understood very broadly. Moreover, they can be explained differently, for example as limits or trumps[7] to certain policies or as expressions of certain interests.[8] Human rights assume a role in law as well in other regulatory frameworks like politics, social justice, equality and others.[9] However, they have slightly different meanings in all these areas. Such iterations of meanings are heavy baggage for any court adjudicating human rights claims. The ECtHR is not an exception in this sense. It is not easy to distil human rights as a legal notion from the additional layers of meaning. This is true not only in relation to the overarching notion of human rights but also in relation to other notions deployed by the ECtHR. They include democracy, rules of law, fair trial and European public order.

This monograph reflects on the inherent dualism of European public order and therefore distinguishes between European public order as a legal category that leads to a particular outcome – and in this case it is expected that it has an identifiable scope – and European public order as a descriptive category that includes multiple layers of meanings and might not have an identifiable content, only vague frontiers and instinctively appreciable scope.

1.2.2 *Minimalist Approach to Human Rights*

This book does not purport to investigate the rationale behind human rights or to change the broader understanding of human rights from the perspective of legal and political philosophy; it is much more practical in its contribution to legal scholarship. This monograph assumes that effective human rights are minimal; they highlight only the most significant and pertinent failures of state authorities. Here, this assumption is applied to the operation of the ECtHR. This idea creates a background principle for the discussion in this monograph.

Relatedly, the role of a human rights court is to ensure that minimal rights are properly protected while avoiding 'human rights inflation',[10] which was defined as 'the tendency to frame any grievance as a rights

[7] See Ronald Dworkin, *Taking Rights Seriously* (Bloomsbury Publishing 2013).
[8] See Joseph Raz, 'On the Nature of Rights' (1948) *Mind* 194, 195–6.
[9] Hurst Hannum, *Rescuing Human Rights* (Cambridge University Press 2019) 8.
[10] Michael Ignatieff, *Human Rights as Politics and Idolatry* (Princeton University Press 2001) 90.

violation'.[11] Such inflation can be presented in plenty of forms; this monograph looks at the Court's desire to frame European public order as one of the representations of human rights inflation by which it contributes to the body of scholarship that rejects the overly expansionist view of human rights.

It is important to explain why human rights inflation is in fact a negative phenomenon. The key reason is that expanded human rights divert attention from the core rights and offer a more fertile ground for backlash. This monograph does not argue that issues that can be included in the scope of human rights should not be protected – perhaps they should – but they should not be labelled human rights. This wrongful labelling removes the sharp focus and stigma from the violations of what can be called a core of human rights. Mendus argued:

> [H]uman rights [are] seen as an expression, not of philosophical optimism, but of political pessimism: they . . . serve rather as a warning against overenthusiastic attempts to create solidarity. [H]uman rights are bulwarks against evil, borne [*sic*] of an acknowledgement of difference, not harbingers of goods consequent upon a commitment to similarity, whether created or discovered.[12]

There is no consensus, even among those theorists who can be called 'human rights minimalists', as to what exactly should be included in the core of human rights. For Ignatieff, they are most fundamental freedoms that are supported by consensus.[13] For Rawls, it is the 'special class of urgent rights'.[14] This monograph does not set out to clearly identify what constitutes the core of human rights; rather, it aims to test the activities of the ECtHR against this understanding of human rights as minimal core legal rights enshrined in the ECHR. From this perspective, the Court's ambition to engage in shaping European public order is excessive and can lead to human rights inflation and inflation of the role and function of the Court as an interpreter of the ECHR. In turn, this would undermine the ability of the Court to defend the core of human rights as it would dilute the stigma of violations.

[11] Dominique Clément, 'Human Rights or Social Justice? The Problem of Rights Inflation' (2018) 22 *IJHR* 155, 155.

[12] Susan Mendus, 'Human Rights in Political Theory' in David Beetham (ed.), *Politics and Human Rights* (Blackwell 1995) 23.

[13] Ignatieff (n. 10). For a more in-depth discussion, see Monique Deveaux, 'Normative Liberal Theory and the Bifurcation of Human Rights' (2009) 2 *Ethics and Global Politics* 171.

[14] John Rawls, *The Law of Peoples* (Harvard University Press 2002) 79.

At the end of the day, it is the states who agreed to comply with some minimal core of human rights and they will determine how far beyond this minimum core they will allow the Court to go. As Posner pointed out: 'Although countries give the ECHR formal power to order them about, they limit its practical power by starving it of resources and limiting the remedies that it may award, and mediating its effects through the Council [*sic*] of Ministers, a political body that can take into account political constraints on the member states' ability or willingness to comply with judgments.'[15]

The ECtHR perhaps needs to leave the development of European public order to the state parties to the ECHR. Ambitious interferences with European public order can be used as an excuse by the states authorities to ignore even those judgments that condemn violations of the core of human rights.

1.2.3 *Diversity of Methods*

Until now, I have tried to explain the overall approach to the subject matter of the monograph. This short section outlines the specific methods that were used to explore European public order from various angles. European public order is a vague and complex notion and it requires a creative and multi-faceted approach for its examination – this monograph aims to offer such an approach. The monograph begins by presenting an exhaustive content analysis of the case law of the Court. Chapter 2 explores all published judgments and decisions of the Court where the formula 'European Public Order' was mentioned and then it categorises the results into six distinct groups. Chapter 3 uses the comparative law method to consider how public order was used in various areas of international and national law. This survey is not comprehensive, but it shows that in every context the notion of public order is vague and unclear and this vagueness is exacerbated when the notion of public order is transferred from the national to the international level.

Chapters 4 and 5 locate the findings of Chapters 2 and 3 in the current debates surrounding the ECtHR. They review the academic debates of the function of the ECtHR and infrastructural innovations developed by the Court and the contracting parties and then consider their implications for the Court's ability to shape European public order. Finally, Chapter 6 uses interviews to establish what the ECtHR judges think about European public order. This chapter is based on a set of semi-structured interviews

[15] Eric Posner, *The Twilight of Human Rights Law* (Oxford University Press 2014) 51.

and tries to establish the rationale behind the deployment of the notion of European public order in the case law of the Court as well as its role in deliberations.

1.3 The Core Arguments

The core argument of this monograph is twofold. First, I argue that it is hardly possible to define European public order and, therefore, using this notion in the Court's judgments is not helpful for the clarity of the Court's reasoning. If one accepts the fact that clarity is one of the factors that affects the legitimacy of Court's judgments, then such fundamentally vague notions can undermine such legitimacy. Second and conversely, European public order can be used as a descriptive notion which is not expected to lead to any legally significant outcomes. Here, European public order is seen as a set of fundamental values shared by the contracting parties to the Convention. In this respect the monograph argues that the ECtHR does impact the understanding of these shared values and standards, but such impact cannot and should not be a strategic aim of the Court.

1.3.1 *The Vague Concept*

The Court cannot shape European public order because the definition of this 'order' is ambiguous. European public order is a very abstract notion that has different meanings in different contexts. In order to re-conceptualise European public order, one needs to look at it from two fairly distinct angles. First, European public order is an analytical tool that helps to explain the impact of the ECtHR on the European standards of human rights protection. To say that the ECtHR shapes European public order would mean that the Court influences the key principles that are shared and accepted by the contracting parties. In this sense, it is less important to know what these principles are precisely; what is more important is to agree that the Court can change the applicable standards of human rights protection. As I have already mentioned, this is perhaps so. The Court's instigated changes, irrespective of how small they are, do impact European standards of human rights protection. The Court has been and will continue to be instrumental in various areas of law and legal practice across Europe.[16] In this sense, European public order offers

[16] See the Report of the Parliamentary Assembly of the Council of Europe: 'Impact of the European Convention on Human Rights in States Parties: Selected Examples' (*Council of Europe Portal*, 8 January 2016) www.coe.int/en/web/execution/-/the-impact-of-the-european-convention-on-human-rights.

a useful tool for analysis of the Court's activities; it can be used to indicate a general set of highly abstract rules that the ECtHR can impact upon. This approach examines European public order from the perspective of an uninvolved observer; any claims that the Court engages with European public order do not have tangible legal consequences in a particular case. For instance, in the case of *Lopez Ostra* v. *Spain*, the ECtHR considered whether the right to a clean environment is relevant to Article 8 of the Convention and decided that it is.[17] One can argue that this novel interpretation of the Convention had consequences for European public order as an analytical concept, but it would make little sense to say that European public order can be used here as a legal justification for this new approach of the Court to the scope of the Convention.

The second meaning of European public order is the legal one: it is deployed by the ECtHR in its case law as a justification for a certain outcome. For example, in some early cases, the Court declared an application inadmissible in accordance with Article 35 of the Convention and then stated that no reasons of European public order would justify declaring it admissible.[18] In these cases, the Court treated European public order as an argument that can justify a departure from the strict interpretation of the wording of the Convention. This meaning requires a lot more precision than the analytical one as the former is used in the Court's reasoning as a justification for a particular outcome of a case. Where the Court uses European public order in a legal sense, it needs to establish some applicable scope and common understanding of this concept; in other words, such utilisation requires a clear meaning.

Although the Court mentions European public order in its case law, often it is used as *obiter dicta* with unclear meaning and vague relevance to the matter at issue. Deployment of vague terms, such as European public order, that can mean almost anything[19] undermines the legitimacy of the Court. To the contrary, deployment of clear reasoning which does not point to numerous meanings can enhance the legitimacy of the Court's judgments.[20] In a legal sense, when the Court mentions

[17] *López Ostra* v. *Spain*, 9 December 1994, Series A no. 303-C.

[18] *De Becker* v. *Belgium*, 27 March 1962, Series A no. 4; *Paez* v. *Sweden*, 30 October 1997, Reports of Judgments and Decisions 1997-VII.

[19] See Chapter 3 for a detailed analysis of the definition of European public order.

[20] Lady Justice Arden lists the qualities that the ECtHR should demonstrate to improve the implementation of the Convention system. 'Quality of reasoning and ability to communicate clearly with their constituents' was one of these qualities. Mary Arden, 'Address at the Seminar "The Convention Is Yours" Organised by the ECtHR', Dialogues Between Judges (Council of Europe 2010) 23.

European public order, it should provide at least some indication of its measurable content. This content might be fairly abstract, but there should be some criteria that can be applicable and testable. I will use another fairly vague concept to illustrate my argument here. Take the doctrine of the margin of appreciation, which has often been criticised for its unclear scope.[21] However, in the case of the margin of appreciation, one can understand how this concept works, just as one can predict what will be taken into account when the Court considers the scope of the margin. If the responding state is acting within the margin, then the Court will not find a violation of the Convention. If the respondent state goes too far then the Court will find a violation. In *S. and Marper* v. *the United Kingdom*, the Court listed a set of criteria for determining the borderline of the margin:

> The breadth of this margin varies and depends on a number of factors, including the nature of the Convention right in issue, its importance for the individual, the nature of the interference and the object pursued by the interference. The margin will tend to be narrower where the right at stake is crucial to the individual's effective enjoyment of intimate or key rights. Where a particularly important facet of an individual's existence or identity is at stake, the margin allowed to the State will be restricted. Where, however, there is no consensus within the member States of the Council of Europe, either as to the relative importance of the interest at stake or as to how best to protect it, the margin will be wider.[22]

When the ECtHR refers to European public order, the indicators that would help establish the scope of this order with at least some degree of certainty are not provided; its consequences are unclear and, when used, it can consist of anything – even mutually exclusive components.[23] European public order can include almost all human rights enshrined in the Convention;[24] it can also relate to the limitation of a qualified right;[25] it can support the extraterritorial application of

[21] See, for example, Jeffrey A. Brauch, 'The Margin of Appreciation and the Jurisprudence of the European Court of Human Rights: Threat to the Rule of Law' (2004) 11 *Colum J Eur L* 113; Anthony Lester 'Universality vs. Subsidiarity: A Reply' (1998) 1 *EHRLR*, 73, 75; Z. v. *Finland*, no. 22009/93, Partly Dissenting Opinion of Judge De Meyer.

[22] *S. and Marper* v. *the United Kingdom* [GC], nos. 30562/04 and 30566/04, ECHR 2008, para. 102.

[23] See Chapter 2 for more detail.

[24] *Deweer* v. *Belgium*, 27 February 1980, Series A no. 35, para. 49; *De Wilde, Ooms and Versyp* v. *Belgium*, 18 June 1971, Series A no. 12, para. 65.

[25] *Ahmed and Others* v. *the United Kingdom*, 2 September 1998, Reports of Judgments and Decisions 1998-VI, para. 52.

the Convention;[26] and it can justify the admissibility of a particular complaint.[27] Therefore, it is central to the line of argument of this monograph to distinguish between the analytical and the legal applications of this concept and to show that deployment of European public order in the latter sense in the judgments of the ECtHR is not particularly effective or helpful. One can, however, argue that, by this notion, the Court merely flags the importance of a particular issue to the contracting parties of the Convention. I would respectfully disagree with such a view. To say that something is part of European public order must mean more than simply highlighting its importance. There are multiple ways of emphasising the value of a particular issue. Saying that such issue is part of European public order means that the Court has the ambition to frame and shape this order in a way that might not be shared by the contracting parties. This brings me to the second line of argument that this book explores in detail.

1.3.2 *Why Should Not the ECtHR Aim to Shape European Public Order?*

The ECtHR should not explicitly or implicitly attempt to impose its view of European public order. At the outset, I need to admit that it is almost impossible to clearly separate those cases where the Court conscientiously tries to influence European public order from those where the Court just cannot avoid formulating a more general rule in order to apply it to the situation at hand. In other words, the latter situation happens when the Court has to define broader rules specifically to explain why a particular case was decided in such a way. By adding explicit references to European public order in its judgments, the ECtHR makes a claim of authority that is superior to that of the contracting parties. Although the judgments of the ECtHR are binding, its authority is tightly constrained by a great number of factors. The Court simply cannot regularly deliver judgments that are explicitly questioned and criticised by the contracting parties,[28] otherwise the Court's effectiveness would be undermined. Of course, this statement requires clarifications. First, in cases concerned with violations of well-established rights, the Court should not 'think' about the states'

[26] *Al-Skeini and Others* v. *the United Kingdom* [GC], no. 55721/07, ECHR 2011, para. 142.
[27] *Korolev* v. *Russia* (dec.), no. 25551/05, ECHR 2010. See similar reasoning in *Finger* v. *Bulgaria*, no. 37346/05, 10 May 2011. Chapter 3 describes all these and some other possible meanings in more detail.
[28] See Shai Dothan, *Reputation and Judicial Tactics: A Theory of National and International Courts* (Cambridge University Press 2014).

reaction. That said, more often the contracting parties negatively react to novel and far-reaching interpretations of the Convention. Second, the states' reactions are not always clear, and their feedback can be unpredictable. However, the Court needs to take the risk of negative reaction into account. When the Court explores far-reaching and innovative ways of interpreting the Convention, such reactions are much more probable. That is why the Court cannot build European public order as it sees fit. What the Court can do is to fine-tune the standards that have already been developed in collaboration with the contracting parties. Yet, this collaborative view on the role of the Court is not shared by everyone in the Court. In his dissenting opinion, Judge Paulo Pinto de Albuquerque stated: 'As administrators of first resort of the Convention, the domestic authorities must therefore be deferential to the final say of the Court, which is entrusted with the uniform upholding of the "constitutional instrument of European public order", whenever the domestic level of human-rights protection is lower than that of the Court.'[29] In practice, the domestic authorities are not always loyal and obedient clients of the ECtHR system. The Court cannot simply ignore that backlash; it could seriously undermine its reputation.

The Court has both explicitly and implicitly stated that its purpose is to shape European public order. Perhaps the most famous and oft-repeated phrase that includes reference to European public order comes from the case of *Loizidou* v. *Turkey* when the Court established 'the special character of the Convention as an instrument of European public order (ordre public)'.[30] Dissenting judges went even further in their ambitious vision of the function of the ECtHR.[31] Judges Dedov and Pinto de Albuquerque opined: 'In Europe, the domestic law of the member States is subordinated to the primacy of the Convention as a constitutional instrument of European public order.'[32] Although, according to the Vienna Convention on the Law of Treaties, the contracting parties to the ECHR cannot use their law as a justification for

[29] *Hutchinson* v. *the United Kingdom* [GC], no. 57592/08, 17 January 2017. Dissenting Opinion of Judge Pinto de Albuquerque, para. 45. This statement was then repeated on a number of occasions; see, for example, *Bosphorus Hava Yolları Turizm ve Ticaret Anonim Şirketi* v. *Ireland* [GC], no. 45036/98, ECHR 2005-VI, para. 156; *Neulinger and Shuruk* v. Switzerland [GC], no. 41615/07, ECHR 2010, para. 133; *Al-Skeini and Others* v. *the United Kingdom* [GC], no. 55721/07, ECHR 2011, para. 141.

[30] *Loizidou* v. *Turkey* (preliminary objections), 23 March 1995, Series A no. 310, para. 93.

[31] Chapter 4 discusses the proper function of the Court.

[32] *Baka* v. *Hungary* [GC], no. 20261/12, 23 June 2016. Dissenting Opinion of Judges Pinto de Albuquerque and Dedov, para. 23.

non-implementation of the ECHR,[33] it is simplistic to argue that there is a direct hierarchy between the Convention and the national law, and especially between the judgments of the ECtHR and the national laws.[34] Here, the Court is one among a number of equals in deciding and fine-tuning European human rights standards. The development of European public order is a common endeavour of all forty-seven contracting parties to the Convention and the ECHR is as much a constitutional instrument of European public order as the constituting documents of any of the forty-seven member states of the Council of Europe. There are at least four reasons why the ECtHR should not put forward the strategic development of European public order as its explicit or implicit purpose.

1.3.2.1 The Reason of Effectiveness and Legitimacy

First of all, the Court's ambition to appear to be more influential than is allowed by its design undermines its legitimacy and effectiveness. I will not be discussing it as a separate issue in this book – I talked about legitimacy before,[35] but it is always at the back of the mind when one assesses the Court's activities and authority. I have argued before that it is almost impossible to clearly establish how to enhance the legitimacy of such an institution as the ECtHR. However, it is possible to test the key challenges to the legitimacy of an institution.[36] Throughout this monograph, I will be arguing that the Court's unilateral attempts to make significant strategic changes to European public order are potentially illegitimate. This statement is perhaps not controversial per se, but what is more controversial is to establish what it actually means to make significant changes to European public order. Before I consider the latter question, I will briefly outline why it is illegitimate to initiate such significant changes. The ECtHR, as well as many other courts adjudicating a bill of rights, is not designed as a representative institution, it is not a parliament and it does not enjoy democratic legitimacy.

[33] Article 27 of the Vienna Convention on the Law of Treaties.

[34] See, for example, Nico Krisch, 'The Open Architecture of European Human Rights Law' (2008) 71 *Mod L Rev* 183; Steven Greer and Luzius Wildhaber, 'Revisiting the Debate about "Constitutionalising" the European Court of Human Rights' (2013) 12 *HRL Rev* 655.

[35] Kanstantsin Dzehtsiarou, *European Consensus and the Legitimacy of the European Court of Human Rights* (Cambridge University Press 2015), ch. 6; Kanstantsin Dzehtsiarou, 'Does Consensus Matter? Legitimacy of European Consensus in the Case Law of the European Court of Human Rights' [2011] *PL* 534.

[36] Dzehtsiarou, *European Consensus* (n. 35) 143.

However, it has been argued that elections are not the only source of legitimacy.[37] Democratic legitimacy is perhaps the 'purest' source of legitimacy and, even if other sources are identifiable, the Court cannot make the claim of the same level of legitimacy as national democratic bodies. As a result, the difference between the Court and national parliaments lays in the nature and form of the decisions that they make. While national parliaments are entrusted with building strategic policy decisions, the vast majority of decisions taken by the Court are judgments in individual cases. The ECtHR was designed as an adjudicatory institution that would prevent the development of dictatorial regimes in the contracting parties. Its case law has developed way beyond this initial design[38] and some of these developments were the result of natural technological or societal developments. In other cases, the Court was blamed for resorting to overly extensive evolutive interpretation.[39] As such evolutive or teleological interpretation is not a problem, sometimes the scope and the degree of evolution can be. It is difficult to defend overly ambitious judgments of the Court as they might not be based on the ordinary meaning of the Convention; these judgments might not lead to obviously better outcomes and the Court cannot draw its legitimacy from morality just because both parties in a case may make convincing moral arguments. In these cases, the Court should defer and allow the issue to develop naturally. Moreover, general rules that the Court adopts should be applicable in all forty-seven contracting parties to the Convention. Certain new solutions might be perfectly sensible in some countries but quite unacceptable in others. However, the Court cannot create different standards for different

[37] See, for example, Aileen Kavanagh, 'Participation and Judicial Review: A Reply to Jeremy Waldron' (2003) 22 *Law and Phil* 451; Or Bassok, 'The Supreme Court's New Source of Legitimacy' (2013) 16 *U Pa J Const L* 153; Basak Cali, Anne Koch and Nicola Bruch, 'The Legitimacy of Human Rights Courts: A Grounded Interpretivist Analysis of the European Court of Human Rights' (2013) 35 *Hum Rights Q* 955; Nienke Grossman, 'The Normative Legitimacy of International Courts' (2013) 86 *Temp L Rev* 61.

[38] See Ed Bates, *The Evolution of the European Convention on Human Rights* (Oxford University Press 2010).

[39] See, for example, Lord Leonard Hoffmann, 'The Universality of Human Rights' (2009) 125 *LQR* 416, 428–9; Jonathan Sumption, 'The Reith Lectures 2019: Law and the Decline of Politics' (2019) 4 *BBC Radio* 18; Koen Lemmens, 'Criticising the European Court of Human Rights or Misunderstanding the Dynamics of Human Rights Protection?' in Koen Lemmens, Patricia Popelier and Sarah Lambrecht (eds.), *Criticism of the European Court of Human Rights: Shifting the Convention System: Counter-Dynamics at the National and EU Level* (Intersentia 2016).

countries and, therefore, the Court needs to consider how a particular standard can be applied in all members states of the Council of Europe where a particular human rights issue exists. As I have already pointed out, it is extremely difficult to define, in abstract, what it actually means to make significant changes in European public order. It seems that this needs to be decided on a case-by-case basis; those examples that come to mind often include the *de facto* adding the rights to the Convention,[40] significant changes to the Court's own case law[41] or rulings that go against a clear consensus.[42] Although these cases are rare, they often attract disproportionate attention to the role and functioning of the ECtHR. This monograph will not give a definitive answer to the question of where the line between an illegitimate revolution of the content of European public order and its gradual evolution is. This answer will likely depend on many factors that may change over time, but the direction of a natural progression in human rights can be recognised through the feedback from the states. The Court receives various signals from the contracting parties through third-party interventions, through its analysis of the state of consensus, through requests for referral to the Grand Chamber. These signals can make the Court aware that the contracting parties are not in a position to accept a particular development. Here, I discuss only new standards or new areas in which the Court is trying to expand. The Court, of course, does not need to consider the opinion of the contracting parties if a prisoner has been tortured or if a clear case of discrimination has occurred. The Court needs to be more deferential to the contracting parties where its standards are not clearly established.

1.3.2.2 The European Court of Human Rights Is Not a Strategic Actor

Although potential illegitimacy is the existential difficulty behind the Court's attempts to revolutionise European public order, there are more pragmatic reasons why attempts to shape European public order are dangerous for the system and distract the Court from making sure that the core rights are protected. So, the second reason why the ECtHR should not put strategic development of European public order as its explicit or implicit purpose is the institutional limitations of

[40] *Young, James and Webster* v. *the United Kingdom*, 13 August 1981, Series A no. 44; *Hirst* v. *the United Kingdom (no. 2)*, no. 74025/01, 30 March 2004.
[41] *Christine Goodwin* v. *the United Kingdom* [GC], no. 28957/95, ECHR 2002-VI.
[42] *A, B and C* v. *Ireland* (n. 2).

strategic actions designed and performed by the Court. These limitations are, to some extent, applicable to all apex courts, but some specific features of the ECtHR exacerbate them. Although Chapter 4 discusses these issues in more detail, I will summarise them briefly here. There are forty-seven judges on the bench of the Court, who are elected for a period of nine years and divided into five sections. This is not like the US Supreme Court or some other national constitutional courts, where the justices are elected for life and can make an important strategic contribution to law; ECtHR judges are elected for nine years and cannot be re-elected.[43] The judges are equal and cannot be forced to decide cases in any particular way. As a result, the Court's ability to strategically make rational changes in European public order is limited.

One can argue that the president and the most senior judges can determine the strategy of the Court, but this is unlikely to be so. Presidents of the ECtHR are elected for only a short period of time with limited and mostly representative competences. The president and the most senior judges can effectively control the Grand Chamber docket, but, although it is an important endeavor, the mere acceptance of a particular issue to the Grand Chamber does not guarantee a particular outcome as seventeen judges are sitting on every Grand Chamber case. It would be possible to act strategically if the bench were formed of very like-minded judges who would agree on the strategic development of European public order. Moreover, this state of affairs would need to continue for a significant period of time. However, this is unrealistic. Judges disagree on the most basic existential questions such as what the meta-function of the Court is.[44] Moreover, it is almost impossible to find forty-seven lawyers who would agree on many heavily morally charged questions. Therefore, it is unlikely that the Court is actually capable of making a strategic consistent and long-term contribution to European public order. Even if it could, it would almost inevitably face the following problem: the third reason why the ECtHR should not aim to shape European public order is because its strategic vision might never be enforced by the contracting parties to the European Convention.

[43] Article 23 ECHR. For a more detailed discussion of the process of election of the ECtHR judges, see Kanstantsin Dzehtsiarou and Alex Schwartz, 'Electing Team Strasbourg: Professional Diversity on the European Court of Human Rights and Why It Matters' (2020) 21 *Ger Law J* 621.

[44] See Chapter 6 for a detailed analysis.

1.3.2.3 Poor Enforcement of the ECtHR Judgments

Even if the Court were to adopt a particular strategy in developing European public order, this strategy might not work due to the nature of the enforcement of the Court's judgments. It seems that when courts rely on strong enforcement mechanisms, they can ensure that even potentially illegitimate decisions are acted upon. This reliance on force, however, makes a system unstable and unlikely to last long. In a system like the one set by the ECHR – where resort to force is not possible – legitimacy is perhaps the key reason for enforcement. The Committee of Ministers of the Council of Europe supervises how the contracting parties execute ECtHR judgments. Although it has some soft sanctions in its toolkit, it rarely goes beyond multiple resolutions demanding execution. The sanction of last resort is expulsion of the member from the Council of Europe, but it has not yet been used.[45] Generally speaking, execution of judgments of the ECtHR is ultimately a voluntary exercise. With such a weak enforcement mechanism, the Court is limited in what changes it can effectively impose.

There are three levels on which most ECtHR judgments need to be executed: monetary compensation, individual measures and general measures.[46] While monetary compensation is self-explanatory, individual measures are those actions that the state should undertake to remedy the violation of the applicant's rights. They usually include a retrial, restitution or other personalised measures depending on the facts of the case. General measures aim to ensure that the same violation does not happen again. These measures usually consist of legislative reform, introduction of a new remedy, improvement of detention facilities, etc. Usually, these measures require significant financial resources and political will. It is the general measures that can potentially 'shape' European public order, but these are the measures which are harder to

45 See Kanstantsin Dzehtsiarou and Donal K. Coffey, 'Suspension and Expulsion of Members of the Council of Europe: Difficult Decisions in Troubled Times' (2019) 68 *Int'l Comp LQ* 443.

46 The supervision process available at www.coe.int/en/web/execution/the-supervision-process. See also Alastair Mowbray, 'An Examination of the European Court of Human Rights' Indication of Remedial Measures' (2017) 17 *HRL Rev* 451; Alice Donald and Anne-Katrin Speck, 'The European Court of Human Rights' Remedial Practice and Its Impact on the Execution of Judgments' (2019) 19 *HRL Rev* 83; Fiona de Londras and Kanstantsin Dzehtsiarou, 'Mission Impossible? Addressing Non-execution through Infringement Proceedings in the European Court of Human Rights' (2017) 66 *Int'l Comp LQ* 467.

implement.[47] It is rare that the Committee of Ministers faces challenges in enforcing judgments when it comes to monetary compensation or individual measures, but compliance with general measures is almost always difficult, lengthy and controversial.

The system of enforcement is such that the contracting parties have quite broad discretion at the stage of implementation. So, even when the Court decides to change European public order strategically, and comes up with a series of judgments to that effect, the requested change might be blurred by different strategies of national implementation. One can argue that a newly implemented policy can come back to the ECtHR and the Court will assess its compatibility with the Conventional standard again. Having said that, it is highly likely that this would be a totally new Court[48] which might opt in to a new 'strategy'. In any event, the states have the last word in defining the policy and the relevant changes happen through the back-and-forth interaction between the Court and the contracting parties. Such changes happen gradually, not by sheer desire of the Court itself.

1.3.2.4 The European Court Is Not a Constitutional Court

The fourth and final reason is that the Court not only lacks the legitimacy to make significant changes to European public order, it is not designed to rule on abstract matters, and consistent abstract rulings are required to impact public order. The Court was not created to undergo abstract constitutional control. This is evident, for example, from the fact that an application should be submitted to the Court by the victim of the violation, not a person who thinks that a particular rule is allegedly against the Convention. Although the Court has diluted the victim requirement over the years,[49] the principle behind this requirement is still intact. One can, however, consider what should be done if the law or even the constitution of a state itself allegedly violates the Convention. Should the Court avoid ruling on such cases to ensure the stability of the Strasbourg system? There are quite a few examples where this is not just a hypothetical suggestion but a real factual background of some of the

[47] See Fiona de Londras and Kanstantsin Dzehtsiarou, *Great Debates on the European Convention on Human Rights* (Palgrave 2018), ch. 8.

[48] It is very likely that adoption and implementation of a particularly controversial judgment will take more than nine years – a lifespan of one judge on the bench of the Strasbourg Court.

[49] See, for example, *Centre for Legal Resources on behalf of Valentin Câmpeanu* v. *Romania* [GC], no. 47848/08, ECHR 2014; de Londras and Dzehtsiarou (n. 47) 54–9.

Court's cases. In *A, B and C* v. *Ireland*, the Court had to decide whether the provision of the Constitution of Ireland, which effectively prohibits medical abortion for almost every reason, violates the ECHR. In this particular case, the Court did not find a violation;[50] however, in a number of other judgments, where constitutional provisions were under review, the Court did find violations. One can argue that the provisions of the national constitutions express the foundations of national public order. Therefore, the Court is effectively stating that some aspects of the national public order are in breach of the ECHR.[51] In *Sejdić and Finci* v. *Bosnia and Herzegovina*, the Court had to consider whether some regulations of the election of the presidents of Bosnia and Herzegovina (and particularly the requirements relating to ethnicities) violate the prohibition of discrimination under Protocol 12 to the ECHR.[52] The Court found a violation of the Convention and Bosnia was obliged to change its constitution – which it has not done yet.[53] In *Baka* v. *Hungary*, the Court considered whether the Constitutional Amendments that effectively removed the president of the Supreme Court of Hungary from his position were in compliance with the Convention and found against the respondent state.[54] Another example is the case *Anchugov and Gladkov* v. *Russia* which was one of the episodes of the prisoner voting saga.[55] Here, the fact that convicted prisoners are disenfranchised in Russia by the provision of the Constitution made finding a violation of the Convention problematic in terms of execution. Although this case was eventually declared by the Committee of Ministers as enforced,[56] it arguably did not result in any significant practical improvements. Effectively, prisoners still cannot vote in Russia. Arguably, as a result of this judgment, the Russian Parliament passed a law empowering the Russian

[50] *A, B and C* v. *Ireland* (n. 2). See also Fiona de Londras and Kanstantsin Dzehtsiarou, 'II. Grand Chamber of the European Court of Human Rights, *A, B & C v Ireland*, Decision of 17 December 2010' (2013) 62(1) *Int'l Comp LQ* 250.

[51] In Chapter 6, the interviewed judges were asked what the consequences are of conflicts between national and European public order. As in relation to many other questions, the judges were not in agreement here.

[52] *Sejdić and Finci* v. *Bosnia and Herzegovina* [GC], nos. 27996/06 and 34836/06, ECHR 2009.

[53] Amra Basic, 'Sejdic-Finci and Pilav: Bosnia-Hercegovina's Road to Implementation of the European Convention on Human Rights' (2019) 28 *Transnat'l L & Contemp Probs* 577.

[54] *Baka* v. *Hungary* [GC], no. 20261/12, 23 June 2016.

[55] For more details, see Kanstantsin Dzehtsiarou, 'Prisoner Voting Saga' in Helen Hardman and Brice Dickson (eds.), *Electoral Rights in Europe: Advances and Challenges* (Routledge 2017).

[56] Resolution CM/ResDH (2019) 240 of the Committee of Ministers https://search.coe.int/cm/Pages/result_details.aspx?ObjectID=090000168097edc2.

Constitutional Court to review the enforceability of ECtHR judgments in Russia[57] and the recent amendments to the Russian Constitution effectively established the supremacy of national law over international.[58] In all these cases, the Court had to consider the compliance of the most fundamental national document – the national constitution – with the ECHR. By the mere fact of deciding whether these provisions violate the Convention, the Court is being dragged into an abstract review. One can consider the practical matter of what the Court should do when the individual case is so closely connected to the national public order. Of course, the Court has to find violations of the Convention irrespective of whence these violations originate, but it does not mean that the Court can simply replace the national public order with its own vision of European public order. The Court's references to European public order in its case law create such an impression. One could argue that every ECtHR judgment should lead to tangible changes, some of which would have an impact only on the victim(s) of the violations and others would change the regulatory framework of the respondent party. The latter judgments arguably interfere with national public order. The logic here is the following: if the violation of the applicant's rights happened as a consequence of a certain legislative provision, this provision needs to be changed to avoid similar violations. If these mechanisms worked, the Court would hardly ever see any repetitive applications. As anyone working with the ECtHR knows, however, the major part of the Court's backlog is 'clone cases.'[59] Therefore, the logic that adjudicatory

[57] Lauri Mälksoo, 'Russia's Constitutional Court Defies the European Court of Human Rights. Constitutional Court of the Russian Federation Judgment of 14 July 2015, No 21-П /2015' (2016) 12 *EuConst* 377; Marina Aksenova, 'Anchugov and Gladkov Is Not Enforceable: The Russian Constitutional Court Opines in Its First ECtHR Implementation Case' (*OpinioJuris*, 25 April 2016) http://opiniojuris.org/2016/04/25/anchugov-and-gladkov-is-not-enforceable-the-russian-constitutional-court-opines-in-its-first-ecthr-implementation-case/; Kanstantsin Dzehtsiarou and Filippo Fontanelli, 'A Primer from the Russian Constitutional Court' [2018] *Eur Yearbook Hum Rights* 319.

[58] See Yulia Ioffe, 'The Amendments to the Russian Constitution: Putin's Attempt to Reinforce Russia's Isolationist Views on International Law?' (*EJIL:Talk*, 29 January 2020) www.ejiltalk.org/the-amendments-to-the-russian-constitution-putins-attempt-to-reinforce-russias-isolationist-views-on-international-law/.

[59] One of the judges interviewed for this project explained the Court's backlog in the following terms:

> If you look at the cases pending before the court today – there are 60,000 of them. [Of those,] 7,000 are single judge cases – in 2011 there were 100,000 single judge cases; 15,000 are ordinary repetitive cases – classic non-execution, excessive length, etc.; 9,000–10,000 are prison conditions – so, not classic repetitive cases because they come from the priority category because they raise Article 3 issues, but, again, you

individual judgments can naturally lead to abstract rectification of the whole problem by the respondent state does not hold up. Hence, one can argue that the Court has to resort to abstract reasoning and specify those measures that could put a halt to the influx of similar applications. There is a direct link between abstract reasoning and European public order as the Court formulates general standards that should be applicable across Europe. Although the Court is often dragged into abstract reasoning, it needs to limit it to the areas where it is strictly necessary without trying to initiate strategic reforms of European public order. The Court should not use individual complaints with a specific challenge at hand as a trigger for more widespread standard-setting.[60] The language of such judgments should clearly indicate their limited application. The Court lacks both the legitimacy and the opportunity to act as a strategic actor. This monograph analyses these four reasons as to why the Court cannot be an architect of European public order. The fact that the ECtHR can unsystematically influence such order does not undermine this claim.

1.4 The Structure of the Book

The book is divided into this introduction, five substantive chapters and a short conclusion. Chapter 2 will explain how the Court has treated European public order; although it has been used quite widely, it has never been defined and its role in the case law is unclear. The chapter offers a typology of cases where the Court uses European public order, but the range of seemingly disconnected areas of deployment shows that it is unlikely that there was a principled reason for the selection of the subject matters. Chapter 3 looks into what European public order means in different circumstances. It has been used in private international law, European Union law and other areas of international

only resolve these issues by getting some solutions on [a] domestic level. In the end, it will not be by processing the individual cases that we actually resolve the problem on the national level. And then you have got 12,000 cases directly linked to frozen cases, perhaps pending the inter-state case, perhaps no, but, in any case, but nothing that the Court can really provide a solution for because it will always be settled in terms of subsequent political discussion and negotiation. So, you are left with 15,000 cases, but if you look into what the Court can do in a given year, it is maybe 2,000. (Interview with Judge 8)

60 For a helpful typology of abstract review of the ECtHR, see Janneke Gerards, 'Abstract and Concrete Reasonableness Review by the European Court of Human Rights' (2020) 1 *Eur Conv Hum Rights L Rev*, 218.

and national law, but it remains vague and its content is impossible to define with any degree of specificity. Chapter 4 considers whether shaping European public order is the meta-function of the ECtHR. It concludes that the Court needs to resort to minimalist effectiveness in its treatment of European public order. Chapter 5 looks into the recent changes in the design of the Court's procedure. It shows that the Court's ambition to shape European public order is quite evident through the new procedures that have been initiated by the Court, including pilot proceedings, more extensive engagement in execution and a broader approach to interim measures. These changes were initiated by the Court itself through amending the Rules of Court. The recent reforms initiated by the contracting parties are a mixed bag of signals. On the one hand, the states allowed the Court to get more involved in execution by introducing infringement proceedings and at the same time reminding the Court that it is a subsidiary body by including reference to subsidiarity and margin of appreciation in the Preamble to the Convention. Chapter 6 tests all the assumptions and conclusions made in the previous five chapters. It is based on interviews with the sitting judges of the ECtHR and summarises the key points of discussion, focusing on the definition of European public order, the role of the Court in defining and maintaining it, as well as the role and the function of the Court. The chapter also touches upon more technical issues of the role of European public order in deliberations and its impact on the outcomes of particular cases.

2 European Public Order in the Case Law of the European Court of Human Rights

2.1 Introduction

The European Court of Human Rights (ECtHR or Court) has used the term 'European public order' in more than a hundred decisions and judgments. This number suggests that its deployment is not a coincidence; the Court seemingly relies on European public order. The Grand Chamber of the ECtHR has been referring to European public order more and more frequently in recent years. However, in none of these judgments has the Court explained what European public order actually means and how it can be conceptualised.

This chapter is the starting point of a detailed analysis of this complex and abstract notion. In Chapter 1 I argued that European public order can be used as an analytical concept or as a legal notion.[1] This chapter attempts to make sense of how the Court uses European public order as a legal formula, which must have some identifiable consequences.

This chapter will examine the Court's references to European public order. This aims to be not only a list of all relevant references but also an attempt to suggest a classification of the ways in which the ECtHR deploys European public order. The chapter is based on a two-step research strategy. The first step was to find all relevant decisions and judgments that referred to European public order. These judgments were identified through searching the Court's case law database 'HUDOC' ('Human Rights Documentation').[2] Two sets of keywords were used: 'European public order' and '*ordre public*'. The search was

[1] See Chapter 1.

[2] The ECtHR case law database (HUDOC) contains all judgments of the Court in English and French (some are available only in English or French) and some of the most important decisions of admissibility, advisory opinions and other documents produced by the Court; it is available at https://hudoc.echr.coe.int.

limited to decisions of admissibility and judgments on merits available in English. Only judgments published in HUDOC before 1 June 2020 were considered. I appreciate that some relevant judgments were missed in this search. For instance, arguably the very first case in which public order was used by the ECtHR in the sense discussed in this book was the case of *Austria* v. *Italy*. The Court stated in that case that:

> it clearly appears ... that the purpose of the High Contracting parties in concluding the Convention was not to concede to each other reciprocal rights and obligations in pursuance of their individual national interests but to realise the aims and ideals of the Council of Europe, as expressed in its Statute, and to establish a common public order of the free democracies of Europe with the object of safeguarding their common heritage of political traditions, ideals, freedom and the rule of law.[3]

In this case the Court came perhaps the closest to defining what European public order means. That said, the Court did not use 'European public order' in the text of the decision. As a result, this particular judgment would not be caught in the automatic search. This is an obvious limitation of this research technique, but there are reasons why it can still offer plausible results. First, in the more recent judgments the Court almost always uses 'European public order' or '*ordre public*' when it talks about vaguely defined commonly accepted standards within European legal space. Second, if the keywords set 'public order' is used then it distorts the result as in the majority of cases the ECtHR uses public order when discussing the limitations of human rights.[4] If this keyword set is added, the number of relevant judgments would not increase significantly but the overall sample grows exponentially.

The second step of this research project was to analyse all the judgments that were identified during the first step. This analysis revealed the following common subject areas in which the Court referred to European public order:

1. territorial jurisdiction of the Court (Section 2.2);
2. interaction between the ECtHR and other international organisations (Section 2.3);

[3] *Austria* v. *Italy*, no. 788/60, admissibility decision of 11 January 1961, 18. It was used in the very first case decided by the ECtHR but in a dissenting opinion by Judge Maridakis. See *Lawless* v. *Ireland* (no. 1), 14 November 1960, Series A no. 1.

[4] The term 'public order' has been used by the Court in 3,252 judgments and decisions in English (as at 22 July 2020).

3. extent of the binding force of the Court's interim measures (Section 2.4);
4. criteria of admissibility (Section 2.5);
5. democracy as a key aspect of European public order (Section 2.6);
6. scope of substantive provisions (Section 2.7).

This chapter shows that the content of European public order as it is understood by the ECtHR is far from homogeneous. Its meaning is changing following the contexts in which it is deployed. It is difficult to identify any uniform conception of European public order deployed by the Court.

At least four distinct roles of European public order in the case law of the ECtHR can be distinguished. First, European public order is used by the Court as a justification for establishing its *espace juridique*. In other words, by including references to European public order, the Court is trying to maintain that the continent of Europe[5] is covered by the European Convention on Human Rights (ECHR or Convention) and there are no geographical gaps in human rights law within Europe. Effectively, here the Court states that European public order dictates that the Court ensure that no territory in Europe that is formally within the geographical borders of its contracting parties can 'escape' the Court's supervision. However, the Court never explains why or what element or meaning of European public order prescribes that. The purpose of this role is comparatively clear, but its content is not. This role of European public order can be called 'jurisdictional'; it justifies the Court's claim of authority on a particular territory. Examples of this role of European public order can be found in the Court's case law related to its territorial jurisdiction and its approach to the interaction between the ECtHR and other international organisations.

The second role of European public order as a legal concept is far less straightforward. It can be called 'substantive' because it is used for interpretation of the substantive rights enshrined in the Convention.[6] In this context, the ECtHR tries to list the elements that are included in the concept of European public order. There are at least two key challenges in such an approach. First, the Court has never explained the rationale behind adding certain phenomena into the ambit of European public order. It seems quite random why certain issues are placed within European public order while others are not. Second, even if

[5] Only Belarus, Vatican City and arguably Kosovo are not parties to the ECHR.
[6] Articles 2–14 ECHR, Articles 1–3 Protocol 1 ECHR, etc.

one assumes that there is some criterion for inclusion of elements in European public order, it is unclear what such inclusion means either for that element or for European public order. One can suggest that if a particular phenomenon is a part of European public order, then it would have an added 'weight' in the balancing exercise[7] conducted by the Court when assessing state interference into qualified rights. However, as the discussion in this chapter shows, this is not always the case. Lack of rationale and unclear consequences of being a part of European public order create the impression of ad hoc reasoning by the Court. Democracy, right to liberty and security, and free elections are among those elements usually mentioned by the Court in connection with European public order. This role of European public order calls for more clarity in how it is applied and what impact it might have on the reasoning of the ECtHR.

The third role of European public order can be called 'procedural'. It is such because it does not directly affect the interpretation of any substantive provisions of the Convention but instead justifies some procedural innovations by the Court that might expand its authority. The Court's uses of European public order in relation to the admissibility criteria or to interim measures are examples of this role. In this context, the Court often mentions that it would not deal with a particular issue or case unless European public order justified the Court's interference.

The fourth role is related to the hierarchy of standards enshrined in the ECHR. I mentioned this role in Chapter 1, where I argued that there are many ways of emphasising the importance of a particular issue without making a claim of authority to build European public order. Having said that, this chapter shows that the Court does use references to European public order to underline the relative importance of the standard discussed by the Court in the case at hand, and to encourage the contracting parties to treat this standard seriously. Whether that is in relation to democracy, interim measures or territorial application of the ECHR, by connecting a standard to European public order the Court emphasises the exceptional value of these concepts for its case law.

This chapter analyses the areas in which European public order has been deployed by the Court. Understanding the Court's approach to and perception of European public order is crucial for establishing the key line of argument of this monograph, namely, that European public

[7] The Court has to weigh competitive rights and public interests within its proportionality analysis.

order is too vague and imprecise to qualify as a legal concept. In this chapter, I will examine the Court's deployment of European public order in six subject areas.

2.2 Territorial Jurisdiction of the Court

According to Article 1 of the ECHR, the contracting parties should secure to everyone within their jurisdiction the rights enshrined in the Convention. Therefore, the ECtHR can only supervise the implementation of the Convention by the contracting parties within their jurisdiction, that is, the jurisdiction of the Court depends on the jurisdiction of the contracting parties. While the vast majority of cases that the ECtHR is dealing with are straightforward from this point of view, as alleged violations have taken place within the geographical borders of the contracting parties, a small fraction of sensitive applications can raise complex legal questions of so-called extraterritorial jurisdiction. This means that when certain conditions are met, the contracting parties can be under an obligation to protect human rights as defined by the ECHR outside their geographical borders. Perhaps the most likely reason for such extraterritorial application is military occupation.

Extraterritorial jurisdiction of the Court is a much-contested issue that has generated heated debate in academia.[8] The contracting parties tend to treat possible claims about their military actions abroad as a very sensitive issue.[9] European public order is mentioned in the

[8] See, for example, Marko Milanovic, 'Jurisdiction and Responsibility: Trends in the Jurisprudence of the Strasbourg Court' in Anne van Aaken and Iulia Motoc (eds.), *The ECHR and General International Law* (Oxford University Press 2018) 97–111; Conall Mallory, *Human Rights Imperialists* (Hart 2020); Stuart Wallace, *The Application of the European Convention on Human Rights to Military Operations* (Cambridge University Press 2019); Sarah Miller, 'Revisiting Extraterritorial Jurisdiction: A Territorial Justification for Extraterritorial Jurisdiction Under the European Convention' (2009) 20(4) *EJIL* 1223; Max Schaefer, 'Al-Skeini and the Elusive Parameters of Extraterritorial Jurisdiction' (2011) 5 *EHRLR* 566; Michael Duttwiler, 'Authority, Control and Jurisdiction in the Extraterritorial Application of the European Convention on Human Rights' (2012) 30(2) *NQHR*137–62; Samantha Besson, 'The Extraterritoriality of the European Convention on Human Rights: Why Human Rights Depend on Jurisdiction and What Jurisdiction Amounts to' (2012) 25 *LJIL* 857.

[9] See, for example, Ian Johnston, 'Theresa May Trying to Protect Soldiers Who Murder Prisoners and Torture Civilians, Says Top Human Rights Lawyer', *The Independent* (5 October 2016) available at www.independent.co.uk/news/uk/politics/theresa-may-left-wing-human-rights-lawyers-cover-up-murder-torture-civilians-armed-forces-a7346846.html; 'UK Troops to Be Protected from "Spurious Legal Claims"', *BBC News* (4 October 2016) available at www.bbc.co.uk/news/uk-politics-37544280;

majority of key cases about extraterritorial jurisdiction, but not in all of them. As pointed out earlier, this meaning of European public order is jurisdictional, which is less problematic than the other senses in which it is understood, but even here the Court's case law is lacking consistency. My research method allowed me to identify that the Court referred to European public order in eleven judgments in this area. However, in important cases related to the territorial jurisdiction of the Court, such as *Ilaşcu and Others* v. *Moldova and Russia*[10] and *Chiragov* v. *Armenia*,[11] European public order was not explicitly referred to. The reasons for this omission will be considered later.

For the purposes of this section, it is necessary to distinguish between two situations of extraterritorial application of the Convention. The first is when military conflict happens between two contracting parties to the Convention and one of them occupies a part of the territory of the other. Although for the occupying state this situation amounts to extraterritorial application, it is not so for the ECHR as its legal space has not been altered by the occupation. In other words, the Convention was applicable to that territory before the occupation and it should be applicable after, albeit through the proxy of a different contracting party.

The second situation takes place when the contracting party to the Convention is acting outside the geographical frontiers of the Council of Europe. In other words, people in that territory were not under the Court's jurisdiction before the occupation took place but after the occupation they obtained a specific right to bring complaints to the ECtHR.[12]

It appears that the Court's references to European public order serve different purposes in these two situations. In relation to the first scenario, European public order justifies prevention of the accountability gaps within the legal realm of the Convention. In relation to the second scenario, European public order prevents the Court from unlimited expansion; in other words, it limits the outreach of the Convention

Kanstantsin Dzehtsiarou, 'Different Human Rights at Home and Abroad: Immunity for British Soldier during Overseas Operations', *Just Security Blog* (5 October 2016) available at www.justsecurity.org/33377/human-rights-home-abroad-immunity-british-soldier-overseas-operations/.

[10] *Ilaşcu and Others* v. *Moldova and Russia* [GC], no. 48787/99, ECHR 2004-VII.

[11] *Chiragov and Others* v. *Armenia* [GC], no. 13216/05, ECHR 2015.

[12] There are cases in which there was no occupation but the contracting parties were acting outside its territory. In this case, the key aspect is whether the actions took place inside or outside the normal frontiers of the contracting parties to the Convention.

unless certain conditions are satisfied. It appears that the Court declares extraterritorial jurisdiction because of European public order in the first scenario and despite it in the second. These two situations will now be considered in turn.

In relation to the first situation, namely when two contracting parties to the Convention are in a state of conflict, the purpose of the Court's reference to European public order appears to be to emphasise that it is crucially important for the effectiveness of the Convention system not to leave any areas of legal vacuum or lawless zones within Europe. The logic seems to be this: if the ECHR is a 'constitutional instrument of European public order',[13] any alleged violation of fundamental rights that takes place within the territory of Europe is covered by this order and, therefore, it should be accounted for.[14] It is less important which contracting party violates the rights of the applicants - it is more important that it is within the realm of the Convention.

The Court referred to European public order in its extraterritorial jurisdiction case law for the first time in relation to the Turkish occupation of Northern Cyprus. In 1974, Turkey occupied a part of Cyprus. In 1983, the Turkish Republic of Northern Cyprus (TRNC) declared independence and was recognised only by Turkey. The TRNC had not ratified the ECHR and therefore the Court did not have direct territorial jurisdiction over it. According to the rules of international law, all human rights violations that happen there should be attributed either to Cyprus, as it is its territory de jure, or to Turkey as an occupying power. Finally, the Court could perhaps pronounce the TRNC a territory beyond the reach of the ECtHR. When Turkey accepted the jurisdiction of the Court and the right to individual petition, it made a reservation which stated that 'the right of petition extends only to allegations concerning acts or omissions of public authorities in Turkey performed within the boundaries of the territory to which the Constitution of the Republic of Turkey is applicable'.[15] The question that the Court had to answer in the context of this occupation was whether it could extend the territorial jurisdiction of Turkey to the TRNC even with a specific reservation stating to the contrary.

This issue first emerged in *Loizidou* v. *Turkey* in which the Greek-Cypriot applicant complained that she was not allowed to access her

[13] *Loizidou* v. *Turkey* (preliminary objections), 23 March 1995, Series A no. 310, para. 75.
[14] *Al-Skeini and Others* v. *the United Kingdom* [GC], no. 55721/07, ECHR 2011, para. 142.
[15] *Loizidou* v. *Turkey* (preliminary objections) (n. 13) para. 15.

property in the territory of the TRNC.[16] She stated that her right to property under Article 1 of Protocol 1 had been violated. Before going into the merits of the case, the Court needed to decide whether Turkey exercised extraterritorial jurisdiction over the TRNC even with the reservation quoted above. Territorial jurisdiction had to be established in two steps. First, the Court had to invalidate the reservation, which it did by referring to European public order. It stated:

> Such a system, which would enable States to qualify their consent [to the jurisdiction of the ECtHR,] would not only seriously weaken the role of the Commission and Court in the discharge of their functions but would also diminish the effectiveness of the Convention as a constitutional instrument of European Public Order (ordre public).[17]

The second step was to establish that Turkey had 'effective overall control' over the TRNC.[18] After considering the military and economic support of Turkey to the TRNC, the Court confirmed the jurisdiction of Turkey over the territory of Northern Cyprus and subsequently found a violation of the applicant's rights. In this case, the reference to European public order was used to ensure that the ECHR was applicable in the territory of one contracting party to the Convention which had been effectively occupied by another contracting party to the Convention.

This issue was further scrutinised by the Court in the interstate case of *Cyprus* v. *Turkey*. Here, the Court emphasised that European public order does not allow the creation of a 'regrettable vacuum in the system of human rights protection'.[19] Those people who appeared to be in the occupied territory should continue to enjoy human rights protection under the Convention because European public order demands it. The Court used the same formula in the more recent case of *Güzelyurtlu and Others* v. *Cyprus and Turkey*.[20]

Another conflict in Europe was between Armenia and Azerbaijan over the Nagorno-Karabakh region which until now remains under the jurisdiction of Armenia.[21] The main hostilities took place before either of the conflicting parties ratified the Convention. Having said that, in 2002

[16] *Loizidou* v. *Turkey* (merits), 18 December 1996, Reports of Judgments and Decisions 1996-VI.
[17] *Loizidou* v. *Turkey* (preliminary objections) (n. 13) para. 75.
[18] *Loizidou* v. *Turkey* (merits) (n. 16) para. 56.
[19] *Cyprus* v. *Turkey* [GC], no. 25781/94, ECHR 2001-IV, para. 78.
[20] *Güzelyurtlu and Others* v. *Cyprus and Turkey* [GC], no. 36925/07, 29 January 2019, para. 193.
[21] This was correct at the moment of drafting in July 2020.

Armenia and Azerbaijan ratified the ECHR and accepted the jurisdiction of the ECtHR; Azerbaijan, however, made a reservation that it would not be able to guarantee human rights in the territory occupied by Armenia. In *Sargsyan* v. *Azerbaijan*,[22] the Court had to consider whether Azerbaijan had jurisdiction over a disputed village which Azerbaijan claimed had been 'rendered inaccessible by the circumstances'.[23] The Court referred to European public order and emphasised that '[w]hen Azerbaijan ratified the Convention on 15 April 2002, the whole of its territory entered the "Convention legal space"'.[24] The Court could not establish effective control over the territory of this village by Armenia, which meant that the only contracting party that remained responsible for the alleged human rights violations in this territory was Azerbaijan. The alternative was for the Court to risk creating an accountability gap, which it was not prepared to do.

To briefly conclude on this first scenario, the Court uses European public order to remind its contracting parties that even if two of them are involved in a military confrontation, the Convention tolerates no gaps in the protection of human rights and the contracting parties will remain responsible for all alleged human rights violations in a disputed territory. Sometimes, the Court makes similar references outside the context of the conflict between two contracting parties, but the idea remains – the Court ensures that European public order secures human rights within the frontiers of its contracting parties.

More recently, the Court referred to European public order in the judgment in *N.D. and N.T.* v. *Spain*.[25] In this case, the Spanish authorities argued that the applicants who jumped over the wall to enter the Spanish territory did not, in fact, do that because they failed to cross a police line. The Court disagreed, pointing out that '[a]s a constitutional instrument of European public order, the Convention cannot be selectively restricted to only parts of the territory of a State by means of an artificial reduction in the scope of its territorial jurisdiction'.[26] While it is correct to argue that the contracting parties should not artificially reduce their responsibility either by creating fully dependent but formally separate entities[27] or by excluding certain territories from the

[22] *Sargsyan* v. *Azerbaijan* [GC], no. 40167/06, ECHR 2015.
[23] Ibid., para. 146.
[24] Ibid., para. 147.
[25] *N.D. and N.T.* v. *Spain [GC]*, nos. 8675/15 and 8697/15, 13 February 2020.
[26] Ibid., para. 110.
[27] As in the case of *TRNC* or the Nagorno-Karabakh Republic.

Court's territorial jurisdiction,[28] it is not entirely clear how references to European public order make this argument any stronger. The Court cannot pretend that it has full jurisdiction over the territory of Europe. It clearly does not have jurisdiction over Belarus as that is not a contracting party to the Convention. Moreover, the role of European public order changes when the contracting parties act outside the borders of the Council of Europe member states. The following analysis examines the second scenario.

In 2001, the Grand Chamber of the Court delivered an admissibility decision in *Banković and Others* v. *Belgium and Others*.[29] The application was brought against the NATO[30] member states that were at the same time contracting parties to the ECHR for alleged human rights violations during the bombings of Belgrade (then Yugoslavia, now Serbia). Sixteen people were killed and another sixteen were seriously injured in the bombing of a TV station. Serbia only ratified the Convention in 2004 and so, at the material time, the ECtHR did not have jurisdiction over this territory. The only way to adjudicate on this case was to establish extraterritorial jurisdiction over the respondent states. It was, in fact, the applicants who first referred to European public order in this case. For them, European public order prevented the Court from leaving 'the applicants without a remedy and the respondent States' armies free to act with impunity'.[31] The Court also referred to European public order but in a different sense, as a limit of the Court's possible supervision outside the borders of Europe. Unlike preventing legal gaps in Europe (the TRNC, for example, was under the de jure ECtHR jurisdiction as part of Cyprus), extraterritorial jurisdiction in *Banković* would result in creating 'islands' of Convention protection outside the territory of the Council of Europe for those people who otherwise would not be under the jurisdiction of the Convention. The Court stated that 'the desirability of avoiding a gap or vacuum in human rights' protection has so far been relied on by the Court in favour of establishing jurisdiction only when the territory in question was one that, but for the specific circumstances, would normally be covered by the Convention'.[32] However, the Court did not rule out the very possibility of extraterritorial application of the ECHR beyond the borders of the Council of Europe

[28] As was done in *N.D and N.T.* v. *Spain* (n. 25).

[29] *Banković and Others* v. *Belgium and Others* (dec.) [GC], no. 52207/99, ECHR 2001-XII.

[30] North Atlantic Treaty Organization.

[31] Banković and Others v. Belgium and Others (n. 29), para. 51.

[32] Ibid., para. 80.

under certain circumstances. According to the ECtHR, in this case, the respondent states did not have 'effective control' over the affected territory. Therefore, the Court declared the application inadmissible for its lack of territorial jurisdiction.

Banković was not the last application in which the Court was asked to look beyond the geographical borders of the Council of Europe. On 20 March 2003, a coalition of armed forces, led by the USA with a large force from the UK and smaller contingents from Australia and Poland, commenced the invasion of Iraq. In a series of cases, the ECtHR had to decide whether European members of the coalition had jurisdiction over the relevant parts of Iraq. In *Al-Saadoon and Mufdhi* v. *the United Kingdom*, the Chamber of the Court decided that the territorial jurisdiction of a contracting party might be extended to a place such as a detention centre even if it was outside the borders of the respondent state.[33] The applicants in this case were arrested by the British troops in Iraq and detained in various detention facilities run by the UK. The British government argued that the fact that the Court was designed to create European public order precluded it from expanding its territorial jurisdiction beyond the legal space of the contracting parties.[34] This argument is akin to what the ECtHR itself stated in *Banković*. In *Al-Saadoon and Mufdhi*, the ECtHR ruled that there were special circumstances under which extraterritorial application of the Convention would be justifiable. The Court established that the UK had effective control over the territory on which these events had taken place. It seems that the Court was prepared to go beyond European public order if there were compelling reasons for it. The Court was more concerned with the fact that the detention facilities were clearly under the control of the UK and therefore declared the application admissible. The Court subsequently found multiple violations of the Convention in this case.[35]

In *Al-Skeini and others* v. *the United Kingdom*, the Court elaborated on its understanding of European public order in the circumstances of extraterritorial application of the Convention.[36] This application concerned the killing of six persons by British soldiers in Iraq. Here, the respondent government emphasised predominantly 'European' and 'territorial' meanings of European public order:

[33] *Al-Saadoon and Mufdhi* v. *the United Kingdom*, no. 61498/08, ECHR 2010.
[34] Ibid., para. 79.
[35] Ibid.
[36] *Al-Skeini and Others* v. *the United Kingdom* [GC] (n. 14).

> [T]he Convention was 'an instrument of European Public Order' and 'a multilateral treaty operating, subject to Article 56 of the Convention, in an essentially regional context and notably in the legal space (*espace juridique*) of the Contracting States'. The essentially territorial basis of jurisdiction reflected principles of international law and took account of the practical and legal difficulties faced by a State operating on another State's territory, particularly in regions which did not share the values of the Council of Europe Member States.[37]

The Court agreed with the argument of the UK government, pointing out that '[t]he Convention is a constitutional instrument of European public order. It does not govern the actions of states [that are] not parties to it, nor does it purport to be a means of requiring the contracting states to impose Convention standards on other states.'[38] This statement seems obvious; the first thing that law students learn about international law is that international treaties traditionally apply only to the states which ratified them (principle of relative effect). However, the Court was quick to acknowledge that European public order does not prevent it from applying the Convention extraterritorially by claiming that it has never ruled 'that jurisdiction under Article 1 of the Convention can never exist outside the territory covered by the Council of Europe Member States. The Court has not in its case-law applied any such restriction'.[39] In this case, the Court suggested that when the contracting party has exercised 'public powers' on the occupied territory, then it has jurisdiction over this territory. This means that European public order does not automatically prevent the Court from going beyond Europe. As such, the Court can set aside the considerations supported by European public order. This is somewhat problematic as, in some other instances, the Court has emphasised that arguments supported by European public order are of the greatest importance. It seems that the Court perceives the value of European public order as uneven: while European public order is of utmost importance for the contracting parties, the Court itself is designed to establish its content and even toss it aside if the Court deems it necessary.

What seems even more problematic is inconsistency in referring to European public order in the context of the first scenario, namely when European public order was used by the Court to 'cement' the legal space

[37] Ibid., para. 109.
[38] Ibid., para. 141.
[39] Ibid., para. 142.

of the Convention, occasionally allowing it to spread outside but never to rupture its fabric. As mentioned, there are important cases of extraterritorial application in which there is no mention of European public order. *Ilaşcu and Others* v. *Moldova and Russia*[40] was decided by the ECtHR after *Loizidou* v. *Turkey*,[41] and the situation in terms of territorial jurisdiction was somewhat similar in these cases. The Moldovan Republic of Transnistria is a *de jure* part of Moldova which was controlled by the Russian troops. While establishing that Russia had jurisdiction over the territory of Transnistria, the Court referred to *Loizidou*. It did not, however, mention European public order which was seemingly quite instrumental in the construction of the jurisdiction of Turkey over the TRNC. In *Ilaşcu*, the Court again avoided creating a legal vacuum and ruled that Russia was responsible for human rights in Transnistria; it then found multiple violations. Similarly, European public order was not mentioned in the subsequent case of *Catan* v. *Moldova and Russia*,[42] although it was referred to in the more recent case on the same issue, *Mozer* v. *Russian and Moldova*,[43] while again it was omitted in *Sandu and Others* v. *the Republic of Moldova and Russia*.[44]

In the case of *Chiragov* v. *Armenia*, which dealt with the Nagorno-Karabakh conflict and was published on the same day as *Sargsyan* v. *Azerbaijan*, there were no references to European public order even though they would have been arguably more appropriate in *Chiragov* than in *Sargsyan*. In the former judgment, the Court established the extraterritorial jurisdiction of Armenia over the Nagorno-Karabakh region – a situation that resembled the Turkish jurisdiction over the TRNC and the Russian jurisdiction over Transnistria. In its reasoning, the Court used the principles of territorial jurisdiction it had established in *Al-Skeini* without considering the implications of European public order. Only Judge Ziemele in her partly dissenting, partly concurring opinion reminded the Court about its ambition to prevent a Convention vacuum in Europe, but neither did she explicitly mention European public order.[45]

[40] *Ilaşcu and Others* v. *Moldova and Russia* (n. 10).
[41] *Loizidou* v. *Turkey* (n. 13).
[42] *Catan and Others* v. *the Republic of Moldova and Russia* [GC], nos. 43370/04, 8252/05 and 18454/06, ECHR 2012.
[43] *Mozer* v. *the Republic of Moldova and Russia* [GC], no. 11138/10, 23 February 2016, para. 136.
[44] *Sandu and Others* v. *the Republic of Moldova and Russia*, nos. 21034/05 and 7 others, 17 July 2018.
[45] *Al-Skeini and Others* v. *the United Kingdom* (n. 14) Dissenting Opinion of Judge Ziemele.

It appears that there are at least three plausible explanations for the failure to refer to European public order in the abovementioned judgments. First, the drafting lawyers did not think it is important or useful to include relevant paragraphs in the judgments and thought that the point about territorial jurisdiction had been well made even without references to European public order. Alternatively, the omissions are merely coincidental. The second explanation is less technical but also less advantageous for the usability of European public order as a legal concept. This explanation indicates that the Court did not really see great legal value in its declaratory statements on European public order and felt that references to it would not change the outcome of the case anyway. I argued in Chapter 1 that the population of judgments with terms that do not have clear consequential value for the Court's reasoning might have a negative effect on the legitimacy of the Court. Finally, one can suggest that it was a principled omission, but it is hard to see the principled reason behind such omission. In any case, it seems that the Court might want to clarify its approach to the jurisdictional meaning of European public order and its role in the reasoning behind it.

European public order is used as the border guard of the Convention, which ensures that it is effective within the boundaries of the Council of Europe and does not spread outside them without good reason. Although this meaning of European public order is comparatively straightforward, some consistency of the Court's reasoning in this area is necessary. Moreover, the Court needs to shed more light on *what* particular aspect or meaning of European public order helps to secure the territorial application of the ECHR.

2.3 Interaction between the ECtHR and Other International Organisations

The Court used references to European public order in its judgments in which the ECHR overlapped with the practice of other international organisations, courts and tribunals. Another aspect of the same challenge occurs when the contracting parties have conflicting obligations under the ECHR and other international treaties. The contracting parties to the Convention are obliged to comply with the rights enshrined in the ECHR and, at the same time, some of the contracting parties have to comply with their obligations as members of other regional (for example, the European Union) or international (for example, the United Nations) organisations or treaties. This state of affairs can cause conflicts when such obligations appear to be in contradiction. Should the ECtHR find a violation of the Convention if the contracting party properly complied with an obligation under another international treaty? The answer to this question is highly contestable and has generated a significant amount of academic commentary.[46] It is somewhat similar to the territorial jurisdiction as it helps to identify the realm of the Court's application – its *espace juridique* – which is concerned not only with its geographical application but also with its prevalence, authority and exclusivity on this territory.

The Court referred to European public order in the context of interaction between the ECHR and other international bodies in thirteen judgments. For example, in *Bosphorus* v. *Ireland*, the Irish authorities implemented the EU sanctions imposed on former Yugoslavia and impounded an aeroplane which was leased by the applicant company from the Yugoslavian airlines.[47] The legal question in this case was whether the respondent state can be responsible for an alleged violation of the Convention right to property by implementing a decision of another international organisation, which in this case was the European Union. The Court established here a presumption in favour of the legality of such actions of a contracting party to the Convention if another international organisation offers an 'equivalent' protection of human rights to the one set under the Convention.[48] This means that the Court would first consider the overall level of protection of human rights that an international organisation can secure. If this level is compatible with the level enforced by the ECtHR, it will apply a 'light

[46] See, for example, Vassilis Tzevelekos, 'When Elephants Fight It Is the Grass that Suffers: "Hegemonic Struggle" in Europe and the Side-Effects for International Law' in Kanstantsin Dzehtsiarou et al. (eds.), *Human Rights Law in Europe: The Influence, Overlaps and Contradictions of the EU and the ECHR* (Routledge 2014); Arman Mansoorian, 'Splitting the Baby: Incidental Review of United Nations Security Council Resolutions by the European Court of Human Rights' (2016) *IOLR* 169; Sébastien Platon, 'The "Equivalent Protection Test": From European Union to United Nations, from Solange II to Solange I (with reference to the Al-Dulimi and Montana Management Inc. v Switzerland Judgment of the European Court of Human Rights)' (2014) *EuConst* 226; Cerric Ryngaert, 'Oscillating between Embracing and Avoiding Bosphorus: The European Court of Human Rights on Member State Responsibility for Acts of International Organisations and the Case of the EU' (2014) 39 *ELR* 176; Johannes Masing, 'Unity and Diversity of European Fundamental Rights Protection' (2016) 41 *ELR* 490.

[47] *Bosphorus Hava Yolları Turizm ve Ticaret Anonim Şirketi* v. *Ireland* [GC], no. 45036/98, ECHR 2005-VI.

[48] Ibid., para. 155.

touch approach' in the assessment of the situation at hand. The Court justified the need for such a presumption by referring to 'the interest of international cooperation'.[49]

European public order in this context is a counterweighing consideration of international co-operation. The Court pointed out that if the protection of human rights by another international organisation is manifestly deficient, 'the interest of international co-operation would be outweighed by the Convention's role as a "constitutional instrument of European public order" in the field of human rights'.[50] This means that international co-operation is a value that should be protected unless such protection goes against European public order. This role of European public order is somewhat similar to how public order is used in private international law.[51] The Court here would allow the application of norms that emanate from other legal orders unless they interfere with the core of protection allowed by the Convention. The key challenge here is how to draw the line of what should be considered as this core. The Court is conveniently ambiguous on that matter.

The Court continued to refer to European public order in its following judgments dealing with EU law. In *Michaud* v. *France*, the Court clarified the rationale behind the *Bosphorus* presumption.[52] It seems that this rationale is similar to the one discussed in relation to the territorial jurisdiction of the Court. The Court's understanding of European public order prevents it from creating gaps in legal protection within the *espace juridique* of the Convention. The Court stated:

> [A]bsolving the Contracting States completely from their Convention responsibility where they were simply complying with their obligations as members of an international organisation to which they had transferred a part of their sovereignty would be incompatible with the purpose and object of the Convention: the guarantees of the Convention could be limited or excluded at will, thereby depriving it of its peremptory character and undermining the practical and effective nature of its safeguards.[53]

This discussion makes a clear connection with the requirement of European public order not to allow any lawless zones in human rights protection in Europe. In the recent case of *Avotiņš* v. *Latvia*, the Court

[49] Ibid., para. 155.

[50] Ibid., para. 156. See also *Behrami* v. *France* and *Saramati* v. *France, Germany and Norway*, 71412/01, (2007) 45 EHRR. SE10, para. 145.

[51] See Chapter 3 for a detailed discussion of public order in private international law.

[52] *Michaud* v. *France*, no. 12323/11, ECHR 2012.

[53] Ibid., para. 102.

further enquired into the mechanism for preventing such zones. The ECtHR stated:

> [If] a serious and substantiated complaint is raised before [the national courts of the contracting parties] to the effect that the protection of a Convention right has been manifestly deficient and ... this situation cannot be remedied by European Union law, they cannot refrain from examining that complaint on the sole ground that they are applying EU law.[54]

This means that the ECtHR exercises a certain degree of deference towards EU law, but European public order does not allow it to give it a carte blanche and leave human rights in some areas without protection.

The EU is not the only international organisation which can impose certain obligations on the contracting parties to the ECHR. In some cases, obligations stemming from their membership in other international organisations or from participation in international treaties can potentially interfere with the rights enshrined in the Convention. In the Court's judgment in the joint case of *Behrami and Behrami* v. *France* and *Saramati* v. *France, Germany and Norway*,[55] the Court considered who was responsible for alleged human rights violations in Kosovo. The UK government, which acted as a third party in this case, made a relevant submission here:

> The application raised fundamental questions about the relationship between the Convention (a regional treaty and 'constitutional instrument of European Public Order') and the universal system for the maintenance of international peace in which the Council of Europe played an important part. To superimpose that regional human rights' structure upon a peace keeping force established by the universal organisation would be inappropriate as a matter of principle and run counter to the *ordre public* to which the Court frequently referred and, further, risked causing serious difficulties to Contracting States in participating in UN and other multinational peacekeeping operations outside the territories of the Convention States.[56]

It is not entirely clear why 'superimposition' of human rights will go against *ordre public*. The UK government failed to explain this or the explanation did not find its way into the final judgment. It appears that the UK authorities tried to emphasise the regional character of European public order, which should not spill over the borders of the

[54] *Avotiņš* v. *Latvia*, no. 17502/07, 25 February 2014, para. 116.
[55] *Behrami* v. *France* and *Saramati* v. *France, Germany and Norway* (n. 50).
[56] Ibid., para. 115.

Council of Europe member states. It used the same tactic in the previously discussed *Al-Skeini* case. In *Behrami* and *Saramati*, the Court referred to European public order but in a slightly different sense than the one used by the UK authorities. The Court effectively repeated the *Bosphorus* presumption, stating that it can be rebutted only if 'the interest of international cooperation would be outweighed by the Convention's role as a constitutional instrument of European public order in the field of human rights'.[57] Having said that, in this case the Court decided that the applications by *Behrami and Saramati* were inadmissible.

The issue of European public order was the centre of attention in the Grand Chamber judgment in *Al-Dulimi and Montana Management Inc.* v. *Switzerland*.[58] In this case, the Court shed some light on the circumstances under which the requirements of European public order can trump the *Bosphorus* presumption. The applicants complained that the so-called 'smart sanctions' that were imposed by the UN Security Council and administered by Switzerland violated the applicants' rights under the ECHR. In execution of these sanctions, Switzerland had frozen the assets of the applicants; this was allegedly done in violation of Article 6 of the ECHR on the right to a fair trial. The Court found a violation of the Convention because the sanctions were imposed in breach of the rule of law which is a 'fundamental component' of European public order.[59] It means that, in this case, the Court found sufficient reasons to trump the international co-operation considerations.

References to European public order played a key role in the concurring opinion by Judge Pinto de Albuquerque, joined by Judges Dedov, Hadjiev and Pejchal. The concurring judges first established that the alleged violation in this case went to the heart of European public order – which consists of 'basic and non-negotiable values'. The concurring judges not only established what the content of European public order was but also examined the consequences of interference of international law with European public order. The judges ambitiously claimed:

> [T]he Convention is subordinated neither to domestic constitutional rules, nor to allegedly higher rules of international law, since it is the supreme law of the European continent. In the Council of Europe's own internal hierarchy of norms, United Nations law is equal to any other international agreement and

[57] Ibid., para. 145.
[58] *Al-Dulimi and Montana Management Inc.* v. *Switzerland*, no. 5809/08, 26 November 2013.
[59] Ibid., para. 145.

subordinated to the primacy of the Convention as a constitutional instrument of European Public Order. From this derives the nature of the Court as the European Constitutional Court . . . .[60]

It appears that, for the concurring judges, the Court's claim that it creates European public order means that it has superior legal status over any other international obligations that the contracting parties to the Convention might have. Such assumption forces the contracting parties to make difficult choices because other international treaties also make claims of superiority and this is especially the case in relation to the EU. These competing claims for superiority weaken the claim of the ECtHR as a constructer of European public order. Moreover, this monograph argues that these claims are problematic from the point of view of the Court's legitimacy. The operation of the Court clearly has a considerable impact on European public order, but this impact is not made by the Court single-handedly; it is produced in collaboration with many other actors such as the contracting parties, the Committee of Ministers, etc.

It appears that the Court claims to have the authority to review the activities of contracting parties to the Convention carried out in execution of their obligations under other international legal regimes in two situations: first, when the provisions of international law allow a certain level of discretion for contracting parties, in which case the Court can consider whether the way that discretion was used is compatible with the Convention;[61] and second, when the overall level of human rights protection provided by the organisation concerned is not equivalent or such protection is manifestly deficient. In both situations, European public order seems to present a justification for the Court's interference in international co-operation. It is perhaps correct

[60] Ibid. Concurring Opinion Judge Pinto de Albuquerque joined by Judges Dedov, Hadjiev and Pejchal, paras. 59–60. One needs to note that Judge Pinto de Albuquerque was a consistent supporter of the ECtHR as ultimate decision-maker of human rights in Europe. For instance, in *Hutchinson* v. *the UK*, Judge Pinto de Albuquerque argued:

> [D]omestic authorities, courts included, must act in a way that coheres with the principle of *pacta sunt servanda* and therefore comply with the letter and abide by the principles underlying the Court's judgments and decisions, including those delivered against other Contracting Parties. As administrators of first resort of the Convention, the domestic authorities must therefore be deferential to the final say of the Court, which is entrusted with the uniform upholding of the 'constitutional instrument of European public order'. (*Hutchinson* v. *the United Kingdom* [GC], no. 57592/08, 17 January 2017. Dissenting Opinion of Judge Pinto de Albuquerque, para. 45)

[61] *Neulinger and Shuruk* v. *Switzerland* [GC], no. 41615/07, ECHR 2010, paras. 133–4.

to argue that contracting parties should not use their obligations under other treaties or stemming from international organisations as a justification for clear human rights violations. However, European public order might not be the best reason for that as the contracting parties might argue that the principle of *pacta sunt servanda* is also a fundamental element of European public order, meaning that they also need to comply with other international treaties. In other words, it seems that European public order does not really help to resolve conflicts of laws in these circumstances.

To sum up, the Court's reasons for deploying European public order in a legal jurisdictional sense are fairly straightforward: the Court leaves no area in which human rights could be violated when it has had no opportunity to review the actions of the government in that area. The Court is fully aware of the fact that the ECHR is not the only international obligation of the contracting parties and therefore it needs to leave the states with a certain margin of appreciation to allow them to comply with all relevant international obligations. However, if a violation creates a threat to European public order, then the Court can act even if the contracting party acted in compliance with its other international obligations. The key challenge of this application of European public order is quite familiar, namely, it is not possible to establish its content or set any parameters that the contracting parties can use to identify what actions would interfere with European public order. As this section demonstrated, sometimes the respondent states use European public order in a sense that contradicts the Court's understanding of the concept;[62] this might not be done *mala fide* but is more likely to be due to the lack of a commonly accepted approach to European public order.

2.4 Extent of the Binding Force of the Court's Interim Measures

The Court uses references to European public order in cases in which the contracting party failed to comply with interim measures given by

[62] Apart from the argument submitted by the UK government in *Behrami* and *Saramati* discussed earlier in this chapter, the judgment in *Garib* v. *the Netherlands* is a useful illustration of a crucially different approach to public order between the judges of the Court and the respondent state. *Garib* v. *the Netherlands [GC]*, no. 43494/09, 6 November 2017, especially in the Dissenting Opinion of Judge Pinto De Albuquerque Joined by Judge Vehabović, para. 9.

the ECtHR. In this context, the role of European public order is to justify the expansion of the ECtHR's procedural competences by stating that otherwise its role as a guardian of European public order could not be effectively undertaken. It seems that the Court considers effective human rights protection to be a key element of European public order and therefore its interim measures, which are not provided for in the ECHR, should be binding on the contracting parties. I will come back to discussing interim measures in Chapter 5.

The Court has referred to European public order in this context in eight cases only, and in all of these cases Russia was a respondent state – although Russia is not the only contracting party to the Convention that has violated interim measures.[63] Before going into the details of how these references were made, this section first gives a brief general overview of interim measures in the case law of the ECtHR.

The key purpose of interim measures is to ensure the effectiveness of human rights adjudication.[64] Interim measures should be used to prevent clearly defined irreparable harm[65] in order to maintain human rights practically and effectively.[66] Such interim measures guarantee that human rights adjudication remains meaningful and leaves the option for the parties to resort to *restitutio in integrum* if acts of the respondent party are found to be in breach of the rights enshrined in the Convention.[67] The vast majority of interim measures are of a negative character; they oblige the respondent state not to worsen the situation of the applicant.[68] More rarely, the contracting parties are asked to undertake certain positive actions such as transferring a prisoner to a civil hospital.[69]

[63] The PACE report has listed those countries which have breached interim measures of the Court; Italy, Russia, the UK and the Slovak Republic are among them. See Council of Europe PACE Report Preventing harm to refugees and migrants in extradition and expulsion cases: Rule 39 indications by the European Court of Human Rights, Doc. 12435 (November 2010).

[64] *Mamatkulov and Askarov* v. *Turkey*, Applications no. 46827/99 and 46951/99, Judgment of 4 February 2005, para. 102. See also Henrik Jorem, 'Protecting Human Rights in Cases of Urgency: Interim Measures and the Right of Individual Application under Article 34 ECHR' (2012) 30 *NJHR* 404, 413.

[65] *Mamatkulov and Askarov* v. *Turkey* (n. 64) para. 104.

[66] Ibid., para. 108.

[67] George Letsas, 'International Human Rights and the Binding Force of Interim Measures' (2003) *EHRLR* 527, 530.

[68] Extradition or deportation.

[69] See *Aleksanyan* v. *Russia*, no. 46468/06, 22 December 2008.

Interim measures can achieve their purpose of ensuring the effectiveness of human rights adjudication only if they are considered legally binding and are routinely followed by the contracting parties to the Convention. For a long time, the question of whether interim measures are in fact legally binding on the contracting parties was disputed. The Court settled this in the case of *Mamatkulov and Askarov* v. *Turkey*.[70] Basing its judgment on the case law of the International Court of Justice,[71] the Inter-American Court of Human Rights,[72] the United Nations Committee against Torture[73] and the Human Rights Committee of the United Nations,[74] the Court ruled that interim measures are legally binding and their violation would almost automatically lead to breach of Article 34 of the Convention. Although that judgment established that the Convention 'creates, over and above a network of mutual, bilateral undertakings, objective obligations which, in the words of the Preamble, benefit from a "collective enforcement"',[75] the Court did not explicitly refer to European public order in this case, although that would be logical if the Court sees interim measures as being crucial for maintaining European public order.

Even before *Mamatkulov*, the Court's interim measures enjoyed a high level of compliance. The compliance rate with interim measures has been more than 99 per cent, while each instance of non-compliance triggered an immediate negative reaction from the Court.[76] This means that the formal legal status of interim measures as binding is not the main reason for their effectiveness. Having said that, the contracting parties might argue that the ECtHR's decision about interim measures does not live up to the standard of a properly reasoned judicial decision,[77] and therefore should not be enforced. Sometimes, state

[70] *Mamatkulov and Askarov* v. *Turkey* (n. 64).

[71] Ibid., para. 117.

[72] Ibid., para. 116.

[73] Ibid., para. 115.

[74] Ibid., para. 114.

[75] Ibid., para. 100.

[76] Yves Haeck, Clara Burbano Herrera and Leo Zwaak, 'Strasbourg's Interim Measures under Fire: Does the Rising Number of State Incompliances with Interim Measures Pose a Threat to the European Court of Human Rights?' (2011) *Eur Yearbook Hum Rights* 375, 380.

[77] Haeck, Burbano Herrera and Zwaak quote the Italian Minister of Internal Affairs:

> We respect the European Court's decisions, and I stress decisions. However, when I receive a fax from an official that says that it is necessary to suspend the expulsion while awaiting the Court's decision, I prefer to continue and expel an alleged terrorist. We cannot await the slowness of the Court, whose decisions we are nonetheless willing

representatives emphasise the lack of formal consent from the contracting parties.[78]

Although interim measures can hardly be regarded as a 'novel instrument' available to the Court, the Court has only recently started to link them with European public order. According to my data, the first judgment in which European public order was mentioned in relation to interim measures was *Savriddin Dzhuraev* v. *Russia*.[79] In this case, the applicant was forcibly removed from the territory of Russia despite the interim measures issued by the ECtHR forbidding his extradition. While the Russian authorities denied their involvement, the Court has nevertheless established that the applicant was kidnapped by the authorities and transferred away from the territory of Russia. In these circumstances, the Court stated that 'utmost importance [should] be attached to the question of the State Parties' compliance with interim measures'.[80] The reference to European public order was seemingly designed to underpin its importance:

> Any laxity on this question would unacceptably weaken the protection of the Convention core rights and would not be compatible with its values and spirit; it would also be inconsistent with the fundamental importance of the right of individual application and, more generally, undermine the authority and effectiveness of the Convention as a constitutional instrument of European Public Order.[81]

The Court used the same reasoning in seven other cases against Russia in which it had violated interim measures. These references to European public order may have been only a rhetorical statement that Russian lawyers of the Court's Registry invented to sound more plausible without delving too much into the meaning of these references. The fact that European public order is mentioned only in cases against Russia, although Russia is not the only contracting party that has violated interim measures instructed by the Court, might substantiate this suggestion. In Chapter 6, I argue that European public order can move randomly from one case and context to another. I call this movement

to receive. However, while awaiting their arrival, we apply our law. We have done so now and will continue to do it. (Ibid., 390)

[78] Eva Rieter, *Preventing Irreparable Harm: Provisional Measures in International Human Rights Adjudication* (Intersentia 2010) 989.

[79] *Savriddin Dzhurayev* v. *Russia*, no. 71386/10, ECHR 2013.

[80] Ibid., para. 213.

[81] Ibid.

the Brownian motion of legal terms; the deployment of European public order in cases related to interim measures is perhaps an example of this motion. European public order is not indispensable to explaining the binding force of interim measures, as my discussion of the judgment in *Mamatkulov and Askarov* v. *Turkey* suggests.[82] Moreover, the fact that these references are present only in the cases against Russia suggests the strong influence of the personality of the drafting lawyers and the section of the Court by which these cases were decided. This, however, is not the only possible explanation.

If one accepts that references to European public order play a role that is more than merely rhetorical, then one needs to consider what this role might be. The most plausible explanation of references to European public order is that here they play the role of a justification that would counter potential claims of the illegitimacy of interim measures. Their role is to emphasise the importance of interim measures. As mentioned, the Court does not have a clear and unambiguous legal mandate to even issue these measures, let alone penalise contracting parties for their non-execution. Interim measures cannot be found in the ECHR and it is not an accidental omission – the contracting parties have discussed it and explicitly rejected their inclusion in the Convention.[83] Although the drafters of new Protocols thought that such an inclusion was not necessary as interim measures already enjoyed a high level of compliance, the contracting parties have not explicitly agreed to be bound by them and, therefore, the member states can claim that they should not be found in violation of the Convention as a result of breaching interim measures. It appears that the Court asserts that references to European public order will justify what one might consider an expansion of its authority.

The Convention needs to be effective to be a 'constitutional instrument of European Public Order'.[84] This raises the question of how exactly unenforced interim measures would undermine European public order. The Court has a separate doctrine of effective human rights

[82] *Mamatkulov and Askarov* v. *Turkey* (n. 64).

[83] The issue of inclusion of interim measures into the text of the ECHR 'was discussed in the late 1940s when the original Convention was drafted and the drafters did not include a provision that would give the power to issue precautionary measures to the Court and/or the Commission. This issue was again discussed in the 1970s but was again rejected by the Committee of Ministers'. Kanstantsin Dzehtsiarou, 'Can the European Court of Human Rights Prevent War? Interim Measures in Inter-state Cases' (2016) *PL* 254, 256.

[84] *Loizidou* v. *Turkey* (n. 13) para. 75.

which one can argue is part of the interpretative toolkit of the ECtHR.[85] It seems that references to European public order do not add much to it. Here, these two doctrines overlap and European public order seems unnecessary.

The Court appears to highlight that ensuring compliance with interim measures is important enough to refer to European public order. Unlike in cases in which the Court shaped the Court's jurisdiction, the interim measures judgments arguably do not have much added value for building the public order of the ECtHR. These judgments are repetitive and deal with issues which are quite well-established under ECtHR case law. All Russian judgments in which European public order was mentioned are about illegal extraditions or deportations. The Court has a very extensive case law on this issue; these cases do not develop the Court's key standards of European public order understood as an analytical concept. At the same time, the Russian cases deal with situations where the authorities not only violate the interim measures but also deny their involvement.

A preliminary conclusion can be drawn from this discussion. There are very few mechanisms available to the Court that allow it to influence ongoing or potential violation of human rights. Usually, the ECtHR comes to the case when the damage is done and the situation has already been considered by domestic authorities. Interim measures are important because they can change the course of events rather than providing a *post factum* remedy. The Court is so concerned with its authority in this area that any action or omission of the contracting parties that could potentially undermine its authority in relation to interim measures might contradict European public order. In this sense, it is not material how important the case at hand is or what is at stake for the applicant. Instead, the reason behind European public order is a claim for authority. However having in mind the vagueness of this term, the foundation of this legal claim is not particularly clear.

2.5 Criteria of Admissibility

According to Article 35 of the ECHR, every application submitted to the Court should comply with certain 'formal' rules. These include that the

[85] The ECtHR stated on a number of occasions that '[t]he Convention is intended to guarantee not rights that are theoretical or illusory but rights that are practical and effective'. *Airey* v. *Ireland*, 9 October 1979, Series A no. 32, para. 24.

applicant must exhaust all domestic remedies before bringing his or her case before the Court; he or she should submit an application no later than six months after the final decision of the national authorities; and such an application should not be repetitive or manifestly ill-founded.[86] If the applicant fails to comply with any one of these rules, the application will be declared inadmissible and the Court proceedings will be discontinued. The decision of inadmissibility is final and cannot be appealed against. Although meeting the admissibility criteria is crucial for success in the ECtHR - up to 90 per cent of applications are declared inadmissible - those criteria rarely come under the spotlight of academic attention.[87] This is perhaps the case because the criteria are considered formal and do not appear to leave much space for discretion or judicial creativity. However, this is not always the case - some decisions on admissibility can easily be confused with the Court's judgments on merits.[88]

In the Court's reasoning concerning admissibility, European public order acts as a trump card that allows the Court to adjudicate an application even when it should be declared inadmissible. I will call this phenomenon the 'trump card assumption'. This is important because the Court in effect uses European public order as a legal source which is superior to the text of the Convention. Let me explain the logic behind this argument. The Court points out that it will be able to depart from the clear wording of the Convention if European public order justifies it. In

[86] Article 35 ECHR.

[87] In 2014 only 7,895 applications were communicated to the respondent parties and more than 56,000 applications were submitted to the Court. In 2015 the statistical data changed due to some administrative reforms, but the number of inadmissible applications is still high: 40,650 applications were registered and 15,965 were communicated to the respondent states. Analysis of statistics 2015 (Strasbourg 2016) available at http://echr.coe.int/Documents/Stats_analysis_2015_ENG.pdf.

[88] In some instances, those cases that are declared manifestly ill-founded and therefore inadmissible by the ECtHR are not only accepted by other international tribunals but violations are found. In the case of *Mann Singh* v. *France* (ECHR, 13/11/2008/, no. 4479/07) the ECtHR considered if the French ban to appear bareheaded on the official photographs is compatible with the freedom of religion of the followers of the Singh religion who are obliged to wear a Turban. The ECtHR conducted a proportionality analysis; it decided that, in the interests of public safety, religious rights can be limited and declared this application manifestly ill-founded. The same applicant brought a complaint about the same matter to the Human Rights Committee (Communication No. 1928/2010 (*Shingara Mann Singh* v. *France*) HRC, 26/09/2013, CCPR/C/108/D/1928/2010) - the UN body that supervises implementation of the International Covenant of Civil and Political Rights. Article 18 of the Covenant contains freedom to manifest religion similar to what Article 9 of the ECHR provides. The Human Rights Committee declared this application admissible and found a violation of the Covenant in this case.

other words, an application can violate the six months rule[89] but still be declared admissible because European public order demands it.

The Court has used European public order in relation to admissibility in two senses. First is when the application is apparently inadmissible but the Court must nevertheless deal with it for reasons of European public order. This sense fits very well with the 'trump card assumption' because the Court adjudicates an application despite it being inadmissible. Second, in the more recent cases, is when the Court justified rejection of applications in which the applicants did not suffer significant disadvantage, as such applications distract the Court from cases which are capable of shaping European public order. This meaning, therefore, sits less comfortably with the 'trump card assumption'. I discuss these two scenarios next.

I identified twenty judgments in which the Court made references to European public order in connection with admissibility criteria. In this context, the Court started referring to European public order from its very early judgments but did so very sporadically. Until 2011, the Court used European public order only as a justification for a possible disregard of inadmissibility of an application, in other words, it used the first scenario outlined earlier. This can be explained by the fact that at the beginning of the Court's history its docket was very limited. The Court needed more cases to start its full operation. In 1962, the Court delivered a decision of admissibility in the case of *De Becker* v. *Belgium*.[90] In this case, the applicant complained that his freedom of expression had been violated by Belgium. The applicant was convicted for collaboration with the Nazi regime and then released under the condition that he would not engage in journalism. However, by the time this case reached the ECtHR, Belgium had already changed its law and these restrictions were effectively lifted. Therefore, the Court accepted the Commission's suggestion that continuation of the proceedings was in the interests of neither European public order nor the applicant.[91] This means that the Commission considered European public order to be a trumping argument that would allow it to continue adjudication even if the formal criteria of admissibility were not met.

Much later, in 1996, the Court used the same formula in the case of *Paez* v. *Sweden*.[92] In this case, the applicant complained that if he was deported back to Peru he would be subjected to inhuman and degrading

[89] Article 35 ECHR.
[90] *De Becker* v. *Belgium*, 27 March 1962, Series A no. 4.
[91] Ibid., para. 25.
[92] *Paez* v. *Sweden*, 30 October 1997, Reports of Judgments and Decisions 1997-VII.

treatment. However, in the meantime, the Swedish authorities granted him permission to stay and he effectively lost his victim status for the purposes of Article 3 of the Convention. The Court stated:

> [T]he Court discerns no reason of *ordre public* (public policy) for continuing the proceedings. In this respect it is to be noted that in several previous cases the Court has had the opportunity to rule on the responsibility under the Convention of a Contracting State where it has been alleged that there are substantial grounds for believing that the person concerned, if expelled or extradited, would face a real risk of being subjected to torture or to inhuman or degrading treatment or punishment in the country of destination.[93]

Here, the Court considered whether there were any reasons that would justify continuation of this case. What could those reasons be? In which circumstances would the Court be happy to continue its proceedings despite the application not being formally in compliance with the admissibility criteria? The Convention does not explicitly allow the Court any discretion over this stage. It appears that the Court sees European public order as a justification for departing from the wording of the ECHR. Having said that, in both cases the Court did not find any reasons to accept a seemingly inadmissible application. In a number of other instances, the Court dealt with the merits of cases that were inadmissible *strictu sensu*, even without any references to European public order.[94] Again, reference to European public order does not have much legal meaning here. First, the Court can depart from the strict rules of admissibility without any reference to European public order. Second, it is unclear what substantive elements of European public order could actually help the Court to turn an inadmissible case into an admissible one.

Between 1962[95] and 2010, the Court mentioned European public order in only three cases. In none of them could European public order trump the Court's conclusion that the application was inadmissible. Moreover, with an increased backlog of applications, the Court opted for simplification, rather than complication, of its admissibility procedure. As such, considering whether an inadmissible application could be admitted for reasons of European public order became unnecessarily burdensome.

93 Ibid., para. 30.

94 See, for example, *Centre for Legal Resources on behalf of Valentin Câmpeanu* v. *Romania* [GC], no. 47848/08, ECHR 2014. In this case the applicant was not strictly speaking the victim of an alleged violation.

95 The judgment in *De Becker* v. *Belgium* was delivered in 1962.

When Protocol 14 came into force in 2010, the Court started using European public order as a justification for rejecting inadmissible applications. This Protocol added a new admissibility criterion to the Convention. According to Article 35(3) of the Convention, the application should be declared inadmissible if the applicant has not suffered a significant disadvantage, unless respect for human rights, as defined in the Convention, requires an examination of the application on the merits. As such, the Court used European public order to justify application of this criterion, which was designed to clear the Court's docket of unimportant applications in order to reserve more resources for more serious ones.

The Court referred to European public order in connection with this admissibility criterion in nine cases between 2010 and 2014. The increased frequency of deployment of European public order in connection with admissibility criteria after Protocol 14 came into force can be explained by the fact that European public order is mentioned in the Explanatory Report to the Protocol. This states:

> [T]he purpose of this amendment is to provide the Court with an additional tool which should assist it in its filtering work and allow it to devote more time to cases which warrant examination on the merits, whether seen from the perspective of the legal interest of the individual applicant or considered from the broader perspective of the law of the Convention and the European Public Order to which it contributes.[96]

The two aspects of European public order appear to be emphasised in this quote. First, European public order can act as a justification if the Court decides to adjudicate on a case, even if an individual did not suffer a significant disadvantage. This understanding is similar to the 'trumping card' role of European public order explained earlier. Second, this admissibility criterion itself allows the Court to reject applications because it prescribes the Court to deal with more important applications through which it can frame European public order. The first aspect is more practical as it allows the Court to declare an application inadmissible unless European public order prevents it. The second aspect justifies rejection because the Court has to prioritise those applications that are somehow connected to European public order. In one of its early decisions after Protocol 14 entered into force, the Court emphasised the second role of European public order to justify the rejection of applications: in *Vladimir Petrovich Korolev* v. *Russia* the ECtHR stated: 'The

[96] Explanatory Report to Protocol 14, para. 77.

High Contracting Parties clearly wished the Court to devote more time to cases which warrant consideration on the merits, whether seen from the perspective of the legal interest of the individual applicant or considered from the broader perspective of the law of the Convention and the European Public Order to which it contributes.'[97] It is clear that this wording has migrated to the Court's judgment from the Explanatory Report to Protocol 14. The Court appears to have reversed the logic that it used in the earlier cases when applications that appeared inadmissible could be considered if they could contribute to European public order. In the more recent cases, the Court has disregarded otherwise seemingly admissible applications if they did not contribute to European public order due to no significant disadvantage being suffered by the applicants.

In *Rinck* v. *France*, the Court mentioned European public order as a reason that would prevent the Court from using the no significant disadvantage criterion, again reverting to the initial meaning of European public order as a 'trump card' against inadmissibility. Having said that, the Court failed to find any reason related to European public order to justify continuation of the proceedings in this case. Among other things, the Court pointed out that the fact that the matter at issue was part of settled case law was a reason not to continue this case.[98]

Dissenting judges have mentioned European public order in the context of admissibility criteria, which has added some confusion about its meaning. For some judges, the admissibility criteria themselves are part of European public order. For example, dissenting Judge Steiner linked the six-month admissibility criterion with European public order and stated that '[t]he six-month rule is, according to our case-law, a question which is linked to observance of the European public order'.[99] As has already been observed, references to European public order usually justify extension of the Court's authority rather than restriction of it, as suggested by Judge Steiner. A similar issue was considered by the concurring judges in *Svinarenko and Slyadnev* v. *Russia*. In this case, the victim status of the applicants was under review and the concurring judges contended that this issue was 'a question of *ordre public* which

[97] *Korolev* v. *Russia* (dec.), no. 25551/05, ECHR 2010. See similar reasoning in *Finger* v. *Bulgaria*, no. 37346/05, 10 May 2011.

[98] *Rinck* v. *France* (dec.), no. 18774/09, 19 October 2010.

[99] *Centro Europa 7 S.r.l. and Di Stefano* v. *Italy* [GC], no. 38433/09, ECHR 2012, Dissenting Opinion of Judge Steiner.

relates to the Court's jurisdiction'.[100] The question was whether the Court was competent to consider admissibility on its own motion without waiting for the respondent party to object on this ground.

The Court's references to European public order illustrate well my argument about its unpredictable content. European public order can justify a departure from admissibility criteria if necessary; European public order can also justify the application of admissibility criteria when that is required; and, finally, admissibility criteria are part of European public order in certain circumstances. It seems that European public order is all and nothing; its lack of detectable content thus makes its deployment as a legal concept highly problematic and can undermine the legitimacy of the ECtHR.

2.6 Democracy as a Key Aspect of European Public Order

This section discusses the substantive role that European public order plays in the reasoning of the Court. Although the Court has used European public order in this sense in many judgments, it has not defined it and never explained on what basis some constitutive elements are included in European public order. The Court made the highest number of references to European public order when claiming that democracy is 'a fundamental feature of the European public order'.[101] The Court referred to European public order in this context in thirty-seven cases.

The Court has emphasised that democracy is the only political regime contemplated by the Convention, and that the Convention was 'designed to promote and maintain the ideals and values of a democratic society'.[102] Moreover, the Preamble to the Convention states that fundamental freedoms are best maintained by an effective political democracy. Although the Convention itself does not define democracy or provide for an individual right to democracy, such rights as freedom of expression and assembly and right to vote and stand for election are fundamental to maintaining effective democratic governance.

There are very few references to democracy as part of European public order in the early cases of the ECtHR. A possible reason for this is that very few of these old cases can be considered to have the issue of

[100] *Svinarenko and Slyadnev* v. *Russia* [GC], nos. 32541/08 and 43441/08, ECHR 2014, Joint Concurring Opinion of Judges Raimondi and Sicilianos, para. 10.

[101] See, for example, *Vona* v. *Hungary*, no. 35943/10, ECHR 2013, para. 71.

[102] *Gorzelik and Others* v. *Poland* [GC], no. 44158/98, ECHR 2004-I, para. 89.

democracy at their heart. 'Old democracies', which were the original signatories to the Convention, gave the Court no need to emphasise the foundations of European public order in this sense. However, after the Council of Europe absorbed more unstable political regimes from Southern and Eastern Europe, the Court had to re-emphasise the importance of democracy in its case law.[103]

The first reference to European public order in the context of democracy was made in *United Communist Party of Turkey and others* v. *Turkey*.[104] In this case, the Turkish authorities had dissolved the applicant party and the ECtHR had to consider whether these actions were compatible with Article 11 of the Convention. The Court pointed out that democracy is a fundamental feature of European public order. This meant that the exceptions set out in section 2 of Article 11 should be construed narrowly and the contracting parties need particularly convincing reasons to justify limiting the freedom of political association. In other words, the fact that the case deals with European public order justifies a stricter test of proportionality.

In this case, the Court made a few suggestions as to how it came to the conclusion that democracy is an element of European public order. First, it is so because 'the Preamble to the Convention ... establishes a very clear connection between the Convention and democracy'.[105] Second, the Court highlighted the fact that Articles 9 to 11 allow only those interferences that are 'necessary in a *democratic* society'.[106] It seems that in this sense European public order must include the most fundamental principles of the European political regime, and democracy is one of those principles.

The positioning of democracy as an element of European public order appears to result in a narrow interpretation of the exceptions to the qualified rights when the subject matter of the application is concerned with safeguarding democracy. In such cases, the Court is reluctant to find measures that restrict participatory democracy through dissolving political parties and civil society associations,[107] restricting voting

103 After the fall of the Berlin Wall in 1989 and the dissolution of the Soviet Union, almost all new independent European states joined the Council of Europe.

104 *United Communist Party of Turkey and Others* v. *Turkey*, 30 January 1998, Reports of Judgments and Decisions 1998-I.

105 Ibid., para. 45. See also *Ahmed and Others* v. *the United Kingdom*, 2 September 1998, Reports of Judgments and Decisions 1998-VI, para. 52.

106 *United Communist Party of Turkey and Others* v. *Turkey* (n. 104) para. 45 (emphasis added).

107 See *Refah Partisi (the Welfare Party) and Others* v. *Turkey*, nos. 41340/98, 41342/98, 41343/98 and 41344/98, 31 July 2001; *Alekseyev* v. *Russia*, nos. 4916/07, 25924/08 and 14599/09, 21 October 2010, para. 62.

rights,[108] prohibiting political rallies,[109] and others as compatible with the Convention.

Conversely, if the actions of the applicants could potentially undermine democracy, the Court might reserve a broader margin of appreciation for the respondent state. The ECtHR has explained it in the following terms:

> Referring to the hallmarks of a 'democratic society', the Court has attached particular importance to pluralism, tolerance and broadmindedness. In that context, it has held that although individual interests must on occasion be subordinated to those of a group, democracy does not simply mean that the views of the majority must always prevail: a balance must be achieved which ensures the fair and proper treatment of minorities and avoids any abuse of a dominant position.[110]

The Court therefore can restrict individual rights in order to maintain effective democracy. For example, in *Ahmed and others* v. *the United Kingdom*, the applicants argued that the reason of protecting a democratic form of governance invoked by the UK authorities cannot justify limiting freedom of expression. In this case, the Court considered whether restricting the political activities of local civil servants violated their freedom of expression when these restrictions were designed to ensure the effectiveness of local democratic administration. The Court ruled that democracy is important because it constitutes an element of European public order and then concluded that democracy does not end with central government.[111] As a result, the authorities can limit freedom of expression in this context, and hence, the Court did not find a violation of the applicants' rights.

The result of democracy being at the heart of European public order is twofold. First, if a state interference undermines the democratic participation of an alleged victim, then the Court will likely restrict the state's margin of appreciation and will require particularly convincing justifications for the interference. Conversely, the contracting parties can restrict human rights in order to protect effective democracy and, as a result, the Court will apply a looser test of proportionality. This also means that the respondent state can enjoy a broader margin of appreciation. Another example of the latter scenario is when the democratic

108 *Sadak and Others* v. *Turkey* (no. 1), nos. 29900/96, 29901/96, 29902/96 and 29903/96, ECHR 2001-VIII.

109 *Primov and Others* v. *Russia*, no. 17391/06, 12 June 2014.

110 *Christian Democratic People's Party* v. *Moldova*, no. 28793/02, ECHR 2006-II, para. 64.

111 *Ahmed and Others* v. *the United Kingdom* (n. 105).

regime is fragile and the country is in a state of transition from totalitarian rule to democracy. Such transitional states can resort to more drastic measures in order to protect their new democratic political regime. In the case of *Ždanoka* v. *Latvia*, the Court considered whether the fact that the applicant was ineligible to stand for election in Latvia on account of her former membership of the Communist Party of the Soviet Union was compatible with the Convention.[112] The Court pointed out that democracy is a fundamental element of European public order:

> It cannot be ruled out that a person or a group of persons will rely on the rights enshrined in the Convention or its Protocols in order to attempt to derive therefrom the right to conduct what amounts in practice to activities intended to destroy the rights or freedoms set forth in the Convention; any such destruction would put an end to democracy.[113]

In this case, the Grand Chamber found no violation of Article 3 of Protocol 1. Curiously, the Chamber also mentioned European public order in its judgment, but, in contrast to the Grand Chamber, it did find a violation. It is not unprecedented that abstract concepts like European public order can, on the facts, justify conflicting results in the same case. This means that the Court needs to engage in a good deal of balancing to resolve such cases even if it is established that democracy plays the key role in them.

Another illustration which shows that European public order does not necessarily unambiguously determine the outcome is *Refah Partisi* v. *Turkey*.[114] In this case, the Grand Chamber of the Court had to consider whether the decision of the Constitutional Court of Turkey to dissolve one of the biggest parties in Turkey was in compliance with the Convention. On the one hand, the issue was about the dissolution of a party which represented a significant proportion of the Turkish electorate. On the other hand, it was claimed that the party was pushing an anti-constitutional and anti-democratic agenda. Although the Court has referred to democracy as an important element of European public order, the references here were more rhetorical than persuasive since democracy-based arguments were presented by both parties to the case. The Court found no violation of the Convention.

[112] *Ždanoka* v. *Latvia*, no. 58278/00, 17 June 2004.
[113] Ibid., para. 99.
[114] *Refah Partisi (the Welfare Party) and Others* v. *Turkey* (n. 107).

Another example that illustrates that references to democracy as one of the elements of European public order do not guarantee a particular outcome is the case of *Cumhuriyet Halk Partisi* v. *Turkey*.[115] Here, the Court confirmed that '[d]emocracy constitutes a fundamental element of the "European public order", [and that] the rights guaranteed under Article 3 of Protocol No. 1 are crucial to establishing and maintaining the foundations of an effective and meaningful democracy governed by the rule of law'.[116] This, however, did not help the applicants, who tried to argue that the referendum in Turkey was held in violation of Article 3 of Protocol 1. The Court pointed out that referenda do not fall within the ambit of this Article and therefore declared this application inadmissible. As I pointed out earlier, the Court stated in the context of admissibility that European public order can be used as a 'trumping card' even when the ECHR text does not support this argument. Interestingly, the fact that democracy is part of European public order failed to trump the fact that Article 3 of Protocol 1 does not cover referenda.

In contrast to human rights which are inherently anti-majoritarian, democracy, at least from a very basic perspective, favours majoritarian decision-making. While both individual rights enshrined in the Convention and democracy as a political model are parts of European public order, it appears that the Court has to define public order in such a way that is capable of reconciling both of these crucially important notions.[117] It seems that democracy as part of European public order does not give conclusive answers to complex dilemmas that the ECtHR has to deal with in its adjudication. Human rights simultaneously protect democracy and restrict it; similarly, democracy enhances human rights as well as limits them. The Court's statement that democracy is a fundamental value of European public order is an abstract notion that can have a limited impact on the practice of the Court as well as on the outcome of the case. Unlike in cases of territorial application of the Convention which settle the *espace juridique* of the Convention, in these cases the Court uses European public order to clarify the substantive meaning of human rights. It is doubtful that the meaning of human rights, which are abstract and open for interpretation, can be explained

115 *Cumhuriyet Halk Partisi* v. *Turkey*, no. 48818/17, 21 November 2017 (Decision of Inadmissibility).

116 Ibid., para. 36.

117 See *Christian Democratic People's Party* v. *Moldova* (no. 2), no. 25196/04, 2 February 2010, para. 21; *Alekseyev* v. *Russia* (n. 107), para. 63.

by reference to the even more abstract and unclear notion of European public order. From the examples discussed here, one can see that references to European public order can indeed justify the contradictory outcomes of a case.

2.7 Scope of Substantive Provisions

Alongside democracy and the rule of law,[118] human rights are a part of European public order. The ECtHR describes the substantive meaning of European public order by saying that some provisions of the ECHR are parts of it. In this context, the Court's references to European public order are predominantly random as they emphasise various aspects of human rights as elements of European public order and these aspects change over time. The following analysis aims to prove this point.

The Court's references to European public order in this context are fairly rare, with only six judgments identified. Also, in many of these judgments the references were made by the dissenting judges, not by the majority. The very first judgment in which European public order was mentioned by the ECtHR was *De Wilde, Ooms and Versyp* v. *Belgium*. In this case, the Court stated that the right to liberty and security enshrined in Article 5 of the ECHR is part of *ordre public*. It was argued by the Belgian authorities that if an individual agreed to detention, then he or she could no longer be protected by Article 5. The Court disagreed, stating that '[w]hen the matter is one which concerns *ordre public* within the Council of Europe, a scrupulous supervision by the organs of the Convention of all measures capable of violating the rights and freedoms which it guarantees is necessary in every case'.[119] References to European public order in this case seem to justify the Court in overriding the will of the applicant to be detained. In other words, the Court was pointing out that an individual cannot willingly agree to his or her rights being violated. It appears that, here, the Court does not emphasise the importance of rights by linking them to European public order; rather, it highlights its role as a guarantor of human rights, irrespective of the will of the applicant to have his or her rights restricted.

[118] In *Aliyev* v. *Azerbaijan* the Court stated that '[o]ne of the fundamental components of European public order is the principle of the rule of law, and arbitrariness constitutes the negation of that principle'. *Aliyev* v. *Azerbaijan*, nos. 68762/14 and 71200/14, 20 September 2018, para. 224.

[119] *De Wilde, Ooms and Versyp* v. *Belgium*, 18 June 1971, Series A no. 12, para. 65.

The Court used a similar strategy in relation to friendly settlements in the early cases it adjudicated. According to Article 39 of the Convention, the parties to a case can secure a friendly settlement on the basis of respect for human rights. In cases such as *Skoogström* v. *Sweden*,[120] *Can* v. *Austria*[121] and *Hatami* v. *Sweden*,[122] the Court considered whether continuation of the proceedings was necessary for reasons of European public order, despite the fact that both parties had agreed to settle. In *Hatami* v. *Sweden*, for example, the Court 'discern[ed] no reason of *ordre public* (public policy) militating against striking the case out of the list';[123] had such a reason existed, the Court could have continued the case. Similarly, the Court used European public order in relation to Article 6 of the Convention, which provides for the right to a fair trial.[124] In *Deweer* v. *Belgium*, the matter at bar was whether accepting payment for settlement can restrict the applicant's access to court. Here, the Court was again considering whether the voluntary actions of the applicant can restrict his human rights. The Court noted:

> [I]n a democratic society[,] too great an importance attaches to the 'right to a court' ... for its benefit to be forfeited solely by reason of the fact that an individual is a party to a settlement reached in the course of a procedure ancillary to court proceedings. In an area concerning the public order (*ordre public*) of the member States of the Council of Europe, any measure or decision alleged to be in breach of Article 6 (art. 6) calls for particularly careful review.[125]

The Court found a violation of Article 6 in this case.

In contrast, in more recent judgments the judges of the Court have expanded this fairly limited understanding of the impact of European public order in a substantive sense comparable to the 'trumping card' argument discussed earlier. Namely, the Court would allow discontinuation of the case unless there were European public order reasons to the contrary. This narrow understanding was extended by concurring judge Cabral Barreto in *Enhorn* v. *Sweden*. He employed the statement used by the Court in *De Wilde, Ooms and Versyp* v. *Belgium*, but gave it a broader meaning. In *Enhorn*, there was no issue of deprivation of liberty upon consent; the concurring judges chose to emphasise the

[120] *Skoogström* v. *Sweden*, 2 October 1984, Series A no. 83.
[121] *Can* v. *Austria*, 30 September 1985, Series A no. 96.
[122] *Hatami* v. *Sweden*, 9 October 1998, Reports of Judgments and Decisions 1998-VII.
[123] Ibid., para. 30.
[124] *Deweer* v. *Belgium*, 27 February 1980, Series A no. 35.
[125] Ibid., para. 49.

importance of the right at hand by linking it to European public order.[126] He pointed out:

The facts of the case relate to a deprivation of liberty in the context of the measures which States are called upon to take in order to protect society from the potential acts of individuals who have contracted an infectious disease such as the Aids virus. The obvious aim of such measures is to prevent the spread of a disease whose consequences are exceptionally serious. The problem is that where such measures entail deprivation of liberty within the meaning of Article 5 § 1 of the Convention, they must be consistent with the Court's settled case-law, which is rightly stringent. I would point out in this connection that 'when the matter is one which concerns *ordre public* within the Council of Europe, a scrupulous supervision by the organs of the Convention of all measures capable of violating the rights and freedoms which it guarantees is necessary in every case'. The aim of Article 5, which relates to individual liberty, is 'to ensure that no one should be dispossessed of this liberty in an arbitrary fashion'. Furthermore, the list of exceptions to the right to liberty secured in Article 5 § 1 is an exhaustive one, meaning that 'only a narrow interpretation of those exceptions is consistent with the aim and purpose of that provision'.[127]

In *Austin* v. *the United Kingdom*, the dissenting judges also tried to attach particular importance to Article 5 by linking it to European public order. Again, no issue of consensual deprivation of liberty was at hand in this case. Instead, the Court was considering whether kettling[128] was compatible with the Convention. The majority ruled that such limitation of liberty did not even fall under Article 5 ECHR. Dissenting judges Tulkens, Spielmann and Garlicki pointed out:

In terms of the principles governing the application of Article 5 of the Convention, a provision which features in all the universal and regional human rights instruments and forms part of the European Public Order, the majority's position can be interpreted as implying that, if it is necessary to impose a coercive and restrictive measure for a legitimate public-interest purpose, the measure does not amount to a deprivation of liberty. This is a new proposition which is eminently questionable and objectionable for two reasons.[129]

[126] *Enhorn* v. *Sweden*, no. 56529/00, ECHR 2005-I. Concurring Opinion of Judge Cabral Barreto.

[127] Ibid.

[128] Kettling is the police tactic for controlling large crowds by separating different sections of demonstrations and keeping the demonstrators within the confined spaces of these sections.

[129] *Austin and Others* v. *the United Kingdom* [GC], nos. 39692/09, 40713/09 and 41008/09, ECHR 2012, Dissenting Opinion of Judges Tulkens, Spielmann and Garlicki, para. 3.

In other cases, the majority of the Court also resorted to similar reasoning and accepted that the principle of non-discrimination is part of European public order. In *Fabris* v. *France*, the Court stated that 'the prohibition of discrimination on grounds of a child's birth "outside marriage" [is] a standard of protection of European Public Order',[130] which made it quite unclear whether the prohibition of discrimination in general or only prohibition of discrimination 'on grounds of a child's birth "outside marriage"' is part of European public order. The Court omitted to clarify this point.

It appears that in more recent cases the judges have changed their approach to European public order in its substantive sense. Earlier, it meant only that the applicant could not consent to his/her rights being violated, but recently it has started to mean that the rights which are part of European public order are of particular importance and should be restricted only in very limited circumstances. The latter understanding is inherently problematic and generates many complex questions, for example, whether it is only Articles 5 and 14 that are constituent parts of European public order or whether all other Articles of the Convention should be included. If some Articles are in European public order and some are not, does this mean that the Court should develop a hierarchy of human rights? What are the exact consequences of being part of European public order for each substantive Article of the Convention involved? The Court has not yet given clear answers to these questions; moreover, it seems that it should not single out any certain right as being part of European public order. Having said that, if all rights are equally part of European public order, then the Court's references to European public order bear no legal effect because it does not prioritise any of the rights enshrined in the Convention and does not assist the Court in its proportionality analysis.

2.8 Conclusion

According to the ECtHR, the Convention is a constitutional instrument of European public order. The ECtHR is a guardian of the Convention rights and participates in creating and shaping European public order. Although there is a fair degree of inconsistency in the application of European public order in the reasoning of the Court, it has at least four identifiable roles: jurisdictional in that it helps the Court to justify and

[130] *Fabris* v. *France* [GC], no. 16574/08, ECHR 2013, para. 57.

secure its *espace juridique* and protect its authority over this territory; procedural as the European public order has been used in relation to interim measures and admissibility; substantive as it assists the Court to clarify the meaning of the rights enshrined in the Convention; and, finally, hierarchical as it has been used to highlight the importance of aspects of the Court's case law. In all contexts, the use of European public order is problematic due to its overly abstract and unpredictable nature. It is impossible to establish its legal effect with any degree of clarity because it can justify contradicting outcomes. In fact, European public order falls well short of a legal notion capable of determining a particular outcome of a case.

Chapter 3 broadens the enquiry and tries to define European public order by looking into various areas in which public order was used. I then try to apply these meanings to European public order as used by the ECtHR.

3 Defining European Public Order: An Impossible Task

3.1 Introduction

This chapter argues that the notion 'European public order' is vague and indeterminate. As a consequence, the ECtHR's claims that the ECHR is a 'constitutional instrument of European Public Order'[1] can have many meanings, and its application in the case law is problematic. This chapter explains why defining European public order is virtually impossible. Unsurprisingly, the ECtHR has failed to define it or to provide an approximate list of its components, and a clear definition of public order is yet to be developed in legal scholarship. This chapter builds upon the argument made in Chapter 2 that the formula 'European public order' is so abstract and open-ended that it can be used to support mutually exclusive arguments. For instance, qualified rights can be limited to protect public order;[2] at the same time, the Court can broaden the scope of those same rights because they are an essential part of European public order.[3] These two options, while in contradiction, could be at stake in the same case. This dilemma illustrates the inherent challenge of vague legal notions to the rule of law and legal certainty.

[1] *Loizidou* v. *Turkey* (preliminary objections), 23 March 1995, Series A no. 310, para. 75.

[2] See Article 9 ECHR, which mentions public order specifically. Morijn argues that 'public policy [in the sense akin to public order] is generally invoked to restrict rather than facilitate the exercise of fundamental rights'. John Morijn, 'Balancing Fundamental Rights and Common Market Freedoms in Union Law: Schmidberger and Omega in the Light of the European Constitution' (2006) 12 *ELJ* 15,39.

[3] See Chapter 2 for more detail. For instance, in *Yumak and Sadak* v. *Turkey* the Court repeated that '[d]emocracy constitutes a fundamental element of the "European public order"'. *Yumak and Sadak* v. *Turkey* [GC], no. 10226/03, ECHR 2008, para. 105. See *Ahmed and Others* v. *the United Kingdom*, 2 September 1998, Reports of Judgments and Decisions 1998-VI, para. 52.

This chapter surveys and analyses various applications of the term 'public order' in national and international judicial practice, arguing that it is vague and abstract in every area of law where it has been used. Having said that, 'vagueness, and resultant indeterminacies, are essential features of law'.[4] Although I agree that vagueness and indeterminacy cannot be eliminated from law, neither can the law be turned into an empty vessel; some commonly accepted meanings are crucial for the effectiveness of legal practice. Marmor gives the following example to explain different types of legal vagueness:

> My teenage daughter is going out on a Saturday night. I want to make sure that she gets back home at a reasonable hour, so I face a choice here: I can either tell her, 'Make sure to be home by no later than [*sic*] 2 a.m.,' or I can be much more vague, and tell her, 'Make sure not to come home too late!' Now, we might think that the vague instruction is more respectful of my daughter's autonomy. It is more educational, in a sense, too, because it makes her more responsible for her own actions, which is generally a good attitude to foster. So far, so good. But now let us suppose that there is a sanction looming here, that is, suppose that my daughter knows that I am the one who gets to determine what would count as 'too late' to come home and that if I decide that she came home too late, I get to impose a penalty. And let us further suppose that she cannot be sure, in fact she only has a vague sense of, what I would consider 'too late' under the circumstances.[5]

Although the task of the ECtHR is much more complex than that of a father trying to instruct his daughter, this allusion can be used to illustrate the challenges of the application of European public order. The ECtHR cannot give precise and clear instructions to states at all times (akin to 'Make sure to be home by no later than [*sic*] 2 a.m.') due to the complexity of interactions among parties and the variety of factors that need to be considered. For instance, the Court cannot prescribe that states hold elections every four years and have at least five political

[4] Timothy Endicott, *Vagueness in Law* (Oxford University Press 2000) 1; see also Jeremy Waldron, 'Vagueness and the Guidance of Action' in Andrei Marmor and Scott Soames (eds.), *The Philosophical Foundations of Language in the Law* (Oxford University Press 2011) 58–82.

[5] Andrei Marmor, 'Varieties of Vagueness in the Law' in Giorgio Bongiovanni et al. (eds.), *Handbook of Legal Reasoning and Argumentation* (Springer Nature B. V. 2018) 561–80, 572. For more on vagueness and law, see Hrafn Asgeirsson, *The Nature and Value of Vagueness in the Law* (Hart 2020); Diana Raffman, 'Vagueness in Law: Placing the Blame Where It's Due' in Geert Keil and Ralf Poscher (eds.), *Vagueness and Law: Philosophical and Legal Perspectives* (Oxford University Press 2016) 49–64; Ralf Poscher, 'Ambiguity and Vagueness in Legal Interpretation' in Peter M. Tiersma and Lawrence M. Solan (eds.), *The Oxford Handbook of Language and Law* (Oxford University Press 2011) 128–44; Geert Keil and Ralf Poscher (eds.), *Vagueness and Law: Philosophical and Legal Perspectives* (Oxford University Press 2016).

parties in Parliament; although this rule would be clear, it would not be reasonable. That said, we know that there are certain parameters of democracy; as long as parameters such as elections and universal suffrage are fulfilled, the most basic requirements of democracy are satisfied and vague details do not undermine the value of the term. Moreover, a balance between vagueness and clarity helps to establish the degree of appropriate interference with state sovereignty. Overly precise and instructive rules could be viewed as undue interference in states' internal affairs, so some vagueness that allows national discretion is not only possible but necessary. However, in the case of European public order, the vagueness is of a different nature. To utilise the same example as before, the father's instruction would be: 'Make sure to come *somewhere at some point in time*.' The notion of European public order has so little normative substance to it that it can hardly have meaningful consequences for the case at hand. For a comparison, consider for example the notion of rule of law. While notoriously vague, it is at least determined by certain conditions.[6] This chapter will substantiate the claim that even such minimal conditions are missing from the definition of European public order.

What makes the notion of European public order even more problematic is the fact that the Court seems to attach fundamental value to it; after all, the Court seems to consider its mandate as being to shape European public order. By claiming that the ECHR is a constitutional instrument of European public order, the Court assumes the role of interpreter of such order. In Chapter 4 of this monograph I argue that this is not the Court's job and that its attempting to undertake such a task can undermine its more straightforward technical function of conflict resolution.

One of the judges I interviewed for this book called European public order an 'essentially contestable concept'.[7] The same judge observed

[6] See Venice Commission of the Council of Europe, 'The Rule of Law Checklist' (The Venice Commission Report), available at www.venice.coe.int/images/SITE%20IMAGES/Publications/Rule_of_Law_Check_List.pdf; Theodore Konstadinides, *The Rule of Law in the European Union* (Hart 2017); Brian Z. Tamanaha, *On the Rule of Law: History, Politics, Theory* (Cambridge University Press 2004); Tom Bingham, *The Rule of Law* (Penguin 2011); Simon Chesterman, 'An International Rule of Law?' (2008) 56 *AJCL* 331; Richard H. Fallon, '"The Rule of Law" as a Concept in Constitutional Discourse' (1997) 97 *CLR* 1.

[7] John S. Dryzek, 'Can There Be a Human Right to an Essentially Contested Concept? The Case of Democracy' (2016) 78 *J Polit* 357; Jeremy Waldron, 'Is the Rule of Law an Essentially Contested Concept (in Florida)?' (2002) 21 *Law and Philosophy* 137; John Gray, 'On Liberty, Liberalism and Essential Contestability' (1978) 8 *Brit J Polit Sci* 385.

that democracy and rule of law are also essentially contestable, but they have some identifiable frontiers, however vague they might be. Moreover, one can define these two terms *a contrario*, by looking into what the lack of democracy and rule of law might mean. European public order can mean almost anything – it can refer to, or include, human rights, democracy, rule of law and many other things. Moreover, it is impossible to define it *a contrario* as there is no such thing as European public disorder – at least in legal parlance. It is also difficult to say what clearly does not fall within the boundaries of European public order. It seems that European public order refers to issues of fundamental importance, but European societies are so diverse and multicultural that such issues can be wide-ranging and present contradictory meanings. Unlike pornography, which famously eludes definition but manifests itself to the beholder,[8] public order is an abstract concept that requires at least some clear benchmarks to be applicable in a legal sense.

This chapter proceeds as follows: it first explains what public order means in various legal contexts and looks at some closely connected concepts like '*ordre public*' and 'public policy'. Section 3.2 also looks at the meaning of these concepts in various contexts of national and international law. It is argued that the vagueness of these concepts is a common feature here. This vagueness, however, increases when regional and international as opposed to national public order is examined. Section 3.3 discusses broad benchmarks that could sketch an understanding of European public order and applies them to the jurisprudence of the ECtHR. Here, I look first into whether the Court exercises supervision over territories that are inhabited by people who share key values. The section concludes that although some values are shared at a high level of abstraction, more concrete views vary greatly on the ground. Moreover, the ECtHR should not impose its own version of these more concrete values on states as this would be problematic from the perspective of constitutional pluralism. The chapter proceeds by looking into whether the Court seeks to protect the autonomy of its order by referring to European public order (Section 3.3.2). It shows that the Court does not protect its order vis-à-vis the contracting parties, as they are supposed to develop in harmony. If the purpose were to protect its order from outside influences, this aim would not be clearly

[8] This is a reference to US Supreme Court Justice Potter Stewart who in 1964 defined the test of obscenity as 'I know when I see it'. *Jacobellis* v. *Ohio*, 378 US 184 (1964), 198.

identifiable from the Court's case law. Section 3.3.3 examines whether the Court's approach to European public order is an attempt to establish a hierarchy of human rights, concluding that only some human rights constitute the core of European public order and, thus, the ECtHR is not trying to set such a hierarchy. Finally, in order to shape public order effectively, a court needs an effective enforcement mechanism, and this is discussed in Section 3.3.4. The ECtHR seemingly lacks a mechanism that would force contracting parties to adopt a public order they might disagree with. This leads to the conclusion that the ECtHR can hardly be seen as an institution that can shape European public order. It can influence it, but there are many actors simultaneously having an impact on European public order.

3.2 The Multiple 'Faces' of Public Order: Various Meanings in Various Contexts

3.2.1 *Public Order as Security and Prevention of Disorder*

The aim of this subsection is twofold. It first illustrates that the references to public order in the text of the ECHR[9] are limited to public order as the ordinary state of affairs in a given society and prevention of disorder. Its meaning is similar to, but not completely the same as, national security. This subsection also argues that this relatively uncontroversial notion of public order is not what the ECtHR means when it claims that the ECHR is a constitutional instrument of European public order. Therefore, the ECtHR case law that interprets public order as a limitation of, for example, the right to freedom of expression (Article 9(2) ECHR) is not particularly helpful in unravelling the meaning of European public order.

The ECHR and its Protocols mention public order three times. The first reference is in Article 6, which provides for the right to a fair trial. It states: 'Judgment shall be pronounced publicly but the press and public may be excluded from all or part of the trial in the interests of morals, public order or national security in a democratic society . . ..'[10] Here, the Court normally interprets public order as the lack of riot and disorderly behaviour, in other words the lack of threat to public safety. In *Campbell and Fell* v. *the United Kingdom* the Court confirmed that public pronouncements of decisions related to disciplinary offences of inmates can

[9] For example, in Article 9(2).
[10] Article 6 ECHR.

constitute a threat to 'public order and security'.[11] Often the Court discusses the terms 'public order' and 'security' as intrinsically linked, although not identical, concepts. State security might include protection of sensitive information that would not lead to any riot but might still justify pronouncement of a judgment in camera.[12]

Second, the expression 'public order' can be found in Article 9(2). Pursuant to it, freedom to manifest one's religion can be limited 'in the interests of public safety, for the protection of public order, health or morals'.[13] Mostly the Court has treated 'public order' as public security, but it has never defined its boundaries. Moreover, the Court's interpretation of this term sometimes goes beyond public security. For instance, the Court has accepted that town-planning regulations which interfere with the right to freedom of religion can pursue a legitimate aim of protecting public order.[14] Another meaning of public order is maintaining religious harmony in society.[15] Although difficult to define, public order in this sense means the normal functioning of a given society and avoidance of crises. Public order and public security are closely connected, but the Court has emphasised their difference. In *Nolan and K.* v. *Russia* the Court stated:

> Unlike the second paragraphs of Articles 8, 10, and 11, paragraph 2 of Article 9 of the Convention does not allow restrictions on the ground of national security. Far from being an accidental omission, the non-inclusion of that particular ground for limitations in Article 9 reflects the primordial importance of religious pluralism as 'one of the foundations of a "democratic society" within the meaning of the Convention' and the fact that a State cannot dictate what a person believes or take coercive steps to make him change his beliefs.[16]

Third, public order is mentioned in Article 1 of Protocol 7, which provides procedural safeguards relating to expulsion of aliens (such as submission of reasons against expulsion, the right to be represented, etc.). Article 1(2) of Protocol 7 provides that state authorities can expel an individual before discharging these duties if 'such expulsion is necessary in the interests of public order or is grounded on reasons of

[11] *Campbell and Fell* v. *the United Kingdom*, 28 June 1984, Series A no. 80, para. 88.

[12] See, for example, *Yam* v. *the United Kingdom*, no. 31295/11, 16 January 2020, paras. 52–7.

[13] Article 9(2).

[14] *Association de solidarité avec les témoins de Jéhovah and others* v. *Turkey*, app 36915/10.

[15] See *Leyla Şahin* v. *Turkey* [GC], no. 44774/98, ECHR 2005-XI, para. 107, *S.A.S.* v. *France* [GC], no. 43835/11, ECHR 2014, para. 127.

[16] *Nolan and K.* v. *Russia*, no. 2512/04, 12 February 2009, para. 73.

national security'.[17] The ECtHR case law on Article 1 of Protocol 7 is quite scarce and fails to shed much light on the meaning of public order in this context. The explanatory report to Protocol 7 tries to distinguish between public order and national security. It provides that '[t]he State relying on public order to expel an alien before the exercise of the aforementioned rights must be able to show that this exceptional measure was necessary in the particular case or category of cases. On the other hand, if expulsion is for reasons of national security, this in itself should be accepted as sufficient justification.'[18] It seems that the drafters of the Protocol realised that public order is a very broad concept and, arguably, offers lesser justification for expulsion than national security.

Although the expression 'public order' is not mentioned in Article 10(2) ECHR, this provision refers to the prevention of disorder as a legitimate aim for state interferences. The Court has had an opportunity to compare prevention of disorders with protection of public order in its case law. In *Engel and others* v. *the Netherlands* the Court pointed out:

> The concept of 'order' as envisaged by this provision [Article 10–2], refers not only to public order or 'ordre public' within the meaning of Articles 6 para. 1 and 9 para. 2 (art. 6–1, art. 9–2) of the Convention and Article 2 para. 3 of Protocol no. 4 (P4-2–3): it also covers the order that must prevail within the confines of a specific social group. This is so, for example, when, as in the case of the armed forces, disorder in that group can have repercussions on order in society as a whole.[19]

In its case law the Court understands public order as an ordinary state of affairs in a particular society, implying measures ranging from prohibition of riots to the requirement of planning permissions. Arguably, this is not the meaning to which the ECtHR alludes when it claims that the ECHR is a constitutional instrument of European public order.[20] Clearly, the Convention has no ambition to serve as the touchstone of European planning laws or even every aspect of European policing. The meaning of public order as it appears in the text of the Convention is also relatively vague and imprecise, but its boundaries can be established and the case law seems to show that the Court has a good idea of

[17] Article 1, Protocol 7.

[18] Explanatory Report to the Protocol No. 7 to the Convention for the Protection of Human Rights and Fundamental Freedoms, 22 November 1984, para. 15, https://rm.coe.int/16800c96fd.

[19] *Engel and Others* v. *the Netherlands*, 8 June 1976, Series A no. 22, para. 98.

[20] See, for example, in the UK the Private International Law (Miscellaneous Provisions) Act 1995, s. 14(3)(a)(i) and in Germany Article 6 of the Introductory Act to the Civil Code.

how to do this. However, the Court's view on European public order has little to do with the statutory expression of 'public order', so the analysis must now turn away from this false friend to better comparators.

3.2.2 *Public Order as a Tool of Private International Law*

This section considers the meaning of public order in private international law. In Chapter 1, I argued that European public order can be used as an analytical concept and as a legal tool. European public order as an analytical concept means that it does not have any precise legal value but describes the whole body of standards applicable across Europe. It is a descriptive concept and its precise meaning does not have any consequences for the outcome of a particular case. To the contrary, European public order as a legal tool used by the Court must mean that it can affect the outcome of a particular case. In private international law, public order can be deployed as a legal tool. This section first briefly outlines the role of public order in private international law. It then shows that it is significantly different from how the ECtHR understands European public order. Finally, even despite these differences, deployment of public order in private international law is also problematic due to the vagueness of its content but perhaps not to the same extent as European public order used by the ECtHR.

Public order[21] exceptions are widely referred to in private international law.[22] Similar exceptions are repeated in relevant national laws.[23] These exceptions allow judges not to apply foreign laws because they contradict national public order when they otherwise would be applicable. The use of public order exceptions can be traced back to the fifteenth century, but their content remains ill-defined. In general terms, public order 'is a device whereby the courts will reject foreign laws or judgments when they are considered contrary to fundamental national cultural values'.[24] While this definition is relatively uncontroversial, and

[21] Also known as '*ordre public*' and 'public policy'.

[22] See, for example, Article 16 of the Convention on the law applicable to contractual obligations, opened for signature in Rome on 19 June 1980, Consolidated at OJ C 027, 26.1.1998 where it is stated that foreign law can be denied application if it is 'manifestly incompatible with the public policy ("ordre public") of the forum'. Yongping Xiao and Zhengxin Huo, 'Ordre Public in China's Private International Law' (2005) 53 *AJCL* 653.

[23] See n. 20 for more detail.

[24] Horatia Muir Watt, 'Evidence of an Emergent European Legal Culture: Public Policy Requirements of Procedural Fairness under the Brussels and Lugano Conventions' (2001) 36 *TILJ* 539, 543. 'The public policy exception was designed as a "safeguard" against the invasion of foreign, unacceptable solutions into the domestic legal order.' Jerca Kramberger Škerl, 'European Public Policy (With an Emphasis on Exequatur

despite centuries of application, the public order exception remains contestable and its scope remains vague and unclear. Almost two centuries ago, Judge Burrough called reliance on public policy reliance on an 'unruly horse';[25] it is never certain where it will get you. Another commentator compared public order to Godot[26] because 'everyone talks about him, waits for him, but no one has ever seen him, or is sure about his existence'.[27] Husserl stated: 'The repeated stubborn efforts, made by Continental writers, to reduce the contents of *ordre public* to a clearly defined category have been altogether unsuccessful.'[28] Despite its unclear contents, national public order as used in private international law was called a 'safety net' to choice-of-law rules and rules governing the recognition and enforcement of foreign judgments; it is a doctrine which crucially defines the outer limits of the 'tolerance of difference implicit in those rules'.[29] To the contrary, it was also argued that '[t]he danger of a doctrine so vague as this is that it may be interpreted to embrace such a multitude of domestic rules, as to provide a fatally easy excuse for the application of the law of the forum and thus to defeat the underlying purpose of private international law'.[30] It seems that public policy or *ordre public* exception is a fertile ground for private international law research and judicial creativity.

Although the terms '*ordre public*', 'public order' and 'public policy' are used almost interchangeably in private international law, they have a noticeable difference in meaning.[31] Public policy is 'an intentional course of action followed by a government, institution, or official for resolving an issue of public concern'.[32] The notion of public policy is most frequently used in Anglo-American law, while 'public order' is the

Proceedings)' (2011) *JPIL*, 461, 461. '[I]n each legal system, there are certain norms which the forum should not dispense with in favor of a divergent foreign law.' Arthur Nussbaum, 'Public Policy and the Political Crisis in the Conflict of Laws' (1940) 49 *Yale LJ* 1027, 1030.

25 *Richardson* v. *Mellish*, (1824) 130 Eng. Rep. 294, 303; 2 Bing 229, 251–2 (Burrough J.).

26 Samuel Beckett, *Waiting for Godot* (New York's Grove Press 1954).

27 Marie Ghantous, 'Ordre Public Protection as Legitimate Aim for Freedom of Expression Restriction in the International Legal Order' (2018) 31 *Rev Quebecoise de Droit Int'l* 243, 248.

28 Gerhart Husserl, 'Public Policy and Ordre Public' (1938–9) 25 *Va L Rev* 40–1.

29 Alex Mills, 'The Dimensions of Public Policy in Private International law' (2008) 4 *Jour PIL* 201, 202.

30 Peter North and James J Fawcett, *Cheshire and North's Private International Law* 106 (Oxford University Press 1999).

31 See ibid., 251.

32 Clarke E. Cochran et al., *American Public Policy: An Introduction* (Cengage Learning 2009) 2.

more common formula in civil law countries. It has been argued that 'public policy in the common-law understanding represents a much broader [than public order] legislative category. In common law, the term also expresses to a certain degree the prevailing political view of societal priorities.'[33] Although, the difference in meaning is noticeable, this chapter treats all these terms as synonyms.[34]

The public order exception protects the sovereignty of national law against external influences. It resists the integration of foreign laws and judgments into the laws of the forum. However, it has been argued that national public order will decline when 'states gradually grow accustomed to resolving conflicts according to a universal standard'.[35] This, however, has not happened yet and national courts continue using public policy exception in their judgments.

Two interrelated features of *ordre public* in private international law make it problematic. First, the scope of national *ordre public* is unclear. Second, this unclear doctrine can prevent foreign laws from application, which can be a significant obstacle for international legal cooperation.[36] The latter is crucial for the outcome of some cases and one of the central issues in conflict of laws:[37] 'it requires courts to ask which rules of the forum are so fundamental that they should override transnational parties' choice of forum'.[38] It has to be interpreted and applied restrictively:

> Public policy clauses may be relied on only restrictively and under exceptional circumstances. Courts are prohibited from applying a public policy clause solely on the ground that there is a discrepancy between the applicable foreign law or

33 Alexander J. Bělohlávek, 'Public Policy and Public Interest in International Law and EU Law' (2012) *CYIL* 117, 118.

34 Although it seems that public order and public policy are seen as synonymous, the ECtHR has mostly referred to European public order. A HUDOC search shows that the phrase 'European public policy' has never been used in Chamber or Grand Chamber judgments. That said, the Court used 'public policy' in a few cases as a synonym of public order. *Paez* v. *Sweden*, 30 October 1997, Reports of Judgments and Decisions 1997-VII, para. 30. See also *Hatami* v. *Sweden*, 9 October 1998, Reports of Judgments and Decisions 1998-VII, para. 30.

35 Kent Murphy, 'The Traditional View of Public Policy and Ordre Public in Private International Law' (1981) 11 *Ga J Int'l & Comp L* 591, 601.

36 See, for example, Peter Kaye, *Civil Jurisdiction and Enforcement of Foreign Judgments* (Professional Books 1987) 1437; Karen E. Minehan, 'The Public Policy Exception to the Enforcement of Foreign Judgments: Necessary or Nemesis' (1996) 18 *Loy LA Int'l & Comp LJ* 795.

37 Mills (n. 29) 201.

38 Liam Harris, 'Understanding Public Policy Limits to the Enforceability of Forum Selection Clauses after Douez v Facebook' (2019) 15 *Jour PIL* 50, 89.

the decision of the foreign court and the law of the forum. A public policy clause must not be used for a revision of a foreign decision on its merits or as a lever to achieve results that are compatible with domestic law in general.[39]

Although public order needs to be applied restrictively, the precise boundaries of its application are not and perhaps cannot be established. It is a vague concept, but national courts are better placed to identify the boundaries of national public order than the ECtHR in relation to European public order. Moreover, when the scope of public order in the context of private international law is identified, its legal effect is quite clear – it can prevent the application of foreign laws. In the context of the ECtHR, this legal effect has not been clearly established by the ECtHR.

Unlike European public order deployed by the ECtHR, private international law understanding of public order is *procedural* rather than *substantive*. It means that private international law is not aiming to create some uniform *substance* of global public order but rather *procedurally* to facilitate the disapplication of foreign laws or judgments that contravene domestic public order but otherwise would be applicable.[40] The content of this public order is established by the local courts and not an international institution. So, effectively, when one examines public order in the context of private international law, one refers to a multitude of national domestic orders rather than a uniform international public order. This distinguishes this understanding from both the ECtHR and the Court of Justice of the European Union, which do not rely on a sum of national public orders but rather aim to create another integrated one, namely European public order.

In Section 3.2.3, I will therefore discuss national public order, in other words, 'a flexible and controversial notion, which is used as a defensive tool that protects the most basic fundamentals of justice and morality of a given state'.[41] I will not only focus on public order as understood by private international law mechanisms but I will spread the net of my analysis to include examples of national public order as used in national administrative, contract and constitutional law. This

[39] Jan Oster, 'Public Policy and Human Rights' (2015) 11 *Jour PIL* 542, 550.

[40] 'Ordre public in private international law or conflict of laws basically is not a concept of international, but of domestic law.' Martin Gebauer, 'Ordre public (Public Policy)' in *Max Planck Encyclopaedia of Public International Law* (2007) available at https://opil.ouplaw.com/view/10.1093/law:epil/9780199231690/law-9780199231690-e1448.

[41] Cornelia Lefter, 'Are the Rules of European Union Public Policy a Reality?' (2015) 5 *Juridical Trib* 254, 254.

is not a comprehensive comparative study and the examples are chosen for illustration purposes only.

3.2.3 *National Public Order and Public Order of the ECtHR*

If public order represents the most fundamental issues in a given society – why then is it so difficult to define? Intuitively, the core values should be self-explanatory. That said, such assumption of clarity is inaccurate because in difficult cases the core values might contradict each other, they can justify confronting results, and sometimes the meaning of this core value depends on the audience to whom a particular decision is speaking. The aim of this section is twofold: it will first examine the reasons why defining public order is challenging and then it will argue that all these reasons become even more pertinent when one examines public order on a regional or international level, such as the level of the Council of Europe.

It seems that there are at least four reasons why *ordre public* is vague and unclear. On the national level, the relatively close proximity of the national courts to this order makes these problems less detrimental to the usefulness of the legal concept of public order than in the case of the ECtHR, but they are nevertheless quite clearly identifiable. The first reason is that the concept of fundamental values that arguably constitutes the core of public order changes over time; it is not stable. As a result, the content of *ordre public* is something of a moving target; while it may seem clear and self-explanatory at some point of time, this view can change and the scope of public order can change too.[42] Second, the core of public order is morally charged, and disagreements are inherent to moral questions. Third, and this reason is a logical consequence of the previous one, is that non-contentious acceptable values of European public order are perhaps possible on a high level of abstraction that is less useful for deciding cases because they require a good deal of interpretation. Finally, *ordre public* is used in multiple contexts on the national level: administrative and contract law come naturally to mind. They have slightly different nuances of meaning and when they are transferred to the level of the Council of Europe, they merge into an unclear and overly vague concept. I will discuss these four reasons in more detail now.

[42] See Elena Rodriguez Pineau, 'European Union International Ordre Public' (1993–4) 3 *SYIL* 43, 50.

First, the content of public order is a moving target that changes over time. Its meaning develops with the society. It was argued that '[t]here is no *ordre public* and no public policy for all times and for all nations. Public policy is necessarily variable. It changes with changing conditions. The *ordre public* is a function of time and place.'[43] All courts, both national and international, that exist for a significant period of time face the challenge of changing conditions and adapting old laws to the new environment.[44] It is hardly possible to avoid evolutive interpretation of laws, especially such fundamentals as constitutions or human rights treaties that cannot easily be changed.[45] The reason is that there are constant social and technological changes that require amended rules and regulations. Do courts have legitimate authority or expertise to establish this meaning? Perhaps they do under certain conditions, namely, when they are not detached from the communities that constitute the society, when these communities are relatively homogenous and when there is a clear policy-maker elected democratically. These three conditions are evidently challenging as far as the ECtHR is concerned. The Court is dealing with diverse societies, the Court is detached from the community – a judge from Malta has very little understanding of the fundamental values that constitute public order in the Ukrainian society. Finally, there is no democratic counterpart to the Court that can correct the Court's understanding of European public order.

43 Husserl (n. 28) 42.

44 See, for example, Kanstantsin Dzehtsiarou and Conor O'Mahony, 'Evolutive Interpretation of Rights Provisions: A Comparison of the European Court of Human Rights and the U.S. Supreme Court' (2013) 44(2) *Colum Hum Rts L Rev* 309. Plenty has been written on the debate between originalist and dynamic interpretation of the US Constitution. See, for example, Bruce Ackerman, 'The Living Constitution' (2007) 120 (7) *HLR* 1738; David A. Strauss *The Living Constitution* (Oxford University Press 2010), Jack M. Balkin, 'Framework Originalism and the Living Constitution' (2009) 103 *Northwest UL Rev* 549; Lawrence B. Solum, 'Originalism versus Living Constitutionalism: The Conceptual Structure of the Great Debate' (2018) 113 *Northwest UL Rev* 1243.

45 Koch and Vedsted-Hansen argued:

> Some legal observers see this dynamic method of interpretation as producing legal uncertainty, because it makes it difficult if not impossible to foresee the state of the law within the near future. It cannot be ignored that interpreting such provisions as those laid down in international human rights treaties may imply a certain risk of lacking foreseeability. This is to some extent an inherent consequence of the established principles of treaty interpretation which generally differ quite much from the tradition of interpretation in domestic legal. Ida Elisabeth Koch and Jens Vedsted-Hansen, 'International Human Rights and National Legislatures – Conflict or Balance?' (2006) 75 *Nord J Int'l L* 311.

For national courts, in order to establish public policy, there should be some degree of societal convergence and a representative body that would be able to describe the directions in which this public policy develops. It has been argued that public policy functions as a general clause of a legal system. 'General clauses may be perceived thus as a technique for the judicial elaboration of rules for the case, particular rules that need further specification by reference to the legislative policies fostered by each branch of the legal system.'[46] At the national level, where parliaments set public policies, the court's power to define rather than interpret them is limited. A recent study confirmed that reliance of the parties on general, undefined public policy 'appear[s] to represent failed attempts to lure a court into discerning public policy where no public policy has been established through political means'.[47] This difficulty increases when there is no clear representative body, as is the case in the Council of Europe. Here, the ECtHR has to define rather than interpret particular public policies.

Unlike a national state which can to some extent justifiably claim the ability to define public policy, I argue that the ECtHR and the Council of Europe do not have sufficient institutional architecture to do so. On the national level, especially in proper democracies, the decision-making is done by the parliament, a representative body that can claim democratic authority in shaping the national public order. To the contrary, in the Council of Europe 'the "ownership" of public problems is often characterized by a policy vacuum'.[48] The Parliamentary Assembly of the Council of Europe (PACE) can hardly be compared to national parliaments. PACE is not directly elected, it does not have any legislative powers and, generally, it does not engage in general policy-making for Europe. Despite the fact that multiple conventions are signed under the umbrella of the Council of Europe, they have varying legal forms[49] and affect only certain areas of European social life. No Council of Europe institution can set some sort of comprehensive and consistent policy that can be legitimately described as European public order. When the

[46] Elena Rodriguez Pineau, 'European Union International Ordre Public' (1993–4) 3 *SYIL* 43, 45.

[47] David Adam Friedman, 'Bringing Order to Contracts against Public Policy' (2012) 39 *Fla St UL Rev* 563, 567.

[48] Diane Stone Global Public Policy, 'Transnational Policy Communities, and Their Networks' (2008) 36 *Policy SJ* 26.

[49] Most of them are soft law mechanisms.

boundaries of public policy are not established by democratic means, the Court's claims of shaping public policy become less persuasive.

The second reason why the concept of public order is very difficult to define, both nationally and internationally, is that it is closely connected to the values and morality shared among the members of a given society.

It seems that, in order to establish public order, national tribunals analysed values which were shared by the majority of persons in a particular territory. The Swiss Federal Tribunal, for example, viewed public policy procedurally and substantively, but both meanings require some level of value convergence. The Swiss Federal Tribunal claimed that 'procedural public policy is breached in case of violation of fundamental and generally recognised procedural principles, the disregard of which contradicts the sense of justice in an intolerable way, so that the decision appears absolutely incompatible with the values and legal system of a state ruled by laws'.[50] A ruling that breaches substantive public policy 'disregards some fundamental legal principles and consequently becomes completely inconsistent with the important, generally recognised values, which according to dominant opinions in Switzerland should be the basis of any legal order'.[51] Both types of public policy require common understanding and a common approach to fundamental values.

In some states, 'good morals'[52] are explicitly listed as part of public order. For instance, the French Council of State[53] in the case of *Commune de Morsang-sur-Orge et Ville d'Aix-en-Provence* ruled:

> Respect for the dignity of a human person is a component of public order. Consequently, the municipal police possesses power to prohibit an attraction which undermines it . . . While public order traditionally covers security, peace and public health, case law has extended the meaning of this concept to take into account, in certain specific circumstances, aspects of public morality . . .[54]

[50] Federal Tribunal, Judgment 4A_490/2009 of 13 April 2010, *Atlético/Benfica*, 2.1.

[51] Federal Tribunal, Judgment 4A_558/2011, 27 March 2012, *Matuzalem*, 4.1. For more discussion, see Daniel Rietiker, 'The European Court of Human Rights and FIFA: Current Issues and Potential Challenges' (2020) 1 *European Convention on Human Rights Law Review* 62; Ádám Boóc, 'Observations on the Definition of Public Policy (Ordre Public) in Swiss Arbitration Law' (2012) 53(3) *Acta Juridica Hungarica* 181.

[52] August Egger, *Schweizerisches Obligationenrecht* (Stampfli 1987) para. 507.

[53] Le Conseil d'État is the highest judicial authority for administrative justice.

[54] Le Conseil d'État a jugé que le respect de la dignité de la personne humaine est une composante de l'ordre public. Par conséquent, l'autorité investie du pouvoir de police municipale peut interdire une attraction qui y porte atteinte, même en l'absence de circonstances locales particulières' . . . Si l'ordre public recouvre traditionnellement sécurité, tranquillité et salubrité publique, la jurisprudence avait étendu l'acception de cette notion pour prendre en considération, dans certaines circonstances spécifiques,

One does not need much evidence to acknowledge that people disagree about morality. Morality is a contentious issue even on the national level, even more so across forty-seven contracting parties to the Convention. That said, many can agree on some very fundamental and abstract maxims, which might be of little use in real-life cases that post much more nuanced and specific questions. Unlike some scholars who argue that making moral choices is the primary function of judges,[55] I am sceptical about the legitimacy of judge-imposed morality within the space of a single state, let alone across the continent of Europe which includes very diverse countries. People have diverging views on difficult moral questions and unification of these views clearly falls outside the mandate of the ECtHR.[56] Here again, the assumption is that the proximity of the national courts to the matters at issue make them better arbiters of morality than the ECtHR. I have argued elsewhere that if the Court can demonstrate a clear trend in accepting a particular moral position and this position is compatible with the core of the Convention, then the Court can rubber-stamp the trend by finding violations in deviant countries.[57] Although this argument is not entirely free from drawbacks, it seems to have a better foundation than morally charged decision-making by the ECtHR judges.

The third reason why it is so complex to define public order is the ambiguity of the level of abstraction at which it can and should be defined.[58] Take, for example, one of the fundamental procedural rights:

des aspects de moralité publique .... (Translated by the author. Commune de Morsang-sur-Orge et Ville d'Aix-en-Provence, Council of State, available in summary at www.conseil-etat.fr/ressources/decisions-contentieuses/les-grandes-decisions-du-conseil-d-etat/conseil-d-etat-27-octobre-1995-commune-de-morsang-sur-orge-et-ville-d-aix-en-provence (in French))

55 See, for example, Letsas who adopted Dworkin's theory of moral reasoning to the ECtHR. George Letsas, *A Theory of Interpretation of the European Convention on Human Rights* (Oxford University Press 2007).

56 Jeremy Waldron, *Law and Disagreement* (Oxford University Press 1999); Jeremy Waldron, 'The Core of the Case Against Judicial Review' (2006) 115 *Yale LJ* 1346.

57 This technique is known as European consensus and used in many judgments of the ECtHR. See Vassilis Tzevelekos and Panos Kapotas (eds.), *Building Consensus on European Consensus: Judicial Interpretation of Human Rights in Europe and Beyond* (Cambridge University Press 2019); Kanstantsin Dzehtsiarou, *European Consensus and the Legitimacy of the European Court of Human Rights* (Cambridge University Press 2015); Luzius Wildhaber, Arnaldur Hjartarson and Stephen Donnelly, 'No Consensus on Consensus' (2013) 33 *HRLJ* 248; Daniel Peat, *Comparative Reasoning in International Courts and Tribunals* (Cambridge University Press 2019) ch. 6.4.

58 Monika Ambrus, 'Comparative Law Method in the Jurisprudence of the European Court of Human Rights' (2009) 2 *Erasmus LR* 353, 365. See also Eva Brems, *Human Rights: Universality and Diversity* (Springer 2001) 417–18.

equality of arms. It generally means that the parties in criminal and civil cases should have similar opportunities to present their case before the court.[59] This principle is arguably an important aspect of European public order.[60] However, what exactly constitutes equality of arms can be contested; it is up to individual states to decide the exact content of this principle. If one assumes that the principle of equality of arms suggests that the defence should have exactly the same set of opportunities as the accusers, then perhaps almost all countries in Europe fall short of this fundamental principle. If certain exceptions are possible, one might wonder where the line that separates acceptable exceptions from violations lies. As I pointed out earlier, it is easier to define commonly accepted elements of public order on a higher level of abstraction, although these definitions can be useless in concrete cases where specific rules are required. Therefore, while public order can perhaps be defined at a very abstract level, this is mostly useless because it would need to be interpreted; conversely, if it were defined on a more precise level, it would suffer from the difficulties of constant changes and moral disagreements.

Even if one defines public order at a very abstract level, one would then face major difficulties in applying it. 'The true meaning of *ordre public* and public policy is revealed to us by its operation in legal reality, as evidenced by the decisions of the Courts, statutory enactments and constitutional provisions.'[61] This difficulty can be illustrated by how public order is used in private international law. As has been established, public order can be used to prevent foreign judgments from application. It has been argued that fundamental rights are the core of public order.[62] Oster points out that '[b]ecause of its openness and flexibility … the concept of public policy … has proven to be a gateway to take on board human rights concerns when applying Private International Law'.[63] It means that national courts should stay

[59] Roger Gamble and Noel Dias, 'Equality of Arms Is a Blessed Phrase: Its Meaning under International Law' (2009) 21 *Sri Lanka J Int'l L* 187; Eva Brems and Laurens Lavrysen, 'Procedural Justice in Human Rights Adjudication: The European Court of Human Rights' (2013) 35 *Hum Rts Q* 176.

[60] In *Deweer* v. *Belgium*, the Court has included the entirety of Article 6 into 'an area concerning the public order (ordre public) of the member States of the Council of Europe'. *Deweer* v. *Belgium*, 27 February 1980, Series A no. 35, para. 49. The principle of equality of arms is explicitly mentioned in Article 6 and one can conclude that it falls at least within the area concerning the public order.

[61] Gerhart Husserl, 'Public Policy and Ordre Public' (1938–9) 25 *Va L Rev* 37, 41–2.

[62] Jan Oster, 'Public Policy and Human Rights' (2015) 11 *Jour PIL* 542, 547.

[63] Ibid., 542.

execution of foreign judgments and decisions if they contravene human rights.[64] The issue of the level of abstractness is crucial here because one needs to decide what human rights should be considered an essential part of public order. We can generally agree that prohibition of torture is part of public order and Article 3 of the ECHR is an authoritative provision containing an absolute prohibition. However, even in the case of Article 3, an academic debate flourishes as to some aspects of its application.[65] If one looks into qualified rights which allow some forms of state interference, the gap between different levels of abstraction in terms of their applicability and relevance to public order will be even more evident. For instance, while freedom of political expression and political debate can be said to be fundamental in a modern democratic society,[66] freedom of commercial expression[67] can hardly be within the core of national public order because of its limited protection by human rights law in general. The challenge here is what human rights should reach the level of public order to prevent application of foreign laws. A similar challenge is applicable to the ECHR: if all rights enshrined in the ECHR are part of European public order, then references to European public order are just rhetorical substitutes for referring to the rights of the Convention, and if they are something else then the level of abstraction is crucial in identifying the utility of this concept.

The final reason why European public order is more unclear and vaguer than national public orders is that it was borrowed by the

64 Gebauer (n. 40).

65 See, for example, Steven Greer, 'Should Police Threats to Torture Suspects Always Be Severely Punished? Reflections on the Gäfgen Case' (2011) 11 *HRL Rev* 67; Natasa Mavronicola, 'Is the Prohibition Against Torture and Cruel, Inhuman and Degrading Treatment Absolute in International Human Rights Law? A Reply to Steven Greer' (2017) 17 *HRL Rev* 479; Neil Graffin, 'Gäfgen v Germany: The Use of Threats and the Punishment of Those Who Ill-Treat During Police Questioning: A Reply to Steven Greer' (2017) 17 *HRL Rev* 681; Stijn Smet, 'Conflicts between Absolute Rights: A Reply to Steven Greer' (2013) 13 *HRL Rev* 469.

66 The Court noted that 'freedom of political debate is at the very core of the concept of a democratic society'. *Rekvényi* v. *Hungary* [GC], no. 25390/94, ECHR 1999-III, para. 26. The 'principle that has been consistently emphasised in the Court's case-law is that there is little scope under Article 10 § 2 of the Convention for restrictions on political expression or on debate on questions of public interest'. *Perinçek* v. *Switzerland* [GC], no. 27510/08, ECHR 2015, para. 197.

67 The breadth of such a margin of appreciation varies depending on a number of factors, among which the type of speech at issue is of particular importance. Whilst there is little scope under Article 10 § 2 of the Convention for restrictions on political speech ... States have a broad margin of appreciation in the regulation of speech in commercial matters or advertising. (*Mouvement raëlien suisse v. Switzerland* [GC], no. 16354/06, ECHR 2012, para. 61)

ECtHR from national law, where it is also quite confusing. Moreover, the ECtHR does not offer much in terms of the role and meaning of European public order in its case law.[68] In these circumstances, the original meaning of this concept is of little help because the Court's application of this formula might make it quite unrecognisable to lawyers working on the national level. Of course, the Court has borrowed many different methods of interpretation of the Convention from national legal systems. The test of proportionality[69] and the margin of appreciation[70] naturally come to mind. However, unlike these concepts, European public order is used by the Court less frequently and is not filled with identifiable meaning.

On the national level, *ordre public* also has slightly different nuances of meaning depending on where the term is used. For example, the above-mentioned case of the French Council of State included human dignity into the ambit of *ordre public*.[71] So, in the area of administrative law, dignity is part of public order, while in the area of French constitutional law, it is not: 'The Constitutional Council, for its part, did not recognise public order as also encompassing human dignity. This can be explained by the fact that there is an independent basis for protecting it.'[72] This term is also used in French civil law. Article 6 of the French Civil Code provides that '[o]ne may not by private agreement derogate from laws that concern public order and good

[68] See Chapter 2 for more detail.

[69] See Fiona de Londras and Kanstantsin Dzehtsiarou, *Great Debate on the European Convention on Human Rights* (Palgrave 2018) ch. 5; Stavros Tsakyrakis, 'Proportionality: An Assault on Human Rights?' (2009) 7 *ICON* 468; Madhav Khosla, 'Proportionality: An assault on Human Rights?: A Reply' (2010) 8 *ICON* 298; Juan Cianciardo, 'The Principle of Proportionality: The Challenges of Human Rights' (2010) 3 *J Civ L Stud* 177.

[70] Among many other sources, see Andrew Legg, *The Margin of Appreciation in International Human Rights Law* (Oxford University Press 2012); Yutaka Arai-Takahashi, *The Margin of Appreciation Doctrine and the Principle of Proportionality in the Jurisprudence of the ECHR* (Intersentia 2001); Petr Agha (ed.), *Human Rights Between Law and Politics: The Margin of Appreciation in Post-National Contexts* (Bloomsbury 2017); George Letsas, 'Two Concepts of the Margin of Appreciation' (2006) 26 *OJLS* 705; Eyal Benvenisti, 'Margin of Appreciation, Consensus, and Universal Standards' (1999) 31 *NYU J Int'l L & Pol* 843; Michael R. Hutchinson, 'The Margin of Appreciation Doctrine in the European Court of Human Rights' (1999) 48 *International and Comparative Law Quarterly* 638.

[71] *Commune de Morsang-sur-Orge et Ville d'Aix-en-Provence* (n. 54).

[72] 'Le Conseil constitutionnel, lui, n'a pas reconnu l'ordre public comme englobant aussi la dignité humaine. On peut expliquer cela par le fait qu'il existe un fondement indépendant permettant de la protéger.' Translated by the author. Vincent Schnebel, 'Histoire d'un grand arrêt: Commune de Morsang-sur-Orge, une blague de juriste pas si drôle' (2012) available at https://chevaliersdesgrandsarrets.com/2012/01/24/morsang-sur-orge/.

morals'.[73] It was argued that the mandatory provisions of the French Civil Code are included in public order as understood by Article 6 of the Code.[74] Article 791 is one of these mandatory provisions which reads as '[o]ne may not, even by an ante-nuptial agreement, renounce the succession of a living person or transfer contingent rights which one may have to that succession'.[75] It is unlikely that this provision constitutes *ordre public* from the perspective of constitutional or administrative law. The concept of *ordre public* has slightly different meanings in the contract law of Germany, Italy, Switzerland and the UK.[76] Therefore, in order for European Public Order to be a legal formula with some identifiable consequences the ECtHR would really need to explain what it means in the context of its case law. It is unlikely that precise meaning can be borrowed from national legal systems as they offer a multiplicity of divergent meanings.

To briefly conclude, the challenges that are known in relation to application of public order in a national legal context grow in scope and intensity when it is migrated to the international level. A problematic and vague concept is unlikely to become clearer and less problematic when it is spread across forty-seven member states.

3.3 The Vague Benchmarks of European Public Order

In Section 3.2, I attempted to show that European public order is hard to define. Several terms are used to refer to public order with different meanings in different contexts, which tend to change over time. In this section, I will try to discuss the benchmarks that could have helped to identify European public order and attempt to see how these work in the case of the ECHR as a constitutional instrument of European public order.[77] These benchmarks are the features of public order which are common to most circumstances in which public order is used. They include a well-defined territory within which people share some common values; the necessity to protect the autonomy of the entity against some externalities; an emphasis of the most important aspects of a particular social structure; and the ability to enforce public order if

[73] Article 6 of the French Civil Code.

[74] Lubos Tichy, 'Ordre Public, Abuse of Rights and Other General Clauses and the New Czech Civil Code' (2014) 9 *ELTE LJ* 15–16.

[75] Article 791 of the French Civil Code.

[76] See Tichy (n. 74) 17–19.

[77] *Loizidou* v. *Turkey* (preliminary objections) (n. 1) para. 75.

that is required. In essence, these features reflect the role of European public order. For instance, public order should be applicable on a particular territory because the ECtHR referred to it in a number of judgments in which the application of the Convention to 'questionable' territories was under consideration.[78] Moreover, European public order must be distinct from a non-European public order which logically should be applicable to any territory that is not covered by the former. In the rest of this section (3.3.1–3.3.4), I explain why these features are necessary for public order and what they mean.

3.3.1 *Common Territory and Values*

Public order is a value-driven concept. When public order is not understood as a normal state of affairs in a particular society,[79] its meaning is closely connected to the values that require protection from interferences and disturbance. It is helpful to identify what values warrant protection; these values are not only expressed in local laws, although these are important indicators. It has been argued:

> In order to approach the content of ordre public the whole system must be studied, taking into account not only its particular legal features but also its philosophy, the policies it pursues, its economic, moral, social and political characteristics. The content of public policy is not to be found listed in legislation. On the one hand, because of the variability of this constantly changing notion, legal systems do not usually provide a fixed set of principles that can be said to be those of public policy.[80]

A quest for common values might be a difficult one. It is safe to suggest that none of the courts in the world could engage in deep societal research in order to clearly identify shared values. They lack time, expertise and finances to do so, and it equally does not fall within their remit. Moreover, such research would most likely be useless because it would reveal people's common disagreement on what values represent. Territory is important in this respect. Although it is not universally true, more disagreements are likely on a more largely populated territory. If it is possible to find some common understanding of certain issues in a given village in the Austrian Alps, the same might be much more difficult across Austria, even harder in the EU and the

[78] See Chapter 2 for a more detailed discussion of the ECtHR case law related to European public order.

[79] See Section 3.2 for more detail.

[80] Elena Rodriguez Pineau, 'European Union International Ordre Public' (1993–4) 3 *SYIL* 43, 50.

Council of Europe, and worldwide. Therefore, larger territories call for public order of a higher level of abstraction, and a higher level of abstraction is less useful in deciding cases. As a result, shared values can be seen as another feature of public order.

The idea of international public order has also been discussed in legal scholarship for quite some time now.[81] Perhaps this public order is only possible at the maximum level of abstraction. Only *jus cogens* norms,[82] a notion which itself has attracted criticism, can perhaps form part of international public order. European societies are more homogenous than societies worldwide, but, still, the diversity is too significant and it is difficult to argue that each and every right of the ECHR is part of European public order.[83] Moreover, it is hard to separate between those rights that fall within the core and those that are outside.

The Preamble to the ECHR states that the contracting parties to the Convention are 'like-minded and have a common heritage of political traditions, ideals, freedom and the rule of law'.[84] In practice, the commonalities are perhaps either overestimated or mentioned as an ideal to be achieved, rather than a portrayal of the present situation. In any event, it is not difficult to prove that there are plenty of human rights issues that cause disagreements in Europe including abortion,[85] proper reasons for extradition and deportation,[86] marriage equality,[87] limits on freedom of expression[88] and many more.

[81] See, for example, Erika de Wet, 'The International Constitutional Order' (2006) 55 *Int'l & Comp LQ* 51, 52; Marie Ghantous, 'Ordre Public Protection as Legitimate Aim for Freedom of Expression Restriction in the International Legal Order' (2018) 31 *Rev Quebecoise de Droit Int'l* 243, 249.

[82] Georg Schwarzenberger, 'International Jus Cogens' (1965) 43 *Tex L Rev* 455; Andrea Bianchi, 'Human Rights and the Magic of Jus Cogens' (2008) 19 *EJIL* 491.

[83] It was argued that 'the idea of a specifically European-based public policy, which would bring European values into play by virtue of a nexus with the territories covered by the European Convention, still remains largely to be elaborated; court practice tends to refer to national, rather than European, connections'. Muir Watt (n. 24) 546; Gennady M Danilenko, 'International Jus Cogens: Issues of Law-Making' (1991) 2 *EJIL* 42; Karen Parker, 'Jus Cogens: Compelling the Law of Human Rights' (1989) 12 *Hastings Int'l & Comp L Rev* 411.

[84] ECHR, Preamble.

[85] *A., B. and C.* v. *Ireland* [GC], no. 25579/05, ECHR 2010; *Tysiąc* v. *Poland*, no. 5410/03, ECHR 2007-I; *P. and S.* v. *Poland*, no. 57375/08, 30 October 2012.

[86] *Othman (Abu Qatada)* v. *the United Kingdom*, no. 8139/09, ECHR 2012; *Saadi* v. *Italy* [GC], no. 37201/06, ECHR 2008.

[87] *Oliari and Others* v. *Italy*, nos. 18766/11 and 36030/11, 21 July 2015.

[88] *Jersild* v. *Denmark*, 23 September 1994, Series A no. 298; *Delfi AS* v. *Estonia* [GC], no. 64569/09, ECHR 2015; *Von Hannover* v. *Germany*, no. 59320/00, ECHR 2004-VI.

It is important to note that there are many countries in which these questions lead to heated debate. Surely, public order can function or be established where there is no agreement in the society as to its key values, under the condition that the national constitutional system establishes a mechanism for legitimately resolving such disagreements. If there is no representative body, the differences in values may seem to be decided arbitrarily.

There is a plurality of values in Europe; arguably, the lack of homogeneity is a value in itself. That said, building a public order as the aim of the ECtHR requires the establishment of a hierarchy of common values. The Court does not seem to have the legitimacy to set this hierarchy. It is much better equipped to facilitate incremental changes in human rights standards rather than force a vague common European public order onto its contracting parties.

If the theory of constitutional pluralism is correct then European and national constitutional structures need to 'somehow accommodate the claims of the others as independent sites of constitutional authority – thereby ensuring the continuing absence of a single dominant authoritative framework'.[89] Although the theory of constitutional pluralism was developed predominantly to describe the constitutional structure of the EU,[90] there were attempts to apply it to the ECtHR.[91] The views on the ECHR as a constitutional element of European public order perhaps presuppose that there is a set of shared values among the contracting parties to the Convention and that the Court has the authority to declare these values. Considering that there is no democratic counterpart on the level of the Council of Europe, the Court might disturb the delicate pluralist balance between the ECtHR and the contracting parties to the Convention.

3.3.2 *The Outer Limits of Public Order and Protection of the ECtHR's Autonomy*

In private international law, a state can protect some aspects of its public order by using the public policy exception to prevent foreign

[89] Neil Walker, 'Constitutional Pluralism Revisited' (2016) 22 *ELJ* 333,334.

[90] See, for example, Alec Stone Sweet, 'A Cosmopolitan Legal Order: Constitutional Pluralism and Rights Adjudication in Europe' (2012) 1 *GlobCon* 53; Matej Avbelj and Jan Komárek, 'Four Visions of Constitutional Pluralism' (2008) 4 *EuConst* 524; Miguel Poiares Maduro, 'Interpreting European Law: Judicial Adjudication in a Context of Constitutional Pluralism' (2008) 1 *Eur J Legal Stud* 13; Neil Walker, 'The Idea of Constitutional Pluralism' (2002) 65 *Mod L Rev* 317.

[91] Steven Greer and Luzius Wildhaber, 'Revisiting the Debate about "Constitutionalising" the European Court of Human Rights' (2013) 12 *HRL Rev* 655.

laws from being applicable on its territory and refusing the recognition or enforcement of foreign decisions.[92] It seems that European public order can potentially be applied vis-à-vis some other orders. I have already argued that European public order and the public order exception in private international law are different in nature, but the former might have some connection to the autonomy of the forum. Meidanis argues that public order is 'the ultimate expression of national sovereignty in a world of gradual convergence (legal and beyond)'.[93] In the case of the ECtHR, autonomy is a better word to capture the essence of my argument because national sovereignty suggests certain elements like governance and external relations that the ECtHR simply does not have. Unlike the values that populate the content of public order, the protection of autonomy is an external function of public order. When national courts use public order, they signal that contradictory foreign values cannot be placed above the national ones. So, what does the ECtHR protect when it discusses European public order?

The Court can use European public order vis-à-vis the contracting parties and, in this sense, European public order is an order that is separable from the sum of the public orders of the contracting parties; alternatively, the Court refers to public order to defend its autonomy from the states or international organisations outside the ECtHR's influence. I will now discuss these two roles of European public order in turn.

In order to describe the relations between European and national public order, their respective scopes need to be established. I have argued already that this is perhaps the biggest challenge for the application of European public order as a legal concept. Here, I will use European public order as an analytical formula and only briefly consider whether the entire ECHR falls within the definition of European public order, or only some core element thereof. Then, I will examine how the separate regime of European public order can be reconciled with national public orders. Pursuant to Article 19, the ECtHR is created to ensure observance of engagements undertaken by the contracting parties to the ECHR.[94] The primary role of the Court is to protect human rights from unjustified interferences by the contracting parties. Some commentators argue that the whole of the ECHR constitutes a part of

[92] Jan Oster, 'Public Policy and Human Rights' (2015) 11 *J Priv Int'l L* 542, 545.

[93] Haris P. Meidanis, 'Public Policy and Ordre Public in the Private International Law of the EU: Traditional Positions and Modern Trends' (2005) 30 *EL Rev* 95, 98.

[94] Article 19 ECHR.

European public order.[95] In that case, the Court's references to European public order make limited sense as the ECtHR is already enforcing all of the ECHR rights anyway. From the legal standpoint, this argument is a circular one because every violation of every right under the Convention is, by extension, an assault on European public order and, therefore, repeating this in the case law does not add anything to the Court's reasoning. However, for argument's sake, in this section, I will assume that all rights of the Convention are included in European public order.

It is difficult to establish what relations European public order has with national public orders because the scope of both orders is unclear. These two vague but similar phenomena overlap to a considerable degree, meaning that European public order cannot be disconnected from national public orders. Most national constitutions include human rights as part of their order and national constitutional or supreme courts create a body of law that can influence the ECtHR.[96] Does this mean that European public order is a sum of the national orders of the contracting parties? Perhaps, no. The Court uses the commonly accepted standards in its jurisprudence through the European consensus doctrine.[97] I argued in the past that European consensus is a rebuttable presumption[98] and because this presumption can be rebutted, it is difficult to maintain that European consensus directly reflects European public order. Moreover, it seems that the Court itself has never made a clear connection between European public order and European consensus in its case law.

Although European consensus is not an exact representation of European public order, the exchange of standards between European and national public orders is constantly happening. Both standards are adjusted through various mechanisms. National public orders feed the ECtHR standards through such mechanisms as European consensus,[99] the Court's presentation and analysis of relevant national legislation in every judgment,[100] the presence of national judges at the bench in Strasbourg and of national lawyers in the Court's Registry,[101] and

95 Muir Watt (n. 24) 551–2; Meidanis (n. 93) 102; Škerl (n. 24) 466–7.

96 Chapter 2 of the Constitution of Russia; Chapter 2 of the Constitution of Poland; Title 2 of the Belgium Constitution.

97 Dzehtsiarou (n. 57).

98 Ibid., 9.

99 Ibid.

100 For example, see *Navalnyy* v. *Russia* [GC], nos. 29580/12 and four others, 15 November 2018, paras. 43–8.

101 See Article 22 ECHR; de Londras and Dzehtsiarou (n. 69) 20–2.

discretion as to how to implement the judgments of the ECtHR. Downwards mechanisms include delivery by the ECtHR of its legally binding judgments,[102] the *de facto erga omnes* effect of the ECtHR rulings,[103] and various soft mechanisms such as judicial training and conferences explaining the standards developed by the ECtHR.[104] The mutual influences of national and European public orders are a 'constant battle', but the resulting changes need to be incremental and acceptable by both sides. Coming back to the key point of this section, the ECtHR needs to defend the autonomy of its order vis-à-vis national orders without significantly undermining the autonomy of the latter. Of course, the key challenge is how to set the acceptable limits of interference of both orders. If the ECtHR is too proactive, it will hit the legitimacy wall and its judgments will not be executed; if the ECtHR is too slow in following the contracting parties, it might lose its influence and fail to protect human rights properly.

Although the view that European public order and national public orders develop in dialogue, collaboration and co-operation[105] is

[102] Article 46 ECHR.

[103] Greer points out:

> Although there may be room for debate about whether or not 'the principle of solidarity' is in fact embodied in the Convention, and whether or not it suggests an erga omnes effect . . . Since the final, authoritative, interpretation of these rights and freedoms lies with the Court, if the Court finds a certain practice in a certain state to be contrary to the Convention, it would be very difficult for another state to argue that precisely the same practice did not constitute a breach of its obligations . . . .
> (Steven Greer, *The European Convention on Human Rights. Achievements, Problems and Prospects* (Cambridge University Press 2006) 280)

Ress points out that, '[n]ormally, judgments of the Court do not have an erga omnes effect, but they have an orientation effect'. Georg Ress, 'The Effect of Decisions and Judgments of the European Court of Human Rights in the Domestic Legal Order' (2005) 40 *Tex Int'l LJ* 359, 374. Helfer also argues that '[t]here is no obligation, however, for government decision-makers to give ECHR judgments this erga omnes effect'. Laurence R. Helfer, 'Redesigning the European Court of Human Rights: Embeddedness as a Deep Structural Principle of the European Human Rights Regime' (2008) 19 *EJIL* 125, 136. For more general debate about *erga omnes* obligations in international law, see Maurizio Ragazzi, *The Concept of International Obligations Erga Omnes* (Oxford University Press 2000); Theodor Meron, 'State Responsibility for Violations of Human Rights' (1989) 83 *Proceedings of the Annual Meeting (ASIL PROC)* 372; Edith Brown Weiss, 'Invoking State Responsibility in the Twenty-First Century' (2002) 96 *AJIL* 798.

[104] The ECtHR has initiated creation of the Superior Courts network. More information available at www.echr.coe.int/Pages/home.aspx?p=court/dialoguecourts/network&c.

[105] Merris Amos, 'The Dialogue between United Kingdom Courts and the European Court of Human Rights' (2012) 61 *Int'l & Comp LQ* 557; ' Judicial Dialogue in the European Court of Human Rights' in A. Müller (ed.), *Judicial Dialogue and Human Rights* (Cambridge University Press 2017).

appealing, there are examples of contracting parties expressing principled disagreement with ECtHR judgments.[106] If the national public order and European public order fail to coincide then three developments are possible: two extremes are unlikely, namely, that the states will either break away from the system or willingly comply with the judgment with which they disagree in principle; a more likely scenario is the gradual merging of the standards. This is what happened in the (in)famous prisoner voting rights confrontation between the UK and the ECtHR.[107] In the case of *Hirst No. 2* v. *the UK*, the Court ruled that blanket disenfranchisement of convicted prisoners is a violation of the ECHR.[108] Then the Court suggested that disenfranchisement should be individually applied by the sentencing Court.[109] The UK authorities expressed significant dissatisfaction with this ruling.[110] The Court loosened its standard[111] and, finally, the UK accepted an even more curtailed version of it.[112] This is a natural development of the standards that allows national public orders and European public order to merge. Although the ECtHR did not explicitly refer to European public order in the cases related to the prisoner voting debate, it is relevant here as an analytical, not a legal, concept.[113] The ECtHR is not created to defend the

106 Marten Breuer (ed.), *Principled Resistance to ECtHR Judgments: A New Paradigm?* (Springer 2019); Fiona de Londras and Kanstantsin Dzehtsiarou, 'Mission Impossible? Addressing Non-execution through Infringement Proceedings in the European Court of Human Rights' (2017) 66 *Int'l & Comp LQ* 467.

107 Brice Dickson and Helen Hardman (eds.), *Electoral Rights in Europe: Advances and Challenges* (Routledge 2017); Ed Bates 'Analysing the Prisoner Voting Saga and the British Challenge to Strasbourg' (2014) 14 *HRL Rev* 503.

108 *Hirst* v. *the United Kingdom (no. 2)* [GC], no. 74025/01, ECHR 2005-IX.

109 *Frodl* v. *Austria*, no. 20201/04, 8 April 2010.

110 The former prime minister of the UK noted that this judgment made him 'physically ill'. 'UK May Be Forced to Give Prisoners the Vote in Time for May Elections' *The Guardian* (1 February 2011) available at www.theguardian.com/society/2011/feb/01/prisoners-vote-may-elections-compensation-claims. During the backbench debate on the issue, MPs were also quite critical of the suggestion. For instance, Mr Philip Hollobone stated: 'It is the settled view of the British people, through their elected representatives in the British Parliament, that prisoners should not have the right to vote, and it has been that way since 1870.' Finally, he questioned the substantive legitimacy of the ECtHR by asking '[h]ow has it come about that we, in a sovereign Parliament, have let these decisions be taken by a kangaroo court in Strasbourg, the judgments of which do not enjoy the respect of our constituents?'. The Backbench Parliamentary Debates, 'Prisoners' Right to Vote', available at www.publications.parliament.uk/pa/cm201011/cmhansrd/cm110210/debtext/110210-0002.htm.

111 *Scoppola* v. *Italy (no. 3)* [GC], no. 126/05, 22 May 2012.

112 *Hirst* v. *the United Kingdom (no. 2)* (n. 108). Status of execution, http://hudoc.exec.coe.int/eng?i=004-2204.

113 See Chapter 1 and Section 3.1 of this chapter where the difference is discussed.

autonomy of European public order against the contracting parties; it is created to develop and adjust it in line with the key developments within the contracting parties.

Since European public order is not used to protect the autonomy of the ECHR system from the member states, it can be utilised to protect such autonomy vis-à-vis external intrusions. I now review a few illustrative examples where the clash between the ECHR and external forces comes into play. The aim of this exercise is twofold: first, to show that the Court does not really understand European public order as a protector of its values; and second, to demonstrate that its deployment is ad hoc, unpredictable and does not follow a clear logic of defending of the autonomy of European public order against external influences.

External interferences in European public order can manifest themselves through various forms. The request to enforce foreign judgments and decisions which might violate the autonomy of such order is one of them. In this context, the Court shows some inconsistency in referring to European public order. When it comes to enforcement of UN or EU sanctions, the Court makes references to European public order. For instance, in *Al-Dulimi and Montana Management Inc.* v. *Switzerland*, the Court was requested to check whether the UN smart sanctions[114] as applied by Switzerland comply with the ECHR.[115] Here, the Court stated that non-arbitrariness is part of European public order and, therefore, the Swiss authorities need to scrutinise the compliance of sanctions with the ECHR.[116] Failure to do so led to finding a violation of the ECHR.

In the case of *Neulinger and Shuruk* v. *Switzerland*, the Court considered whether the decision of a national court to enforce a foreign judgment was compatible with the Convention. Here, the Grand Chamber stated:

> [T]he Court must ... bear in mind the special character of the Convention as an instrument of European public order (*ordre public*) for the protection of individual human beings and its own mission, as set out in Article 19, 'to ensure the observance of the engagements undertaken by the High Contracting Parties' to the Convention. For that reason the Court is competent to review the procedure followed by domestic courts, in particular to ascertain whether the domestic courts, in applying and interpreting the provisions of the Hague Convention, have secured the guarantees of the Convention and especially those of Article 8.[117]

[114] See David Cortright and George A. Lopez (eds.), *Smart Sanctions: Targeting Economic Statecraft* (Rowman and Littlefield 2002).

[115] *Al-Dulimi and Montana Management Inc.* v. *Switzerland*, no. 5809/08, 26 November 2013.

[116] Ibid., paras. 145–7.

[117] *Neulinger and Shuruk* v. *Switzerland* [GC], no. 41615/07, ECHR 2010, para. 133.

Here, the Court found a violation of Article 8. However, in an earlier case of *Maumousseau and Washington* v. *France*,[118] the Court had to deal with a similar set of circumstances considering whether a foreign judgment should be executed. The Court did not find a violation of Article 8 and also made no reference to European public order.[119] The Court does not seem to see that references to European public order act as a mechanism to protect the internal order of the ECtHR from undue outside influence. If this was the idea, it is not executed consistently or persuasively by the Court.

Another example of interference from outside the Council of Europe in the Convention public order is related to extradition requests. The Court can rule that the ECHR will be violated if an applicant is extradited to a country where she or he can be ill-treated or killed.[120] Extradition requests present a challenge to the Court because it needs to compare the requirements of European public order with the public orders that exist outside its jurisdiction. It seems that the extradition context is very appropriate for references to public order. Despite the fact that European public order has been mentioned a couple of times in the extradition context,[121] it has never been used as a reason to prevent extradition. For example, in *Savriddin Dzhurayev* v. *Russia*, the Court referred to European public order while discussing the failure of the Russian authorities to comply with interim measures prescribed by the Court.[122] However, when discussing the substance of this extradition request, the Court referred only to Article 3 of the Convention without expressing the need to back it up with European public order. This lack of a direct link between extradition and public order is quite telling. The ECtHR does not see the need to refer to European public order when an external order is seemingly interfering. It means that the Court does not really consider European public order as a concept that protects the autonomy of the ECtHR system.

[118] *Maumousseau and Washington* v. *France*, no. 39388/05, 6 December 2007.

[119] For more detailed discussion of this case, see, Louwrens Rienk Kiestra, 'The Recognition and Enforcement of Foreign Judgments: The Obligation to Recognize and Enforce Foreign Judgments' in *The Impact of the European Convention on Human Rights on Private International Law* (T.M.C. Asser Press 2014).

[120] See *Soering* v. *the United Kingdom*, 7 July 1989, Series A no. 161; *Chahal* v. *the United Kingdom*, 15 November 1996, Reports of Judgments and Decisions 1996-V.

[121] As was explained in Chapter 2, the Court mentioned European public order when dealing with interim measures and admissibility of complaints in the area of extradition but not when it comes to substance.

[122] *Savriddin Dzhurayev* v. *Russia*, no. 71386/10, ECHR 2013, para. 213. See Chapter 2 for more detail.

Similarly, the Court could have used European public order as a protector of its autonomy when referring to legal sources in its reasoning. The Court has never used European public order to justify the priority of internal legal sources over external sources.[123] Effectively, there is no clear hierarchy of sources applied by the Court. In some cases, the Court was prepared to accept the development of human rights standards outside Europe as a reason for the higher level of protection of human rights afforded under the Convention.[124] It seems that the ECtHR does not use European public order as a justification for its preference for internal sources over sources from outside the Council of Europe.

To conclude, the Court does not see European public order as a replacement for national orders. These orders coincide in the core and the peripheral standards gradually develop to merge. The ECtHR also does not use it to protect its autonomy from external influences. Here, the Court uses European public order quite inconsistently.

3.3.3 *Setting the Human Rights Hierarchy*

Another benchmark for European public order is as an indicator that can separate the core set of rights and standards that enjoy particular protection under the ECHR from other peripheral standards. In the following paragraphs, I will assess whether the Court has the ambition to use European public order as a label for the most important rights.

The Court refers to some rights as part of European public order, but it does this inconsistently. If one assumes that there are some core human rights among others, then such an approach creates a whole series of challenges.[125] It means that some rights are worthier than others and more stringent tests of proportionality should be applied to these rights. Of course, ECHR rights are not all the same – some rights are absolute, some qualified, some derogable and some non-derogable – but Chapter 2 suggests that the Court does not only mention European public order in relation to rights of a particular type. Another possible

[123] For a more detailed discussion of the sources used by the ECtHR, see Kanstantsin Dzehtsiarou, 'What Is Law for the European Court of Human Rights?' (2017) 49 *Georgetown J Int'l Law* 89.

[124] *Christine Goodwin* v. *the United Kingdom* [GC], no. 28957/95, ECHR 2002-VI; *Hirst* v. *the United Kingdom (no. 2)* (n. 108).

[125] Tereya Koji, 'Emerging Hierarchy in International Human Rights and Beyond: From the Perspective of Non-derogable Rights' (2001) 12 *EJIL* 917; Theodor Meron, 'On a Hierarchy of International Human Rights' (1986) 80 *AJIL* 1; Eckart Klein, 'Establishing a Hierarchy of Human Rights: Ideal Solution or Fallacy' (2008) 41 *Isr L Rev* 477.

explanation of the selection of rights is that these rights are selected randomly by some non-strategic choice of arguments made by the drafting lawyers of the Court. In other words, the references to European public order occur haphazardly, irrespective of the ECHR provision applied. Once this formula ends up in a judgment, it starts its own life being repeated in other judgments, sometimes in similar contexts, at other times in quite different contexts, and sometimes the Court stops using references to European public order in a particular context after a certain period of time.

As Chapter 2 shows, references to public order were common in the context of admissibility decisions in the early days of the Court.[126] Applications to the Court were sparse at that time and the Court would assess whether an inadmissible application should nevertheless be adjudicated in the interests of public order. More recently, the Court has had no shortage of applications and these references have ceased to exist. Moreover, they have not been used as a counterbalance to non-admissibility for a prolonged period of time.

The case of *Loizidou* makes perhaps the most well-known reference to European public order.[127] After *Loizidou*, this reference re-emerged in many (but not all) cases dealing with the extraterritorial application of the Convention. I call this phenomenon the 'Brownian motion'[128] of legal terms because often it randomly resurfaces in certain contexts, then it appears in subsequent judgments, some of which are relevant and others not.[129] This inconsistent application makes it difficult to substantiate the point that the ECtHR actually signals that some rights are more important because they belong to European public order.

It is almost impossible to clearly establish a ground on the basis of which human rights can be divided between those within and those outside European public order. Here, it suffices to say that in the earlier case law the Court stated that the right to liberty and security (Article 5 of the Convention)[130] and the right to a fair trial (Article 6 of the Convention)[131] fall within the ambit of European public order. In the

[126] See, for example, *Paez* v. *Sweden* (n. 34).
[127] *Loizidou* v. *Turkey* (preliminary objections) (n. 1) para. 75.
[128] Ioannis Karatzas and Steven E. Shreve, 'Brownian Motion' in *Brownian Motion and Stochastic Calculus* (Graduate Texts in Mathematics, vol. 113) (Springer 1998).
[129] I will discuss 'Brownian motion' of European public order in more detail in Chapter 6.
[130] *De Wilde, Ooms and Versyp* v. *Belgium*, 18 June 1971, Series A no. 12, para. 65.
[131] *Deweer* v. *Belgium*, 27 February 1980, Series A no. 35.

more recent cases, the Court started saying that those rights that can be associated with the protection of democracy are linked to European public order.[132] All these rights are fairly different in nature; while the right to liberty and security under Article 5 ECHR can be interfered with by the authorities only under certain clearly defined conditions, Article 11, for instance, allows a much broader range of interferences. The Court does not often mention European public order in relation to absolute rights which one would assume must be part of European public order. The lack of a clear purpose for its deployment and the scattered occurrence of these references throughout the history of the ECtHR both point to the conclusion that the Court does not seek to set a hierarchy of rights and supports the suggestion about the Brownian motion of this term through the case law of the ECtHR.

The Court has not used European public order to establish some sort of hierarchy of the rights enshrined in the Convention. The Court's references to European public order are inconsistent: they migrate between different rights which are often not logically connected.

3.3.4 *Proper Enforcement Mechanisms*

Finally, if a court has the ambition to enforce its vision of public order, it needs to have a proper mechanism of enforcement. This benchmark is a pragmatic one because a court not only needs to declare a particular form of public order, it also needs to enforce it. Otherwise, the court's vision of public order would remain a theoretical construct. This issue is discussed in more detail in Chapter 5.

It is widely acknowledged that the ECtHR has a weak system of enforcement.[133] Its impact mostly relies on persuasion rather than enforcement *stricto sensu*. The Committee of Ministers of the Council of Europe is entrusted with supervising the implementation of the ECtHR's judgments. This body comprises representatives of the ministries of foreign affairs of the member states of the Council of Europe. The range of tools that the Committee of Ministers can use is rather limited. They can issue resolutions condemning the resisting states for their lack of enforcement; then they can send the cases back to the ECtHR, declaring that they have not been properly

[132] See *United Communist Party of Turkey and Others* v. *Turkey*, 30 January 1998, Reports of Judgments and Decisions 1998-I, para. 45.

[133] See Başak Çali and Anne Koch, 'Foxes Guarding the Foxes? The Peer Review of Human Rights Judgments by the Committee of Ministers of the Council of Europe' (2014) 14(2) *HRL Rev* 301.

enforced;[134] finally, the Committee of Ministers can suspend and expel states for failing to co-operate in the area of human rights.[135] Resolutions and returning cases back to the Court can cause some reputational damage, but this damage is hardly substantive. The nuclear option of suspension and expulsion is hardly an option at all. Even when a member state occupies part of another member state, the Council of Europe fails to initiate these mechanisms.[136] If the violation is less serious than occupation, then it is naïve to expect the Committee of Ministers to expel. So, some reputational damage is all that can be done by the Committee of Ministers. If the Court tries to enforce its vision of European public order, in other words, its vision of the most important aspect of the normal functionality of the society, and if some states resist, then some reputational damage will unlikely persuade these states to accept this new vision of public order. This again shows that the Court should not apply European public order vis-à-vis contracting parties. Moreover, and as I have already pointed out, states have a wide area of discretion at the stage of implementation and can adjust the judgment of the ECtHR to the vision of public order that they maintain locally.

3.4 Conclusion

Section 3.2 showed that it is effectively impossible to clearly define public order. It is used in a variety of contexts, and what unites each of these contexts is that public order is vague and imprecise. It is used in the sense of social security and preservation of normalcy in a given society, but it is unlikely that the ECtHR means this when referring to European public order. It is widely used in private international law and here it means the core values of a given forum. But despite the term having been used for more than a few hundred years, a proper definition of such public order is not possible. It is also used in national contract, administrative and public branches of law. This section concludes that it is hardly possible to define international or regional

134 See, for example, *H46-42 Kaverzin group* (Application No. 23893/03); *Afanasyev group* (Application No. 38722/02); and *Belousov* v. *Ukraine*. (Application No. 4494/07) CM/Notes/1377bis/H46-42 available at https://search.coe.int/cm/Pages/result_details.aspx?ObjectId=09000016809e9230.

135 Article 8 of the Statute of the Council of Europe.

136 See Kanstantsin Dzehtsiarou and Donal K Coffey, 'Suspension and Expulsion of Members of the Council of Europe: Difficult Decisions in Troubled Times' (2019) 68 *Int'l & Comp LQ* 443.

public order on a level of abstraction which is meaningful for practical adjudication.

Section 3.3 identified four key benchmarks that reveal the role and features of European public order: reflecting the values of the peoples living on a particular territory, protecting the autonomy of the forum, setting a potential hierarchy of these values and, finally, enforcing these values among the stakeholders. One might conclude that European public order can reflect common values only on a very high level of abstraction. European public order is not used by the ECtHR as a protector of the autonomy of the Strasbourg system vis-à-vis the contracting parties. The Court's application of European public order vis-à-vis external actors is haphazard and inconsistent. European public order does not and should not indicate a hierarchy of human rights. Finally, due to the weak enforcement mechanism, the Court cannot make the contracting parties adopt the Court's view on European public order if it is not shared by the state authorities.

4 The Function of the European Court of Human Rights

4.1 Introduction

This monograph aims to establish whether the European Court of Human Rights (the ECtHR or the Court) can effectively shape European public order. The Court claims that the European Convention on Human Rights (the ECHR or the Convention) is the constitutional instrument of European public order;[1] since the Court is the sole official interpreter of the Convention,[2] it is implied that the Court's role is to build European public order. Moreover, some ECtHR judges in their dissenting opinions or extrajudicial writing have suggested just that. The present chapter examines whether this is indeed the case, that is, whether the regulation of European public order is one of the functions that the ECtHR has been entrusted with and what this function might entail.

First, the functions of the ECtHR should be considered by comparing the ECtHR with other international tribunals. Assessment of the effectiveness of any organisation depends on how well it achieves its aims.[3] Thus, if shaping European public order is not a function of the ECtHR, then the Court's failure to shape it does not say much about its effectiveness. Alternatively, if this is the core function of the Court then it needs to show that its case law frames and defines European public order. This chapter does not look into the Court's ability to impact European public order;[4] rather, it explores whether the Court should

1 *Loizidou* v. *Turkey* (preliminary objections), 23 March 1995, Series A no. 310, para. 93.
2 Article 32 of the ECHR.
3 See Yuval Shany, *Assessing the Effectiveness of International Courts (International Courts and Tribunals Series)* (Oxford University Press 2012) 14; see also Chester Barnard, *The Functions of the Executive* (Harvard University Press 1951) 20; and James L. Price, 'The Study of Organizational Effectiveness' (1972) 13 *Sociol Q* 3, 3–7.
4 This is done in Chapters 5 and 6.

be under pressure to do so. It asks not whether the Court *can* shape European public order but whether it *should* shape it.

This latter question does not have a single correct answer and often it depends on who is being addressed. Some state representatives would likely subscribe to a minimalist view on the function of the Court; to the contrary, some human rights defenders would adopt an exceptionally wide conception of its function. There is no agreed view on the function of the Court even among the ECtHR judges.[5] Therefore, the first part of this chapter looks into what is often included in the 'shopping list' of functions of international courts and tribunals. It is argued that international tribunals are entrusted with two sets of functions: their technical function suggests that they are designed only to resolve conflicts in a particular case; their more controversial meta-function suggests that they are created to develop the law in the area they are set to supervise. It is argued here that the latter function is more abstract and difficult to determine. Moreover, the fact that the ECtHR can hardly be conceptualised as a strategic actor makes the development of its meta-function an ad hoc exercise susceptible to being described only on a very abstract level. With this assumption in mind, this chapter proceeds by analysing what might be included in the meta-function of the ECtHR.

I argue that the academic debate surrounding this issue captures the crux of the matter incorrectly. Calling the meta-function of the Court a 'constitutional function' adds an unnecessary layer of complexity. I then argue that the debate is mainly concerned with whether the meta-function of the Court *should* have priority over its technical function. I approach this debate by trying to identify a precise content of the Court's meta-function, which is a complex task because it changes over time and depends on a multiplicity of factors. I conclude that, since the content is vague and hardly possible to determine, it would be illogical for the meta-function to take priority over the Court's technical adjudicatory function, which is easier to define. As I have pointed out in Chapter 3, vagueness as such is not an insurmountable difficulty for

[5] Some judges interviewed for this monograph saw the Court's function very restrictively. Judge 18 pointed out: 'The primary role for the protection of human rights is on national institutions. That is why one of the main principles based on which this Court functions is the principle of subsidiarity and the doctrine of the margin of appreciation. Domestic institutions are better located for establishing facts, assessing facts and providing social balance.' Interview with Judge 18. To the contrary, Judge 24 opined: 'I think that the Court to a certain extent should act as a constitutional court. I would be somebody who would say that the living instrument is alive.' Interview with Judge 24.

some legal terms or phenomena. However, when one considers the function of a court like the ECtHR, clarity is of existential importance. If the Court implicitly or explicitly declares its priority to be a vaguely defined meta-function, and there is significant disagreement about the meaning of this function, then such a declaration might destabilise the Court. This argument is substantiated by looking at how the Court's meta-function is seen and presented in academic writing, the Court's case law and the extrajudicial speeches of the presidents of the ECtHR.

There is disagreement as to what the meta-function of the Court is. Academics, majorities of the Court, dissenting judges and ECtHR presidents have significantly varying understanding of the content of the Court's meta-function. Moreover, there are major divergences within each of these groups. For instance, some dissenting judges argue in favour of a restrictive view on the meta-function of the Court; at the same time, others point out that the Court needs to be more active and expansive in order to enhance its impact. So, what does this conclusion about diverging views on the meta-function of the Court mean for European public order? If there is no clear view on what the meta-function of the Court is, then it is highly unlikely that the Court can legitimately claim that it should strategically and conscientiously shape European public order. These grandiose claims need to be legitimate; if there is no clear and supported anchor to them, they are destined to remain empty rhetorical phrases.

4.2 What Are International Courts For?

One can suggest that the core purpose of international tribunals is to settle disputes in contentious cases peacefully and to explain international law through various comments and advisory opinions. That said, this adjudicatory aim fails to explain a court's role that goes beyond 'simple' conflict solving and interpretation. I argue that most international courts have two types of function: a technical one and a meta-function. The former function covers a court's adjudication and decision-making in the cases under its consideration. The latter one is a secondary function that furthers the strategic goal of a particular tribunal. The meta-function 'uses' judgments and advisory opinions not as self-sufficient phenomena but as means by which to help tribunals realise their ideal version of law and society in their specialised area. I will discuss these two types of function in turn.

4.2.1 *Technical Function*

The technical function is relevant to a court's 'immediate' adjudication; it explains the court's role in delivering a particular judgment in a particular case. Traditionally, tribunals were seen as mere instruments for resolving legal disputes[6] and the technical function facilitates the achievement of this aim. Shelton classifies the key functions of a court as being

> to (1) interpret the submissions of the parties to isolate the issue(s) in the case and identify the object(s) of the claim; (2) determine whether the court is competent to hear a particular matter; (3) determine whether the court should refrain from exercising [the] jurisdiction that it has; and (4) decide all issues concerning the exercise of its jurisdiction, including ruling on questions about evidence, burden of proof, due process, and questions of law relevant to the merits of the dispute.[7]

In other words, these functions help the court to make a justified decision based on the evidence at hand. They do not include any strategic purposes that an international court might strive to achieve in the long run and only support its immediate decision-making. The technical function is crucial for an international court or tribunal, but it is not concerned with broad implications of a judgment beyond the immediate outcome of a case. This technical function of a court is closely connected to the process legitimacy of a tribunal.[8] For example, if tribunals select meritorious applications transparently and consistently, explain properly the reasons for their judgments and come up with clear, fair and executable decisions, then they ensure that the stakeholders have sufficient reasons to comply with those judgments. That said, it seems that the key strategic role of an international tribunal is consolidated in its meta-function.

4.2.2 *Meta-function*

The rulings of an international tribunal aim to put an end to conflicts, but, beyond that, some judgments are means by which

[6] Geir Ulfstein, 'International Courts and Judges: Independence, Interaction, and Legitimacy' (2014) 46 *NYU J Int'l L & Pol* 849, 860.

[7] Dinah Shelton, 'Form, Function, and the Powers of International Courts' (2009) 9 *Chi J Int'l L* 537, 545.

[8] Process legitimacy has been widely discussed in academic literature. See Kanstantsin Dzehtsiarou, 'Does Consensus Matter? Legitimacy of European Consensus in the Case Law of the European Court of Human Rights' [2011] *PL* 535; Thomas M. Franck, 'Why a Quest for Legitimacy' (1987) 21 *UC Davis L Rev* 535, 543; J. L. M. Gribnau 'Legitimacy of the Judiciary' (2002) 6 *EJCL*; see also Max Weber, *Wirtschaft und Gesellschaft* (J.C.B. Mohr (Paul Siebeck) 1972) 19; Joseph Raz, *The Authority of Law* (Clarendon Press 1979).

to achieve a more fundamental end. If understood from this perspective, conflict resolution is just an immediate or tactical outcome which contributes to a much grander agenda of shaping a particular body of law. This, in turn, contributes to a strategic purpose of shaping stakeholders' behaviour in a way that complies with the core purpose of a tribunal. This is especially true when a tribunal is not a technical interpreter of the detailed provisions of a treaty but is entrusted with populating abstract norms with applicable meaning. The ECtHR clearly falls within the latter category.[9] The open-ended provisions of the Convention allow wide judicial discretion and the outcome of a case sometimes depends mostly on its interpretation rather than on its text *strictu sensu*.

This meta-function has been examined by international law scholars for some time now. According to von Bogdandy and Venzke: 'International courts stabilize normative expectations, which includes the reassertion of international law's validity and its enforcement; they develop normative expectations and thus make law; and they control and legitimate the authority exercised by others'.[10] In other words, the meta-function of an international tribunal is to develop the body of law in the area it is supposed to safeguard.[11] Talking about international courts and tribunals, Geir Ulfstein identifies the following meta-functions: '[d]etermine an authoritative interpretation of a legal norm beyond the relevant case (precedential or *erga omnes* effect); [d]evelop international legal norms through their interpretation ("lawmaking"); [c]ontribute to the operation and legitimation of related legal regimes and institutions; [and p]romote compliance with specialized and general international legal norms, as well as the rule of law in the international society'.[12] Almost none of these functions is predominantly concerned with the immediate resolution of conflict between the parties to the case; rather, they represent an ambition of tribunals to shape the law.

[9] Judge Paulo Pinto de Albuquerque stated that 'the Convention is a law-making treaty and not a mere contract treaty'. Paulo Pinto de Albuquerque, 'Plaidoyer for the European Court of Human Rights' (2018) 2 *EHRLR* 119, 121.

[10] Armin von Bogdandy and Ingo Venzke, 'On the Functions of International Courts: An Appraisal in Light of Their Burgeoning Public Authority' (2013) 26 *LJIL* 49, 49.

[11] See also Daniel Terris et al., *The International Judge: An Introduction to the Men and Women Who Decide the World's Cases* (Oxford University Press 2007) 229.

[12] Ulfstein (n. 6) 860.

4.3 Can the European Court of Human Rights Act Strategically?

This section argues that, in order to fulfil its meta-function, the Court needs to be able not only to set some strategy but also to act strategically. It is important to define what I mean by strategy. Unlike many political scholars, I do not examine whether the Court can change its case law to enhance its political legitimacy. It has been argued that 'judges strategically attempt to set precedents that they believe will be followed and implemented by other actors, including political actors'.[13] Here, acting strategically refers to the ability of the Court to set long-term policy objectives and consistently work towards their realisation. Such strategy is not set in stone and changes over time, but the Court needs to operate as a strategic actor to update and streamline this detailed strategy. I argue that the design of the Court does not suggest that it can build a long-term strategy and lead the contracting parties towards its realisation. However, this ability to act as a strategic actor is crucial for the Court's claim that it can shape European public order.

It is quite rare for a tribunal to continue operating in the same environment for the whole duration of its existence unless it functions only for a very short period of time. If a tribunal is effective and remains in existence for a significant period of time, then the context of its existence inevitably changes. Therefore, the content of a court's meta-function changes over time too: tribunals are not stable; they evolve.[14] For example, take the main meta-function of the ECtHR; it was created to safeguard the rights enshrined in the ECHR by interpreting said

[13] Yonatan Lupu, 'International Judicial Legitimacy: Lessons from National Courts' (2013) 14 *Theo Inq L* 437, 447. There is plenty of research considering national courts as strategic actors, especially in the context of the US Supreme Court. See, for example, Lee Epstein and Jack Knight, *The Choices Justices Make* (Congressional Quarterly Press 1998); Forrest Maltzman, James F. Spriggs II and Paul J. Wahlbeck, *Crafting Law on the Supreme Court: The Collegial Game* (Cambridge University Press 2000); Lee Epstein and Tonja Jacobi, 'The Strategic Analysis of Judicial Decisions' (2010) 6 *Annu Rev Law Soc Sci* 341; Jeffrey R. Lax and Charles M. Cameron, 'Bargaining and Opinion Assignment on the US Supreme Court' (2007) 23 *J L Econ & Org* 276; Richard L. Revesz, 'Environmental Regulation, Ideology, and the D.C. Circuit' (1997) 83 *VA L Rev* 1717; David W. Rohde, 'Policy Goals, Strategic Choices, and Majority Opinion Assignments on the U.S. Supreme Court' (1972) 16 *Midwest J Polit Sci* 652; Jeffrey K. Staton and Georg Vanberg, 'The Value of Vagueness: Delegation, Defiance, and Judicial Opinions' (2008) 52 *AM J Polit Sci* 504.

[14] See David D. Caron, 'Towards a Political Theory of International Courts and Tribunals' (2006) 24 *Berkeley J Int'l L* 401, 411.

Convention.[15] This aim was the same when the Convention was created in the 1950s and the Court was not effectively operating; the same aim was predominant in the 1960s, 1970s and 1980s during the so-called 'sleeping beauty'[16] period of the Convention; it was the same in the 1990s and 2000s when huge support for human rights allowed the Court to develop the key aspects of its jurisprudence;[17] and it is the same now when the Court and the Convention are getting a much colder reception.[18] While the formal description of this function has stayed the same, its content has changed significantly. As I argued in Chapter 2, the content of European public order is vague and changes over time. The Court's role cannot be clarified if its vague meta-function can be fulfilled by shaping the vague notion of European public order.

Understanding the meta-function through the notion of public order suggests that international tribunals, in particular the ECtHR, are strategic actors. This means that their judges effectively consider what context presently exists in international law and politics, and determine the strategy that they need to undertake in order to further the aims of a given court.[19] This strategic vision is crucial because without it the Court cannot intentionally shape European public order; it can only coincidentally influence it. The impact of the Court on European public order can be described as a collateral effect of its technical function. In other words, strategic vision is needed to create a picture from the multiple pieces of the puzzle: the picture being European public order and the pieces being the judgments of the Court. Having said that, this strategic approach to the ECtHR is problematic on a number of practical levels. First, the judges of international courts frequently change[20] and it is often difficult to decide on a particular long-term strategy within the relatively

[15] See the Preamble to the Convention, as well as Article 19 of the Convention.

[16] See Ed Bates, *The Evolution of the European Convention on Human Rights* (Oxford University Press 2010) 172–388.

[17] Robert Spano, 'The Future of the European Court of Human Rights – Subsidiarity, Process-Based Review and the Rule of Law' (2018) 18 *Hum Rights L Rev* 473, 477.

[18] Mikael Rask Madsen, 'The Challenging Authority of the European Court of Human Rights: From Cold War Legal Diplomacy to the Brighton Declaration and Backlash' (2016) 79 *LCP* 141, 167–75.

[19] There is plenty of literature that considers whether international tribunals are strategic actors. Among others, see Lee Epstein and Jack Knight, 'Toward a Strategic Revolution in Judicial Politics: A Look Back, a Look Ahead' (2000) 53 *Political Res Q* 625; Shai Dothan, *Reputation and Judicial Tactics: A Theory of National and International Courts* (Cambridge University Press 2014).

[20] For instance, in the ECtHR they are elected for a period of nine years.

short period of a judicial tenure. Second, the judges might have different views on the meta-function of the Court. For example, it is no secret that some judges of the ECtHR see the Court as the constitutional court of Europe capable of imposing its will on national states,[21] while others have a very different approach which focuses on subsidiarity.[22] All important judgments are deliberated by the judges collectively[23] and therefore, depending on the composition of the Court, the outcomes of different cases may point in different directions.[24] Moreover, the views of the judges on the meta-function of the Court differ significantly.[25] Third, the retrospective nature of the Court's adjudication means that it almost always assesses past situations which likely have only a limited impact on the future. Although the Court can influence the outcome in similar cases in future, this influence can be restricted by the specificity of the facts of the initial case. Fourth, the ECtHR has a very limited role in supervising the execution of its judgments and often the message that the Court attempts to convey is diluted after the judgment is enforced.

One can, of course, suggest that the role of the Court judges is limited and the key strategies are developed by the Registry of the ECtHR. Indeed, the Registry is an important element of the Strasbourg Court. The Registry lawyers represent the Court's institutional memory and often it is the Registry lawyers who draft judgments, assist judges in preparing cases and suggest solutions. However, the role of the Registry should not be overestimated. Although the Registry is very influential in running everyday operations of the Court, the most important strategic decisions of the behaviour of the Court are made, or at least should be made, by the Court judges.

The judges of the ECtHR interviewed for this monograph have confirmed that they do not normally discuss the abstract matters that stem from a particular case. Instead, they attempt to uncover a proper solution to

[21] See Dissenting Opinion of Judge Pinto de Albuquerque, Joined by Judges Hajiyev, Pejchal and Dedov. *Al-Dulimi and Montana Management Inc.* v. *Switzerland* [GC], no. 5809/08, 21 June 2016.

[22] Rober Spano, 'Universality or Diversity of Human Rights?: Strasbourg in the Age of Subsidiarity' (2014) 14 *Hum Rights L Rev* 487.

[23] Important meritorious cases are adjudicated by either the Chamber of seven judges or the Grand Chamber of seventeen judges.

[24] There is an institute of jurisconsult at the Court. According to the Rules of Court, for the purposes of ensuring the quality and consistency of its case law, the Court shall be assisted by a jurisconsult (Rule 18B). However, jurisconsult can only point to possible inconsistencies and cannot force judges to take a particular decision.

[25] See Chapter 6 for an overview of the interviews with the judges, who expressed quite divergent views on what the key purpose of the Court is.

the case at hand.[26] Therefore, the meta-function can be a coincidental consequence of a set of decisions rather than a well-thought-through strategy. Another possible explanation for the perception that the ECtHR is a strategic actor is that the commentators might see some trends while ignoring cases pointing in another direction, thus expressing academic confirmation bias.

The meta-function of international tribunals is to develop the body of law in the area they are designed to safeguard. Arguably, in the context of the ECtHR, this body of law is related to European public order. That said, the limited capacity to act strategically makes this meta-function of the Court abstract and overly ambiguous.

Section 4.4 considers, in more detail, what technical and meta-functions the ECtHR is designed to fulfil. I begin by looking into legal scholarship and then examine the case law and the extrajudicial writing of the judges of the ECtHR. The view of the contracting parties of the Convention has been omitted from this analysis, but it will be discussed in detail in Chapter 5 of this monograph.

4.4 What Is the European Court of Human Rights For?

The scholarly analysis of the function of the ECtHR does not focus on the question of whether the Court has a meta-function at all. The fact that the Court does not only resolve the conflict in a particular case but also influences European human rights standards is generally accepted.[27] The debate concentrates on the question of whether the meta-function of the Court should have a priority over the more technical function of conflict resolution. The legal discourse here is framed around the issue of the constitutional role of the ECtHR, in other words, whether the Court should prioritise its constitutional function over a so-called

26 See Chapter 6 discussing the interviews with the judges.

27 Certain judges of international human rights tribunals were '[a]sked what their institutions are ultimately for, [and they gave] a variety of answers. Despite the many differences among the types of court they sit on and [the] cases they hear, their responses fall into three areas: the establishment of a community of law, the preservation of the dignity of the individual, and the prevention of violence and war.' Daniel Terris et al. (n. 11) 229. All these categories fall within the broader category of meta-function of an international court. Perhaps with the exception of the preservation of dignity of the individual, which can be found on both the technical and the meta-level, other functions fall squarely within the meta-function of an international tribunal.

adjudicatory function.[28] I argue here that this conceptualisation is misleading and the discussion needs to be arranged in terms of the meta-function and technical function of the Court; the latter terminology captures the crust of this challenge better. After showing that 'meta-function' is a better term than the 'constitutional role of the Court', I demonstrate that the indeterminate nature of this meta-function can make the attempts to prioritise it futile and undermines a more straightforward technical function.

The debate about the function of the ECtHR should be built around the cleavage between meta-function as opposed to technical function rather than between the constitutional and the adjudicatory nature of the Court. The arguments about the priority of the constitutional model of the ECtHR[29] might be misunderstood and they can mislead such debate. The very term 'constitutional justice' is borrowed from national law and its application to the ECtHR is problematic. Depending on what is meant by a constitutional court, the ECtHR both *is* and *is not* a constitutional court. If a constitutional court is one that deals with the interpretation of a bill of rights, then the ECtHR must be a constitutional court because the substantive provisions of the Convention[30] are similar to the human rights norms of many national constitutions.[31] Alternatively, the question might relate to the ability of constitutional courts to determine the structure of power-sharing in a state, for example by determining the particularities of

[28] Steven Greer and Luzius Wildhaber, 'Revisiting the Debate about "Constitutionalising" the European Court of Human Rights' (2013) 12 *HRL Rev* 655; Luzius Wildhaber, 'A Constitutional Future for the European Court of Human Rights?' (2002) 23 *HRLJ* 161; Stephen Greer, *The European Convention on Human Rights* (Oxford University Press 2006); Alec Stone Sweet, 'On the Constitutionalisation of the Convention: The European Court of Human Rights as a Constitutional Court' (2009) 80 *RTDH* 923; Kanstantsin Dzehtsiarou and Alan Greene, 'Restructuring the European Court of Human Rights: Preserving the Right of Individual Petition and Promoting Constitutionalism' [2013] *PL* 710; Fiona de Londras, 'Dual Functionality and the Persistent Frailty of the European Court of Human Rights' [2013] *EHRLR* 38; Oddný Mjöll Arnardóttir, 'The Brighton Aftermath and the Changing Role of the European Court of Human Rights' (2017) 9 *JIDS* 223.

[29] See, for example, Shelton arguing that '[s]ome courts focus more on the public, even constitutional aim of the regime in which they operate than they do on dispute settlement'. Shelton (n. 7), 564. Greer points out: 'The European Court of Human Rights has effectively become the Constitutional Court for greater Europe, sitting at the apex of a single, transnational, constitutional system.' Steven Greer, 'What's Wrong with the European Convention on Human Rights?' (2008) 30 *HRQ* 680, 701.

[30] By this I mean the Articles which enshrine human rights, e.g. Articles 2–14 of the Convention, Articles 1–3 of Protocol 1, etc.

[31] For instance, Articles 3–17 of the Basic Law of the Federal Republic of Germany, Articles 17–64 of the Constitution of Russia and Articles 13–54 of the Constitution of Italy.

electoral or administrative laws; such competencies fall within the scope of jurisdiction of many national constitutional courts. In this case, the ECtHR is not a constitutional court. Moreover, the term 'constitutional' can have many connotations that diverge the debate. Namely, it presents the Court as an ultimate authority shaping power within Europe which can be seen as a major interference with national sovereignty and damage the Court's ability to resolve conflicts. This unnecessary layer of uncertainty overshadows the core question of whether the ECtHR should prioritise a technical function of conflict resolution or its meta-function of impacting European public order.

The scholarly debate in this area can be described as the following: one group of scholars argue that the Court must prioritise its meta-function or, as it is commonly called, 'the constitutional function of the Court'. They suggest that the Court must focus on enhancing human rights protection on a strategic level.[32] In other words, the aim of the Court must be to deliver judgments that can move human rights forwards rather than to restore the human rights of the particular applicant. The commentators belonging to this group maintain that individual applications are just a means to an end. The national authorities are then required to effectuate the standards that are established by the Court. Restoring the rights of a particular applicant is effectively 'useless' if it does not lead to strategic changes in the respondent state and/or in Europe more generally. There are many ideological and practical consequences of this suggestion. From the ideological perspective, the Court should not concentrate on small, insignificant and perhaps repetitive meritorious applications. In practice, this means that the Court needs to have a significant degree of discretion in the selection of individual applications to maximise its impact on the 'grand picture' of human rights protection in Europe.[33]

The second group of academics, while accepting the value of the meta-functions of the ECtHR, argue that it should not completely overshadow

[32] See, for example, Wildhaber (n. 28).

[33] See Helen Keller, Andreas Fischer and Daniela Kühne, 'Debating the Future of the European Court of Human Rights after the Interlaken Conference: Two Innovative Proposals' (2010) 21 *EJIL* 1025, 1037. This paper refers to the report by the Steering Committee on Human Rights (CDDH) which concluded that the 'proposal to decline cases for examination which raise no substantial issue under the Convention would give too wide a discretion to the Court enabling it to pick and choose the cases it would wish to deal with. It would also entail an important restriction of the right of individual application'.

the technical function and that deciding individual cases is, at least, equally important.[34] The then president of the ECtHR, Dean Spielmann, eloquently explained the approach of this group of academics:

> [T]he European Court has certain similarities with constitutional courts, [but] that is only part of the picture. Our Court also deals with cases that do not raise new issues of principle or interpretation, but are important nonetheless. They are the cases that have made the reputation of the Convention system – cases of torture and ill-treatment, cases of illegal detention, of arbitrary interferences with property rights, etc. For me, then, maintaining the dual function of the European Court is crucial.[35]

As mentioned earlier, this debate is not purely theoretical; it can have a number of tangible consequences for the design, composition and *modus operandi* of the Court.[36] For instance, if the function of conflict resolution in a particular case is not that important, then the Court might invest more resources into dealing with Grand Chamber cases which deal with the most complex and controversial issues,[37] rather than 'wasting' its time on thousands of repetitive applications which may not further the Court's meta-function.

I have argued that the Court's meta-function is rather impossible without its main task of technical conflict resolution.[38] The Court gets an idea of what is important and what is not from dealing with hundreds of individual applications. Moreover, the Court can have a proper impact on the standards of human rights protection when a particular point is repeated in a major number of judgments and decisions. Although the discussion of the priority of a technical or meta-function is an important one, the key question this chapter asks is how the meta-function can be articulated. These various competing meta-functions can be illustrated by the following example.

[34] See, for example, Dzehtsiarou and Greene (n. 28); Marie-Benedicte Dembour, '"Finishing Off" Cases: The Radical Solution to the Problem of the Expanding ECtHR Caseload' [2002] *EHRLR* 604, 621.

[35] A speech by President Spielmann, 'Address' (Meeting with the Supreme Court and the Supreme Administrative Court, Stockholm, 19 May 2014) available at www.echr.coe.int/Documents/Speech_20140519_Spielmann_ENG.pdf.

[36] Geir Ulfstein, 'International Courts and Judges: Independence, Interaction, and Legitimacy' (2014) 46 *NYU J Int'l L & Pol* 849, 864.

[37] Fiona de Londras and Kanstantsin Dzehtsiarou, 'Managing Judicial Innovation in the European Court of Human Rights' (2015) 15 *HRL Rev* 523, 532–4.

[38] Dzehtsiarou and Greene (n. 28).

It is useful to consider two cases dealing with Article 3 violations: *Buntov* v. *Russia*[39] and *Bouyid* v. *Belgium*.[40] In both cases, the Court found a violation of Article 3 that prohibits torture, inhuman and degrading treatment. In *Buntov*, the Court dealt with a brutal case of torture in prison which constituted an obvious violation of Article 3. To the contrary, in *Bouyid*, the Court considered the borderline situation of whether a slap on the face by a police officer falls within the ambit of Article 3. If the meta-function of the Court is to define the standards and deal with complex cases, then *Bouyid* should take priority; however, if the key meta-function of the Court is to eliminate grave violations of human rights, then the *Buntov* case is an obvious choice. This shows that defining the meta-function is not only a theoretical exercise but can additionally have significant practical consequences.

The Court's Rules of Procedure[41] do not help to identify the Court's priorities or to define its meta-function. Although the ECtHR has published its priority policy,[42] it mostly arranges applications depending on the urgency of the case and what Articles of the Convention are involved. Only priority category II can be said to reflect a potential meta-function of the Court; this category includes '[a]pplications raising questions capable of having an impact on the effectiveness of the Convention system (in particular a structural or endemic situation that the Court has not yet examined, pilot-judgment procedure) or applications raising an important question of general interest (in particular a serious question capable of having major implications for domestic legal systems or for the European system)'.[43] Even here, this definition leaves a broad area of discretion to the decision-makers based on their concept of the meta-function of the Court, thus placing its definition in the eye of the beholder. This policy does not determine the meta-function of the Court but rather the meta-function can determine the content of this policy.

The Court described its binary function in *Rantsev* v. *Cyprus and Russia*:

[39] *Buntov* v. *Russia*, no. 27026/10, June 2012.

[40] *Bouyid* v. *Belgium* [GC], no. 23380/09, ECHR 2015. For a detailed commentary, see Natasa Mavronicola, 'Bouyid v Belgium: The "Minimum Level of Severity" and Human Dignity's Role in Article 3 ECHR' (2020) 1 *Eur Conv Hum Rights L Rev* 105.

[41] They include the Rules of Court available at www.echr.coe.int/documents/rules_court_eng.pdf as well as other official policies.

[42] ECtHR, 'The Court's Priority Policy' available at www.echr.coe.int/Documents/Priority_policy_ENG.pdf.

[43] Ibid.

> [Its] judgments serve not only to decide those cases brought before it but, more generally, to elucidate, safeguard and develop the rules instituted by the Convention, thereby contributing to the observance by the States of the engagements undertaken by them as Contracting Parties. Although the primary purpose of the Convention system is to provide individual relief, its mission is also to determine issues on public-policy grounds in the common interest, thereby raising the general standards of protection of human rights and extending human rights jurisprudence throughout the community of the Convention States.[44]

Here, the Court seems to prioritise its technical function while acknowledging its broader meta-function. Former president of the ECtHR Guido Raimondi has also identified the meta-function of the Court's judgments: '[A]lthough the judgments naturally have a concrete impact on the situation of the individual applicant, their value goes beyond that by virtue of this interpretative role of the Court.'[45] Section 4.5 looks at the precise scope of the meta-function of the ECtHR.

4.5 What Is the Court's Meta-function?

There is a general agreement among legal scholars and practitioners that most international courts do not simply resolve conflicts between parties but contribute somewhat to the development of the body of law they are designed to apply.[46] A challenge is to define the more precise content of the meta-functions of the ECtHR. This section examines the relevant legal scholarship and extrajudicial writing of the Court judges. It is safe to conclude that there is no agreement here and that meta-functions often depend on the views and preferences of a particular commentator.

4.5.1 *The View on the Court's Meta-function from Academia*

Greer and Wildhaber have identified the challenge of defining the precise content of the Court's meta-functions by distinguishing between the meta-functions from the perspective of activists as opposed to those in favour of judicial self-restraint. They argue:

> 'Judicial activists' and 'perfectionists' are likely to consider the Court's mission to be, first, the steady expansion of human rights on a widening front, second, the abandonment of notions such as subsidiarity and margin of appreciation in

[44] *Rantsev* v. *Cyprus and Russia*, no. 25965/04, ECHR 2010, para. 197.

[45] Guido Raimondy, 'Debate Following the Presentation by Luzius Wildhaber – The Old Court, the New Court and Paul Mahoney' (2016) 36 *HRLJ* 297, 299.

[46] See von Bogdandy and Venzke (n. 10), 49; Shelton (n. 7) 564.

favour of ambitious standard-setting, and, third, the renunciation of the distinction between those cases which, on the one hand, require 'routine adjudication' or 'fine-tuning', and, on the other, those relating to 'grave breaches'. The implication is that all these distinctions would be replaced by the simple concept of 'human rights violations writ large'. On the other hand, advocates of 'judicial self-restraint', 'realism', and 'minimalism' would go less far. For them the ECtHR's inescapable dependence upon, and interconnectedness with, the various national courts, parliaments and governments, necessarily involves a sense of proportion and prioritisation.[47]

This quote underpins two main points that I am attempting to make. Firstly, there is no unanimity in what is understood by the meta-function or meta-functions of the Court and the Convention. Both academics and judges alike might lean towards restraint, activism, or anything in between or outside of this measuring scale. Moreover, these views are not stable and each judge can be an activist in the context of one case and a supporter of restraint in another. Imagine that a judge, who is generally an activist and thinks that the Court is capable of law-making, has particular views on the issue of regulating of religions; she thinks that, in this area, states should have a wide margin of appreciation. This makes advancing a strategic view on the meta-function of the Court extremely difficult because of the inability to agree on what the Court needs to achieve by virtue of its case law. Moreover, academic attempts to describe a strategy of the Court will almost inevitably be incomplete as it is virtually impossible to take all potential variations of the case law into consideration. For example, one can argue that the Court retracted its activist approach to prisoner voting rights after this line of case law was severely criticised by the contracting parties.[48] However, this strategy on reducing the rights in this area does not explain the case of *Söyler* v. *Turkey* which effectively goes against the identified trend.[49] Either the trend is not identified correctly or the Court does not necessarily rationally follow a particular trend.

Secondly, it shows that the views on the meta-function change over time. Bates showed that the role of the Court has changed significantly from what was anticipated by the drafters. It has made a journey from

[47] Greer and Wildhaber (n. 28) 679.

[48] See Ed Bates, 'Analysing the Prisoner Voting Saga and the British Challenge to Strasbourg' (2014) 14 *HRL Rev* 503, 537. See Chapters 3 and 5 for a more detailed discussion of prisoner voting case law of the ECtHR.

[49] See *Söyler* v. *Turkey*, no. 29411/07, 17 September 2013; Kanstantsin Dzehtsiarou, 'Prisoner Voting Saga' in Helen Hardman and Brice Dickson (eds.), *Electoral Rights in Europe* (Routledge 2017).

being an institution that was supposed to act only in extreme situations, preventing the contracting parties from sliding to dictatorship, to being a court that adjudicates a bill of rights. Considerable developments happened in relation to the Court's interpretation of human rights. The Court was much more open to the idea of limiting the margin of appreciation[50] of the contracting parties two decades ago than it is now. The content of its meta-function also changed when many newly established democracies joined the Council of Europe in the 1990s. Moreover, the meta-function of the Court is now changing with the rise of illiberal democracies and in response to the COVID-19 pandemic. It seems that the Court is often expected to get involved in current affairs relevant to human rights protection, but the exact degree and depth of this involvement are far from being clear.

The confusion over the meta-function of the Court intensifies because such meta-functions can be identified on a different level of abstraction. Prioritising subsidiarity or standard-setting occupies a higher level of abstraction, but it does not mean that more precise meta-functions cannot be articulated. Çali identified four purposes of the ECtHR: '(1) to hold states parties to account; (2) to protect minority groups and views; (3) to trigger reform; and (4) to uphold a model of rights-bearing based on individuals rather than citizens'.[51] These purposes are perhaps more precise than the purpose of 'prioritising subsidiarity' but are nevertheless detached from immediate conflict resolution between parties.

Some commentators argue that the embeddedness of the Convention in national legal systems is the key meta-function of the Court.[52] According to Judge Spano, the Court should make sure that the contracting parties comply with the standards that have already been developed by the Court.[53] Although this approach is acceptable in general terms, its problems become apparent when its practical

[50] The margin of appreciation doctrine has generated a lot of scholarship. See, for example, Andrew Legg, *The Margin of Appreciation in International Human Rights Law* (Oxford University Press 2012); George Letsas, 'Two Concepts of the Margin of Appreciation' (2006) 26 *OJLS* 705; Janneke Gerards, 'Pluralism, Deference and the Margin of Appreciation Doctrine' (2011) 17 *ELJ* 80.

[51] Basak Çali, 'The Purposes of the European Human Rights System: One or Many?' [2008] *EHRLR* 299, 299.

[52] Spano (n. 17); see also Laurence R. Helfer, 'Redesigning the European Court of Human Rights: Embeddedness as a Deep Structural Principle of the European Human Rights Regime' (2008) 19 *EJIL* 125.

[53] Spano (n. 17).

application is considered. First, this approach is far from being universally accepted. For instance, Judge Pinto de Albuquerque argued extra-judicially that the 'the Convention is a law-making treaty and not a mere contract treaty'[54] and therefore the meta-function of the Court is not merely to embed the standards that have already been established but to continue developing such standards. Of course, Judge Spano does not suggest that the Court should not engage in developing standards at all, but the priority should be pushing for what has already been achieved. Even when conceptualised in that way, Spano's approach might not be generally accepted. Second, Judge Spano acknowledges that ensuring embeddedness is a fairly recent stage in the Court's history. That means that the Court might develop further and its meta-function might continue changing. Spano points out that 'in the last decade or so an important shift in the Court's case law started to manifest itself. The Court began reformulating its case law to increase further the embeddedness of Convention principles'.[55] Moreover, often human rights standards are developed by application and the crude differentiation between application and development might be difficult in practice. Finally, often the Court can be forced by circumstances to develop its body of law rather than simply ensuring that the already developed standards are properly applied by the contracting parties.

This short overview shows that the Convention commentators do not manifest a clear vision as to what the meta-function of the Court is and how this meta-function can be achieved. The conceptualisations of the Court's meta-function are limited, some of them overestimating the Court's ability to act as a strategic actor. Moreover, the Court's priorities change over time. Section 4.5.2 describes how the Court sees its function and defines it in its case law.

4.5.2 *Meta-function of the Court in the Court's Case Law*

4.5.2.1 The Views of the Majority

The Court does not often engage with the existential questions of what the Court is for in its reasoning; therefore, it does not often analyse its own meta-function. Much more frequently do the dissenting and concurring judges touch upon these issues in their opinions. This section looks into how the majority define the purpose of the Court, then Section 4.5.2.2 considers the dissenting and concurring opinions.

[54] Pinto de Albuquerque (n. 9) 121.
[55] Spano (n. 17) 477.

The Court's discussion of its function predominantly focuses on defining the boundaries of the Court's jurisdiction. It is mostly defined in technical terms, namely, the Court identifies whether a particular issue falls within its jurisdiction or, in other words, whether it is the function of the Court to deal with a particular human rights issue. Although the terminology is overwhelmingly technical, it sheds some light on what meta-function the majority had in mind when deciding a particular case. For instance, if the Court agrees not to check the correctness of the interpretation of the national law, it will not assume a meta-function as the ultimate interpreter of the national law. Therefore, it is not the function of the Court to act as the fourth instance court. In other words, by curtailing its jurisdiction, the Court signals that it considers that dealing with this particular subject matter, territory or authority is not part of its meta-function. It does not mean that jurisdiction is the same as the meta-function of the Court, but it is useful to demonstrate the outer boundaries of the meta-function.

The Court normally limits its jurisdiction in two different ways. First, it may consider that a certain issue is not within the Court's scope of review. For instance, the Court cannot review alleged human rights violations that took place in Belarus as it is not a party to the Convention. I call this an 'unconditional limitation' as no factor except a fundamental change of circumstances[56] can change the Court's approach. Second, there may be a 'conditional limitation', meaning that the Court will not review a ruling or decision of a particular body unless, for example, it is manifestly disproportionate. I will attempt to illustrate these two types of limitations and link them to how the Court understands its meta-function.

There are plenty of examples of the unconditional limitation of the Court's jurisdiction. However, even if this limitation is presented as unconditional, the reality might be more complex. On a number of occasions, the ECtHR ruled that it does not deal with social problems *in abstracto*;[57] the Court, instead, requires a person (victim) who is affected by the issue and the ECtHR deals with this individual case. In this case an abstract application should be perceived as an unconditional limitation of the Court's jurisdiction. By way of illustration, in *Beuze* v. *Belgium*, the Court pointed out that 'the role of the Court ... is

[56] In the Belarusian example, the ratification of the ECHR will be such a fundamental change of circumstances.

[57] See, for example, *Roman Zakharov* v. *Russia* [GC], no. 47143/06, ECHR 2015, para. 164.

not to adjudicate in the abstract or to harmonise the various legal systems but to establish safeguards to ensure that the proceedings followed in each case comply with the requirements of a fair trial, having regard to the specific circumstances of each accused'.[58] It seems that this approach, although oft-repeated in the case law, stands in contradiction to the aspiration of the Court to act as a constitutional instrument of European public order which requires at least some abstract reasoning. Moreover, it has been convincingly argued[59] that the Court engages in abstract reasoning contrary to the above statement from the *Beuze* judgment.

The case of *Ališić* is another example of an unconditional limitation of the Court's scope of review. Here, the ECtHR stated that 'it is primarily for domestic courts to resolve problems of interpretation of domestic law so that the role of the Court is confined to ascertaining whether the effects of such an interpretation are compatible with the Convention'.[60] The Court has effectively rejected the role of the 'fourth instance' Court, leaving interpretation of national law to the domestic courts. However, there are plenty of examples where the Court considers the interpretation of domestic law and suggests that the contracting party should interpret it in a way that is compatible with the Convention.[61]

In some cases, the Court excluded certain facts from its analysis by arguing that it is not its role to examine these facts. For instance, in *Giniewski* v. *France*, the Court stated:

58 *Beuze* v. *Belgium* [GC], no. 71409/10, 9 November 2018, para. 148. See also *Jalloh* v. *Germany* [GC], no. 54810/00, ECHR 2006-IX, para. 95; *Ibrahim and Others* v. *the United Kingdom*, nos. 50541/08 and three others, 16 December 2014, para. 254; *Gäfgen* v. *Germany* [GC], no. 22978/05, ECHR 2010, para. 163.

59 Sadurski argued that '[u]ntil the pilot judgments, the Court resorted to a shrewd legal drafting technique by disguising the fact that it was the law which often was the target of its scrutiny. Indeed, the consideration of the more general, systemic directives was placed in the "reasoning" part of the judgments, while the operative part of the judgments focused strictly on the individualised violations'. Wojciech Sadurski, 'Partnering with Strasbourg: Constitutionalisation of the European Court of Human Rights, the Accession of Central and East European States to the Council of Europe, and the Idea of Pilot Judgments' (2009) 9 *HRL Rev* 397, 413. See also Janneke Gerrards, 'Abstract and Concrete Reasonableness Review by the European Court of Human Rights' (2020) 2 *Eur Conv Hum Rights L Rev* 218.

60 *Ališić and Others* v. *Bosnia and Herzegovina, Croatia, Serbia, Slovenia and the former Yugoslav Republic of Macedonia*, no. 60642/08, 6 November 2012, para. 113. See also *Times Newspapers Ltd* v. *the United Kingdom (nos. 1 and 2)*, nos. 3002/03 and 23676/03, ECHR 2009, para. 43; *Miragall Escolano and Others* v. *Spain*, nos. 38366/97 and nine others, ECHR 2000-I, para. 33; *Angel Angelov* v. *Bulgaria*, no. 51343/99, 15 February 2007, para. 34.

61 *Anchugov and Gladkov* v. *Russia*, nos. 11157/04 and 15162/05, 4 July 2013, para. 111.

> [T]he action for defamation brought against the applicant was lodged by an association, the General Alliance against Racism and for Respect for the French and Christian Identity. It is not for the Court to comment on whether this group is representative, nor on its task of defending the Catholic Church or Christianity in general. Nor is it the role of the Court, short of taking the place of the domestic courts, to evaluate whether the article in question directly undermined the complainant association or the interests it seeks to defend.[62]

The Court excluded these facts from its consideration and dealt only with its consequences; therefore, such exclusion is unconditional.

When considering conditional limitations of its jurisdiction, the Court stated that its function is to intervene but only in the most extreme cases. In other words, it conditionally excludes certain issues from its review. The ECtHR defines its function by stating that the parties are competent to decide, but the Court reserves the right to review the results of such decision-making. The so-called *Bosphorus* presumption[63] is one of the better-known areas in which the Court decided to apply a conditional limitation of its jurisdiction. In that case, the Court considered whether the EU sanctions implemented by Ireland violated the applicant's right to property under Article 1 of Protocol 1 to the Convention. The Court ruled that it can only assess legal rules and regulations emanating from another international organisation with a comparable level of human rights protection if these standards are manifestly unreasonable. The ECtHR opined that it was not its role to review all such rules and regulations and, therefore, limited the scope of its jurisdiction.

In some cases, the Court states that it is its role to review the results of the tests of proportionality performed by national authorities. Although these statements are relevant to the function of the Court, they seem uncontroversial and do not shed any light on how the Court perceives its meta-function. In *Scoppola No. 3* the Court considered whether the prisoner disenfranchisement laws adopted in Italy are in compliance with the Convention.[64] The Court stated:

> [I]t will be for the legislature itself to balance the competing interests in order to avoid any general, automatic and indiscriminate restriction. It will then be the role of the Court to examine whether, in a given case, this result was achieved

62 *Giniewski* v. *France*, no. 64016/00, ECHR 2006-I, para. 48.

63 *Bosphorus Hava Yolları Turizm ve Ticaret Anonim Şirketi* v. *Ireland* [GC], no. 45036/98, ECHR 2005-VI.

64 *Scoppola* v. *Italy (no. 3)* [GC], no. 126/05, 22 May 2012. For an in-depth discussion of the issue, see Dzehtsiarou (n. 49); Bates (n. 48).

and whether the wording of the law, or the judicial decision, was in compliance with Article 3 of Protocol No. 1.[65]

Here, the Court has reiterated its role; however, if it was not up to the Court to consider the proportionality of the measures, then what would the Court's role be? It is only in relation to negative obligations under absolute rights that the Court's role might be different, but here the Court conceptualised its most basic technical function of conflict resolution. Similarly, in *Ireland* v. *the United Kingdom*, the Court acknowledged that the states are better placed to assess the existence of emergency, but it nevertheless pointed out that '[t]he Court . . . is responsible for ensuring the observance of the States' engagements, is empowered to rule on whether the States have gone beyond the "extent strictly required by the exigencies" of the crisis'.[66] These statements show the Court's attempts to describe its scope of review, which is essential for the technical function of conflict resolution.

To briefly conclude, the majority of the Court does not clearly state what the function of the Court is. The majority hints at what the outer limits of the Court's function might be occasionally while dealing with this issue in the context of its scope of jurisdiction. The Court's approach here is predominantly negative; namely, it states what is not the role of the Court. When the Court points out what the role of the Court is, it is mostly obvious and uncontroversial and cannot shed much light on the content of its meta-function. I will now look at the dissenting and concurring opinions, which are usually less formalised and offer a more fertile ground for analysis.

4.5.2.2 Dissenting and Concurring Views

Dissenting and concurring opinions give a better insight into the Court's view of its meta-function for a number of reasons.[67] First, the dissenting judges can write their opinions individually and therefore do not need to find a compromise, which is required for the collective judgment of the majority. Second, arguably the dissenting and concurring opinions are less authoritative and, therefore, the judges can be less careful about the reaction of the contracting parties to a particular expression or statement. Finally,

65 *Scoppola* v. *Italy (no. 3)* (n. 64) para. 102.

66 *Ireland* v. *the United Kingdom*, 18 January 1978, Series A no. 25, para. 207.

67 For a detailed discussion of the separate opinions in the ECtHR jurisprudence, see Robin White and Iris Boussiakou, 'Separate Opinions in the European Court of Human Rights' (2009) 9 *HRL Rev* 37.

as dissenting opinions are usually written by the judges themselves and are less rigidly reviewed by the members of the Court's Registry, they can contain more explicit views of a particular judge.

The disagreement that was identified while analysing the academic commentaries of the function of the Court mentioned earlier can again be illustrated here by reference to the dissenting judges: they too do not agree as to what the meta-function of the Court is. I will demonstrate two approaches that are evident from the analysis of the ECtHR case law: a restrictive approach and an expansive one. Under the restrictive approach, the dissenting judges remind the majority about the subsidiary nature of the Court; they believe that the Court's meta-function is fundamentally limited. If a judge applies an expansive approach, she emphasises the role of the Court as being to develop the standards of human rights protection or to expand the scope of its jurisdiction. These two approaches present themselves in different contexts but can be clearly identified.

Dissenting and concurring judges usually describe the role of the Court in much more detail than the majority does. As in the case of the majority, their opinions are often linked to the jurisdiction of the Court but also touch various other aspects of adjudication of the Strasbourg Court. I will start by examining the opinions of those who are in favour of a more restrictive view on the meta-function of the Court. They argue that the Court is not free to 'invent' new rights and arbitrarily increase the level of protection of the existent rights. According to the judges who fall within this category, the Court is restricted to considering only those facts that are in front of it without assuming anything beyond written submissions. Moreover, the judges argue that the Court should not engage in abstract interpretation of the Convention. Among other things, the judges imply that it is not within the meta-function of the Court to promote certain abstract economic and social policies that the respondent state is required to implement. Finally, it was pointed out that the Court's role in the execution of its judgments is limited and, therefore, its meta-function should not include dealing with issues relating to execution. These points are now illustrated in turn.

Dissenting judges argue that the Court cannot add new rights to the catalogue of rights that exists in the Convention. Judge Wojtyczek pointed out:

> [T]he mandate of the European Court of Human Rights has been defined in a restrictive way by Article 19 of the Convention. The role of the Court is to

> ensure the observance of the engagements undertaken by the High Contracting Parties to the Convention and the Protocols thereto. Therefore the Court remains the guardian of a limited catalogue of rights as protected under the minimum standard set forth in the Convention and the additional Protocols. It is also necessary to bear in mind that human rights are interrelated in different ways. Quite often different human rights may collide in specific circumstances. In such situations, heightening the standard of protection of one right may lead to lowering the standard of protection of other fundamental human rights.[68]

It seems that Judge Wojtyczek reflected on the long-standing criticism of the ECtHR that it goes beyond the text of the Convention and adds new rights to it.[69] According to Judge Wojtyczek, this approach is not part of the meta-function of the Court.

Another example of the restrictive interpretation of the Court's meta-function relates to how existing rights are interpreted. If one concludes that the Court should not abide by any strict rules of interpretation then the Court is perhaps given carte blanche in interpreting the Convention as it sees fit. As a consequence, one can suggest that this interpretation can even reach the level of policy-making and such policy-making is the real meta-function of the Court. For instance, if it is assumed that the Court is not at all bound by its previous judgments then it is free to change its approach at any time without any need to justify itself. On a number of occasions, the Court confirmed that it should be somewhat bound by its previous case law and that compliance with the rules of interpretation adds legitimacy to the Court's pronouncements. This was the key point of the dissenting opinion of Judges De Gaetano and Wojtyczek in *S., V. and A.* v. *Denmark*. They stated:

> The Court, in the exercise of its mandate as defined and delimited by Article 19 of the Convention, has a special role to play in developing European legal culture. An important element of legal culture is the culture of interpretation. The latter presupposes clear and precise rules of interpretation. In many legal

[68] Concurring Opinion of Judge Wojtyczek. *National Union of Rail, Maritime and Transport Workers* v. *the United Kingdom*, no. 31045/10, ECHR 2014.

[69] See Lord Leonard Hoffmann, 'The Universality of Human Rights' (2009) 125 *LQ Rev* 416, 428–9. Evolutive interoperation of the Court is often wrongly confused with judicial law-making. There is a lot of scholarship dealing with evolutive interpretation. See, for example, Alastair Mowbray, 'The Creativity of the European Court of Human Rights' (2005) 5 *HRL Rev* 57; Dragoljub Popovic, 'Prevailing of Judicial Activism over Self-Restraint in the Jurisprudence of the European Court of Human Rights' (2009) 42 *Creighton L Rev* 361; Alastair Mowbray, 'An Examination of the European Court of Human Rights' Approach to Overruling Its Previous Case Law' (2009) 9 *HRL Rev* 179; Lisa Sonnleitner, 'The Democratic Legitimacy of Evolutive Interpretation by the European Court of Human Rights' (2019) 33 *Temp Int'l & Comp LJ* 279.

systems there exists a coherent set of rules of interpretation, usually unwritten but clearly explained and applied in judicial decisions, with judgments often containing extensive and precise considerations concerning the interpretative rules underpinning the reasoning. European human rights law has not yet reached the level of development and refinement of domestic legal systems on this point and the European Court of Human Rights not only has not developed a sufficiently coherent interpretative methodology within the scope of the discretion left to it by the general rules of treaty interpretation, but has often overlooked, or shied away from, the applicable customary rules of treaty interpretation codified in the Vienna Convention on the Law of Treaties. Viewed from the domestic perspective, the role of the Court in building up a culture of interpretation is far from satisfactory.[70]

These judges were not satisfied with how rigidly the Court applies its rules of interpretation. In other words, the Court could set them aside if the result would justify that and this approach might stretch the meta-function of the ECtHR beyond what Judges De Gaetano and Wojtyczek could subscribe to.

In line with what has often been repeated by the majority of the Court, some judges urge the ECtHR not to engage in an abstract assessment of the legislation, claiming that this is not the role of the ECtHR. For instance, in *Biao* v. *Denmark*, dissenting Judges Villiger, Mahoney and Kjølbro argued that '[t]he role of the Court is not to review the contested domestic legislation *in abstracto*, but to assess its specific application to the applicants' situation'.[71] It was argued that it is not a proper role of the Court to substitute national organs in substantive decision-making when all necessary procedural guarantees are satisfied. Judge Sajó stated:

[T]he role of the Court is to satisfy itself that a proper balance has been struck in the case ... [T]he role of the Court is supervisory. Where the balancing exercise has been undertaken by the national authorities in conformity with the criteria laid down in the Court's case-law, the Court would require strong reasons to substitute its view for that of the domestic courts.[72]

The described views are relevant to the Court's role in relation to European public order. The Court has fewer tools with which to impact European public order if it cannot decide issues in abstract, second-guess the substantive decision-making of the contracting parties or set

[70] Joint Partly Dissenting Opinion of Judges De Gaetano and Wojtyczek. *S., V. and A.* v. *Denmark* [GC], nos. 35553/12 and two others, 22 October 2018.

[71] Dissenting Opinion of Judges Villiger, Mahoney and Kjølbro. *Biao* v. *Denmark* [GC], no. 38590/10, 24 May 2016, para. 38.

[72] Dissenting Opinion of Judge Sajó. *Godelli* v. *Italy*, no. 33783/09, 25 September 2012.

aside the rules of interpretation. If all these restrictions are taken seriously then the Court can hardly strategically shape European public order.

Some judges point out that it is not the role of the Court to consider facts that have not been submitted by the parties to the case. In other words, these opinions try to limit the breadth of the Court's scope of review. For example, Judge Serghides pointed out:

> The Court's task is to judge according to the facts before it and not to imagine facts, as a novelist has the right to do to make his story better ... In the present case the Court was not in a position to make predictions as to how the result of the trial would have been affected if the applicant had had a lawyer during the first three days of his detention, because: (a) that was impossible; (b) that was not its role; and (c) that would amount in the abstract to negating or diminishing the role of every lawyer.[73]

This view confirms that the ECtHR should not interpret abstract and hypothetical facts but only limit itself to the circumstances of an individual case.

The ECtHR judges also imply that it is not the meta-function of the Court to decide broad issues of social and economic policy in the member states of the Council of Europe. In the case of *Hatton* v. *the United Kingdom* concerning an alleged violation of Article 8 as a result of noise pollution from Heathrow Airport, dissenting Judge Kerr pointed out:

> If Convention standards are not met in an individual case, it is the role of the Court to say so, regardless of how many others are in the same position. But when, as here, a substantial proportion of the population of south London is in a similar position to the applicants, the Court must consider whether the proper place for a discussion of the particular policy is in Strasbourg, or whether the issue should not be left to the domestic political sphere.[74]

This view suggests that the Court's meta-function is limited and it should not undermine domestic political processes. Therefore, this view can be classified as restrictive.

Finally, another example of this restrictive approach can be found in the concurring opinion of Judge Turković in *Khamtokhu and Aksenchik* v. *Russia* on the role of the Court in enforcing its own judgments. This case concerned alleged discrimination embedded in a Russian law

[73] Partly dissenting opinion of Judge Serghides, para. 58. *Simeonovi* v. *Bulgaria* [GC], no. 21980/04, 12 May 2017.

[74] Dissenting opinion of Judge Kerr. *Hatton and Others* v. *the United Kingdom*, no. 36022/97, 2 October 2001.

according to which all women and men under eighteen and over sixty years of age cannot be sentenced to life imprisonment while men older than eighteen but younger than sixty can. She stated:

> [D]iscretion as to the manner of execution of a judgment reflects the freedom of choice attaching to the primary obligation of the Contracting States under the Convention to secure the rights and freedoms guaranteed ... In other words it reflects the subsidiary role of the Court. This applies even more to situations in which a member State voluntarily guarantees a right which is not a Convention right itself, as any preference for extension of benefits should in principle fall within the competence of the domestic authorities, who are, as often emphasised by the Court, better placed than an international judge to appreciate what is in the public interest ... This is especially true in situations in which the remedy of a violation involves statutory rules.[75]

The dissenting judge reminded that it is not the role of the Court to determine the exact manner in which the judgment of the Court should be executed. This particular point is the subject of heated academic debate.[76] Overall, many judges see either a very limited role or no role at all for the Court to rationally influence European public order.

There are many examples of the expansive approach to the meta-function of the Court. In other words, dissenting judges think that the Court's scope of review should increase, giving the Court more of an impact on European public order. One of such examples can be found in the case of *Parrillo* v. *Italy*. It is widely known that the Court applies only light scrutiny to the matter of whether there is a legitimate aim of interference with qualified rights; therefore, it concludes that the legitimate aim was absent only in extreme cases.[77] The Court more often

[75] Concurring opinion of Judge Turković. *Khamtokhu and Aksenchik* v. *Russia* [GC], nos. 60367/08 and 961/11, 24 January 2017.

[76] Chapter 5 of this monograph will look into how weak execution undermines the attempts of the Court to determine European public order. See Fiona de Londras and Kanstantsin Dzehtsiarou, 'Mission Impossible? Addressing Non-execution through Infringement Proceedings in the European Court of Human Rights' (2017) 66 *Int'l & Comp LQ* 467; Helen Keller and Cedric Marti, 'Reconceptualizing Implementation: The Judicialization of the Execution of the European Court of Human Rights' Judgments' (2015) 26 *EJIL* 829; Alice Donald and Anne-Katrin Speck, 'The European Court of Human Rights' Remedial Practice and Its Impact on the Execution of Judgments' (2019) 19 *HRL Rev* 83; Başak Çalı, 'Explaining Variation in the Intrusiveness of Regional Human Rights Remedies in Domestic Orders' (2018) 16(1) *ICON* 214; Philip Leach, 'Rach to Remedies' in Andreas Føllesdal, Birgit Peters and Geir Ulfstein (eds.), *Constituting Europe: The European Court of Human Rights in a National, European and Global Context* (Cambridge University Press 2013) 142.

[77] See *Catan and Others* v. *the Republic of Moldova and Russia* [GC], nos. 43370/04 and two others, ECHR 2012; *Bayev and Others* v. *Russia*, nos. 67667/09 and two others,

finds that a measure was not 'necessary in a democratic society' rather than it not having a legitimate aim.[78] In *Parillo*, dissenting Judge Sajó pointed out that '[f]ailure to undertake a serious scrutiny of a State's purported aim in imposing the restriction will undermine the potential for rights to be protected from any proportionality analysis. The scrutiny of the aim of a measure is part of the supervisory role of the Court'.[79] Curiously, I also mentioned Judge Sajó's opinion to illustrate the restrictive views on the meta-function of the Court. For Judge Sajó, the Court is not doing enough in one case or context and it is doing too much in a different one. This also substantiates the earlier point that a judge can express significantly different views in regard to the meta-function of the Court depending on the context in which the meta-function is discussed.

Judge Pinto de Albuquerque is perhaps the most vocal supporter of the expansive meta-function of the Court. On a number of occasions in his dissenting opinions, he warned that the restrictive approach taken by the majority is damaging the position of the Court vis-à-vis some member states. In *Hutchinson* v. *the United Kingdom*, the Court considered whether lifelong parole for prisoners violates Article 3.[80] In this case, the Court significantly reconsidered its judgment on the same issue in *Vinter* v. *the United Kingdom*.[81] Judge Pinto de Albuquerque pointed out:

> [T]he present judgment may have seismic consequences for the European human-rights protection system. The majority's decision represents a peak in a growing trend towards downgrading the role of the Court before certain domestic jurisdictions, with the serious risk that the Convention is applied with double standards. If the Court goes down this road, it will end up as a non-judicial commission of highly qualified and politically legitimised 47 experts, which does not deliver binding judgments, at least with regard to certain Contracting Parties, but pronounces mere recommendations on 'what it would be desirable' for domestic authorities to do, acting in a mere auxiliary capacity, in order to 'aid' them in fulfilling their statutory and international obligations. The probability of deleterious consequences for the entire

20 June 2017; Fiona de Londras and Kanstantsin Dzehtsiarou, *Great Debates on the European Convention on Human Rights* (Palgrave 2018) 97–8.

78 There are plenty of examples; see *S. and Marper* v. *the United Kingdom* [GC], nos. 30562/04 and 30566/04, ECHR 2008; *Christine Goodwin* v. *the United Kingdom* [GC], no. 28957/95, ECHR 2002-VI.

79 Dissenting Opinion of Judge Sajó. *Parrillo* v. *Italy* [GC], no. 46470/11, ECHR 2015.

80 *Hutchinson* v. *the United Kingdom* [GC], no. 57592/08, 17 January 2017.

81 *Vinter and Others* v. *the United Kingdom* [GC], nos. 66069/09 and two others, ECHR 2013.

European system of human-rights protection is heightened by the current political environment, which shows an increasing hostility to the Court.[82]

In the same fashion, Judge Pinto de Albuquerque, this time joined by Judge Dedov, in his dissenting opinion in *Ilnseher* v. *Germany*, argued that '[b]y rubber-stamping the Karlsruhe court's [German Constitutional Court] stance, against the crystal-clear and longstanding standards of customary international and treaty law and the consensus reigning in comparative law, the Court is taking one step more towards the legal periphery in Europe'.[83] It seems that for Pinto de Albuquerque, the Court must assume the role of a standard-setter in Europe with a very broad set of competences. Still, this position is the one that many would not fully subscribe to.[84]

This brief illustration of the views of dissenting judges clearly shows that there is no commonly agreed meta-function of the Court. The judges perceive the role of the Court differently; this role is often case dependent and it is hardly possible to extract any clear and uniform strategy behind these views. This is not surprising as the Court consists of forty-seven lawyers who do not share a common ideology or educational and cultural background and who also change every nine years. A quest for the meta-function of the Court is a never-ending story and if this quest is given priority in the operation of the Court, it can undermine a much more precise and clearer technical role of adjudication.

4.5.3 *The Views of the Presidents of the ECtHR*

Finally, it is useful to look at what the presidents of the Court said extrajudicially. While I have already discussed some of their opinions, labelling them as academics, the speeches given by the presidents of the Court can be useful here too. These speeches are of a particular genre which allows the presidents to explain their view on the role of the Court. This section is based on an analysis of the speeches of the presidents of the Court starting from Luzius Wildhaber (1998) and

[82] Dissenting Opinion of Judge Pinto de Albuquerque. *Hutchinson* v. *the United Kingdom* (n. 80).

[83] Dissenting Opinion of Judge de Albuquerque and Dedov. *Ilnseher* v. *Germany* [GC], nos. 10211/12 and 27505/14, 4 December 2018. See also Partly Dissenting and Partly Concurring Opinion of Judge de Albuquerque in *G.I.E.M. S.R.L. and Others* v. *Italy* [GC], nos. 1828/06 and two others, 28 June 2018.

[84] There are plenty of examples of opinions calling for a restrictive view on the competence of the ECtHR. For example, see, Lord Hoffmann's view on the Court's expansive jurisprudence in Hoffmann (n. 69) 428–9.

which are available on the official website of the Court.[85] It is acknowledged that this analysis is not comprehensive and, therefore, the results are illustrative only. The key narrative related to the meta-function of the Court in the presidents' speeches focuses on the relations between the contracting parties and the Court. One of the key areas of discussion here is who is the principal contributor to European public order – the states or the Court. In the last thirty years, the balance has shifted from the Court to the states and this dynamic is detectable in the speeches of the presidents of the Court too.

One necessary caveat should be made before I present my analysis. The presidents' speeches are their official and very polished views on the Court. It is obvious that the presidents cannot openly express their 'uncensored' views as this might undermine the position of the ECtHR. Moreover, it is the opinion of the institution of the president of the Court rather than their personal views. As the presidents of the Court represent an international judicial body, they are much more restrained in their speeches than, for example, are politicians. The relevant narratives need to be carefully extracted from innuendos, references and hints, rather than clear articulations.

Although the key points mentioned in all of the speeches of the presidents are compatible, their tones and subtle messages are different. Towards the end of his tenure, President Wildhaber already felt the backlash against the Court and tried to defend its principled position. He emphasised that the key role of the Court is to resolve social conflicts and that this will not be accepted positively by all contracting parties. However, he argued that the democratic countries agreed to be bound by the Convention and the Court, and, thus, this is the price they pay for being within the family of democratic nations.[86]

Jean-Paul Costa, who became the president of the Court after Wildhaber, was also concerned with the role of the Court vis-à-vis the contracting parties. Judge Costa pointed out:

> While the Court has clearly been able to extend its role in its whole history, we should on no account underestimate the role which the national authorities must play in implementing the Convention. In practice, the States and the Court pursue the same goal: securing the rights and freedoms defined

[85] Only speeches in English were considered for this project.

[86] Luzius Wildhaber, 'Solemn Hearing of the ECHR on the Occasion of the Opening of the Judicial Year' (19 January 2007) available at www.echr.coe.int/Documents/Speech_20070119_Wildhaber_JY_ENG.pdf, 3.

in the Convention and its Protocols and, where the Court is concerned, ensuring their observance in accordance with its function under Article 19.[87]

He continued by saying that '[o]ne of the fundamental principles underpinning the whole system is that of subsidiarity. The task of securing respect for the rights enshrined in the Convention falls first to the authorities of the Contracting States rather than to the Court.'[88] The rhetorical narrative shifted from the ECtHR as an ultimate authority in Europe, with the contracting parties obliged to accept the rulings if they wish to continue being part of the family of democratic states, to a much more moderate approach to the relations between the contracting parties and the Court.

Judge Costa also emphasised the role of the states in more practical terms. He stated:

[T]he Court reveals the cause of the violation of the applicant's rights - this is frequently a gap in the domestic law or in the domestic system. It may, where appropriate, give indications or guidance to the State authorities regarding the steps they might take. But it cannot fill the gap. Nor can it fully redress the harm done to the applicant, having no remedial powers apart from the discretion to make an award of compensation.[89]

The Court then elected Judge Bratza to act as its president for a short period of time. The emphasis on the contracting parties continued and intensified under President Bratza. He, for instance, pointed out that the existence of the Court depends upon the support of the contracting parties to the Convention.[90] The Strasbourg system is based on a shared responsibility which runs through the Convention.[91]

87 Jean-Paul Costa, 'The Role of the National Authorities, Especially the Courts, and the Future of Human Rights Protection in Europe' (Kiev 1 July 2011) available at www.echr.coe.int/Documents/Speech_20110701_Costa_Kiev_ENG.pdf, 2.

88 Ibid, 4.

89 Jean-Paul Costa, 'Speech by Mr Jean-Paul Costa, President of the European Court of Human Rights, at the Ceremony to Mark the 15th Anniversary of the Constitutional Court of the Slovak Republic' (Kosice 3 April 2008) available at www.echr.coe.int/Documents/Speech_20080403_Costa_Kosice_ENG.pdf, 2.

90 'The Court is then a dynamic institution, but also in many respects a fragile one, which ultimately relies heavily on the support and good faith of the Council of Europe member States.' Meeting of the Ministers' Deputies CoE - Address by Sir Nicolas Bratza (24 October 2012) available at www.echr.coe.int/Documents/Speech_20121024_Bratza_ENG.pdf, 4.

91 Sir Nicolas Bratza, High Level Conference (Brighton 18–20 April 2012) available at www.echr.coe.int/Documents/Speech_20120420_Bratza_Brighton_ENG.pdf, 5 and Sir Nicolas Bratza 'Solemn Hearing of the ECHR on the Occasion of the Opening of the

Dean Spielmann was then elected as the president of the ECtHR; during his presidency, the Court was often criticised for trying to fulfil a function that was not in the minds of the contracting parties. Unlike his predecessors, who emphasised the shared responsibility to protect human rights, President Spielmann often called on the contracting parties to stop damaging the Court by constantly criticising it. For example, he stated:

> States tend to accuse us of activism when we find against them, while applicants reproach us for showing restraint if we do not find a violation. To provide the best possible response, our Court necessarily treads a narrow path. We face a constant challenge as regards the acceptability of our decisions. This question is all the more sensitive as our legitimacy is conferred on us by the States that we find against, and our position is therefore far from easy. We do not follow a particular judicial strategy, but it goes without saying that we do think about how our judgments will be received. However, such considerations are circumscribed by our obligation to ensure compliance with the European Convention on Human Rights. The rhythm imposed by our Court is not necessarily the same as that of the member States. Sometimes we go further and advance more quickly.[92]

The idea of dialogue between the ECtHR and the contracting parties, as well as the non-hierarchal structure of the Convention, became more pronounced in the speeches of President Spielmann.[93] It seems that the presidents of the Court emphasise the subsidiary nature of the Court more and more, seeming to suggest that the meta-function of the Court is not to build European public order but to reflect and discuss such order, which has already been built by the contracting parties.

Judge Raimondi then replaced Judge Spielmann as the president of the Court. His public addresses show a slightly different view on the meta-function of the Court. Although Judge Raimondi continued talking about subsidiarity, he was prepared to defend the position of the Court more eagerly. For instance, he emphasised:

Judicial Year' (27 January 2012) available at www.echr.coe.int/Documents/Speech_20120127_Bratza_JY_ENG.pdf, 5.

92 President Dean Spielmann 'Solemn Hearing for the Opening of the Judicial Year: Opening Speech' (Strasbourg 30 January 2015) available at www.echr.coe.int/Documents/Speech_20150130_Solemn_Hearing_2015_ENG.pdf, 3.

93 Spielmann pointed out that '[t]he paramount concern is effectiveness, not uniformity. And so there is an important place for dialogue within the system, among its multiple levels'. 'Judgments of the ECHR Effects and Implementation' (Göttingen 20 September 2013) available at www.echr.coe.int/Documents/Speech_20130920_Spielmann_Gottingen_ENG.pdf, 4.

> The Court and the Member States are together in a partnership with a common goal . . . yet they have distinct roles. In recognising their separate missions in this context, it is worth stressing the fundamental principle of judicial independence and the need for respect for the lawful authority of the judiciary, which underpins the Court's role . . . While it is, of course, open for Member States to discuss the development of the Court's case-law, this must be done in a way that is consistent with full respect for the Court's independence and the binding nature of its judgments.[94]

President Raimondi also insisted that the Court has created 'a new legal landscape'.[95] He also tried to re-conceptualise the principle of subsidiarity by shifting the focus from the Court to the contracting parties. He pointed out that 'subsidiarity represents a deepening, and not a dilution, of human rights protection in Europe. It lays a just emphasis on the role of the national authorities – above all the national courts – in safeguarding fundamental rights'.[96] Perhaps this is not what the contracting parties meant when they included mention of the margin of appreciation and subsidiarity into Protocol 15.[97] It seems that they had in mind that the Court should be more deferential and show more 'respect' for decisions made on the national level. President Raimondi's public addresses give the impression that he is much more in favour of an 'activist court' than his predecessor.

In 2019, Judge Sicilianos was elected as the president of the ECtHR. There are few publicly available speeches at the moment of writing (January 2020) to engage in their proper analysis. However, it seems that President Sicilianos continues the line set by President Raimondi. He pointed out, for example, that '[o]ver the last 60 years the Court has acquired a well-established place on the European legal landscape justifying its position as an essential pillar of

94 President Guido Raimondi, 'Continued Reform of the European Court of Human Rights Convention System – Better Balance, Improved Protection' at the High-Level Conference (Copenhagen 12 April 2018) available at www.echr.coe.int/Documents/Speech_20180412_Raimondi_Copenhagen_ENG.pdf, 3.

95 President Guido Raimondi at the presentation of the Nijmegen Medal 2016 (18 November 2016) available at www.echr.coe.int/Documents/Speech_20161118_Raimondi_Nijmegen_ENG.pdf, 3.

96 President Guido Raimondi, 'Speech to the Supreme Court of the Netherlands' (18 November 2016) available at www.echr.coe.int/Documents/Speech_20161118_Raimondi_Supreme_Court_Netherlands_ENG.pdf, 2.

97 Protocol 15 amends the Preamble to the Convention by including the margin of appreciation and subsidiarity into it. Protocol No. 15 amending the Convention for the Protection of Human Rights and Fundamental Freedoms, available at www.coe.int/en/web/conventions/full-list/-/conventions/treaty/213.

European construction and unity'.[98] President Sicilianos reserves a significant meta-function for the Court: 'The challenge for the Court today is to ensure that the European continent remains a single legal space, founded on common values, in order to protect Europeans from instability and division, serving the cause of peace and democracy.'[99] It is unclear whether the Court has the capacity and infrastructure and can properly act as a strategic actor to achieve this ambitious task.

This section showed that even the very sterile public addresses by the presidents of the Court reveal significant differences in their understanding of the role of the ECtHR. The challenges and emphases change over time and remain abstract and vague.

4.6 Conclusion

Understanding the function of an institution is the key to understanding its effectiveness. If an institution is reformed, the reform efforts need to improve the institution's capacity to fulfil its core function. There should additionally be at least a general agreement as to what function an institution is supposed to fulfil and then the institution can rationally attempt to fulfil this function. If such agreement is absent, the actions of the institution might point in different directions and seem contradictory. International tribunals perform two intrinsically connected functions: the technical one and the meta-function. The technical function of the ECtHR is rather straightforward: it has to resolve cases and put a legal end to conflicts between parties. The meta-function is much more complex and controversial: the Court's meta-function is to develop the body of law and bring about the version of international society it was designed to ensure. Although the meta-function is detectable on a high level of abstraction, it is much harder to pinpoint its precise content.

There is a general agreement among the Convention commentators that the ECtHR has a meta-function. The challenge is to define this function as it changes over time and its content depends on the political ideology of those who define it. The main part of this chapter

[98] President Linos-Alexandre Sicilianos, 'The European Court of Human Rights Marks 60 Years of Work for Peace, Democracy, and Tolerance' (2019) available at www.echr.coe.int/Documents/Speech_20190930_Sicilianos_60_years_ECHR_ENG.pdf, 2.

[99] Ibid.

demonstrated that there is a variety of views on the meta-function of the Court. If the Court's meta-function is to build European public order, then at least two sets of challenges can be identified. First, the vagueness of this meta-function creates unsatisfiable expectations and perhaps undermines the legitimacy of the Court as it is not clear what the Court is building and how it is going to build it. Second, there is no agreement as to whether this is at all a mission of the Court. In this sense, the Court's references to European public order might be seen by the contracting parties as an illegitimate interference into the domain that is reserved for the contracting parties themselves to regulate.

This chapter focused on the individual views of various stakeholders on the meta-function of the ECtHR. Chapter 5 will consider whether institutional reform can suggest any meta-function of the Court. In other words, it will see if one can indeed detect the ambition to shape European public order through the institutional reforms initiated by the Court and the contracting parties to the Convention.

5 Institutional Infrastructure of the European Court of Human Rights and Its Ability to Shape European Public Order

5.1 Introduction

In the previous chapters, I have shown that the European Court of Human Rights (ECtHR or Court) should refrain from relying on the legal concept of European public order in its reasoning as it is vague and unprecise and distorts the meaning of the function of the Court. However, European public order can be useful as an analytical concept describing the activities of the Court. This chapter looks at European public order as an analytical concept. In order to influence European public order in that sense, it seems that the Court needs to be able to formulate rules of general application. These rules should comply with a few basic conditions. First, they should be abstract enough to be applicable beyond the individual circumstances of the case and, second, they should not deal with a problem that is exclusive to a particular member state. On top of that the Court should be able to ensure that these rules are properly implemented; thus, the Court's increased role on the stage of implementation is a sign of a deeper involvement with European public order. Finally, the Court's activities should not be exclusively *post factum*; it should be able to influence ongoing situations when this is possible and necessary.

This chapter looks away from the Court's reasoning and considers whether the Court has an ambition to build European public order. In this chapter, I examine the institutional evolution of the Strasbourg system of human rights protection. To do that I evaluate the key reforms of the ECtHR. I divide the reforms into two categories. The first includes those reforms that were initiated by the ECtHR and adopted through amendments of the Rules of Court that the contracting parties have not explicitly endorsed. It seems that the main innovations that were developed by the ECtHR clearly enhance the Court's ability to influence European public order. It seems that the Court's intention behind such innovations as the pilot judgment procedure and the interim measures is quite straightforward: they allow the Court to have a more immediate impact on European public order. The second category includes those amendments that were explicitly agreed by the contracting parties through Protocols. These reforms are not pointing in one direction and give a mixed bag of signals. While the emphasis on subsidiarity and the margin of appreciation seems to curtail the Court's ability to formulate rules of general application, the addition of extended advisory opinions and infringement proceedings points in a different direction.

This chapter starts with the consideration of pilot judgments and interim measures. Both of these institutional developments aim to increase the Court's ability to make effective general rules and implement them in relation to the situation at hand. These developments, however, are not always successful and the failures show that the Court might not always need to engage in framing rules of general application and ambitiously aim to shape European public order. The chapter continues by analysing the institutional reforms initiated by the member states. It is argued that the states did give the Court some tools that would also help it to shape European public order, while other reforms point in a completely opposite direction. Ultimately, this section shows that the contracting parties to the Convention are unsure as to what the proper function of the Court is and their feedback to the Court might often seem quite confusing.

5.2 The Court's Institutionalisation of Its Strategic Impact

This section argues that the Court has tried to institutionalise its role as a producer of rules and regulations of general application in recent years. These developments show that the Court has an ambition to build European public order and sees its meta-function as impacting the laws of the contracting parties. Here, I will not consider the developments in interpretation of the ECHR; I will look only into the institutional innovations. These innovations need to satisfy three basic conditions simultaneously. First, in some form they need to be reflected in the Court's internal regulations such as the Rules of Court; it is not enough for these innovations to be developed in the Court's case law only. The following example shows what innovation would not satisfy this condition. One can argue that over the years the Court has developed various degrees of abstract review within the test of proportionality. For instance, when a particular measure was applied to the applicant, the Court could not only assess this measure in isolation but more generally consider the necessity of the legislation according to which this measure was adopted.[1] Although relevant, such a way of abstract reasoning is not clearly institutionalised and codified so as to be included in my analysis here. Second, the aim of these institutional innovations should be to give the Court more legitimacy to act beyond the dispute; they should assist the Court in formulating rules of general application beyond the case at hand. Finally, the contracting parties should not have given an explicit consent to these innovations. In other words, these innovations are not included in the text of the European Convention on Human Rights (ECHR or Convention) through the Protocols. Those innovations which were initiated or consented to by the states are considered in Section 5.3. Here, I will look at only two illustrative examples: the pilot judgments and the interim measures. I would argue that these two procedures satisfy the above-mentioned conditions.

5.2.1 *Pilot Judgments*

In 2011, Alan Greene and I argued that '[i]deally, each and every one of its [the ECtHR's] judgments should be a "pilot", which means that the respondent party and effectively all other High Contracting Parties should amend their practice to be in compliance with the ECHR'.[2] Our key intention was to emphasise that although the Court deals with the individual facts of the case, when a judgment logically results in a rule of general application requiring to change the applicable law, the respondent state has to make sufficient changes. The states are free to choose the means by which these changes are to be effectuated at the

[1] Judge Pinto de Albuquerque explained: 'The abstract review of "conventionality" is the review of the compatibility of a national law with the Convention independently of a specific case where this law has been applied.' *Vallianatos and Others* v. *Greece* [GC], nos. 29381/09 and 32684/09, ECHR 2013, Partly Concurring, Partly Dissenting Opinion of Judge Pinto de Albuquerque.

[2] Kanstantsin Dzehtsiarou and Alan Greene, 'Legitimacy and the Future of the European Court of Human Rights: Critical Perspectives from Academia and Practitioners' (2011) *German LJ* 1707, 1708–9.

national level. We thought that there is no need for the Court to emphasise that in a pilot judgment. Around the same time, Stuart Wallace also argued that the pilot procedure is nothing more than 'a modicum of honesty about the role the court is playing and the power it is exercising over contracting states. While the court's judgments have historically entailed legislative changes, it is only now that the court is expressly demanding change in its judgments.'[3] It appears now, however, that this new approach of the Court was more than merely technical. Markus Fyrnys explained:

> The very fact that pilot judgments are focused on the identification of systematic malfunctioning of the domestic legal order and on the indication of appropriate general remedial measures normatively extends the binding effect of the Court's judgments and changes their legal nature, accentuating the Court's constitutional function.[4]

Symbolically, the pilot procedure shows that the Court's open demands to change legislation are not subtle and logical outcomes of a given judgment any longer but a clear request explicitly stated in the judgment. By developing the pilot proceedings, the Court has institutionalised its role as a body that can demand a uniform approach to a human rights issue from the contracting parties and by doing so contribute to European public order.

In this subsection, I will focus on three interrelated aspects. First, I will briefly explain the most important features of the pilot judgment procedure. Then I will offer a couple of telling examples that explain what pilot judgments are capable of achieving. Finally, I will try to consider whether pilot judgments are appropriate as a means of involvement with European public order. The first two aspects were under a lot of scrutiny by the Convention commentators and therefore I will only briefly summarise the relevant points; the final aspect, however, has featured much less prominently in the academic discussion and it is the central question related to the Court's ability to shape European public order.

The pilot judgment procedure was developed by the Court and was not initially reflected even in the Rules of Court.[5] Subsequently, the

[3] Stuart Wallace, 'Much Ado about Nothing? The Pilot Judgment Procedure at the European Court of Human Rights' (2011) *EHRLR* 71, 81.

[4] Markus Fyrnys, 'Expanding Competences by Judicial Lawmaking: The Pilot Judgment Procedure of the European Court of Human Rights' (2011) 12 *German LJ* 1231, 1233.

[5] See David T. Björgvinsson, 'The "Pilot-Judgment" Procedure of the European Court of Human Rights' in Gudmundur Alfredsson et al. (eds.), *International Human Rights Monitoring Mechanisms: Essays in Honour of Jakob Th Möller* (Brill | Nijhoff 2009) 537.

Court 'codified' this procedure and now its regulations are enshrined in Rule 61 of the Rules of Court. It is not mentioned in the Convention and therefore it is purely a Court-made tool. The pilot judgment procedure received a mixed reception from academics. Some of them argued that it is damaging to human rights protection in certain cases,[6] while others called it 'the most creative tool the Court has developed in its first fifty years of its existence'.[7] Another commentator pointed out that 'the Court's judicial elaboration of the so-called "pilot judgment procedure" is an innovative response to the problem of repetitive cases and rests on the idea of the Court's constitutional function'.[8]

What makes the regulations of the pilot judgment proceedings important for the discussion of European public order? The very first sentence of Rule 61 explains that a pilot judgment should be used where 'the facts of an application reveal in the Contracting Party concerned the existence of a structural or systemic problem or other similar dysfunction which has given rise or may give rise to similar applications'.[9] The Court here is acting outside the scope of an individual case and pushes the respondent state to do something beyond the immediate outcome of the case. The Court's decision on the matter at issue becomes the rule that is designed to change the accepted standard in the respondent state. The infamous set of judgments related to prisoner voting rights can illustrate this argument well.[10]

The prisoner voting saga began with the case of *Hirst No. 2* v. *the United Kingdom* in which the ECtHR ruled that a blanket ban on prisoner voting violates Article 3 of Protocol 1.[11] Although, *Hirst No. 2* was not a pilot

[6] It was argued, for example, that the pilot judgment procedure should not be applied 'where the underlying "systemic" problem is not a particular law or policy, but discriminatory state ideologies rooted in national history'. Dilek Kurban, 'Forsaking Individual Justice: The Implications of the European Court of Human Rights' Pilot Judgment Procedure for Victims of Gross and Systematic Violations' (2016) 16 *HRL Rev* 731, 733.

[7] Antoine Buyse, 'The Pilot Judgment Procedure at the European Court of Human Rights: Possibilities and Challenges' (2013) 3 *Law of Ukraine: Legal J* 303, 303.

[8] Fyrnys (n. 4) 1232.

[9] Rule 61 of the Rules of Court.

[10] For a more detailed analysis of the prisoner voting debate, see, for example, Ed Bates, 'Analysing the Prisoner Voting Saga and the British Challenge to Strasbourg' (2014) 14 *HRL Rev* 503; Danny Nicol, 'Legitimacy of the Commons Debate on Prisoner Voting' (2011) *PL* 681; Helen Hardman, 'In the Name of Parliamentary Sovereignty: Conflict between the UK Government and the Courts over Judicial Deference in the Case of Prisoner Voting Rights' (2020) 15 *Br Polit* 226; Sandra Fredman, 'From Dialogue to Deliberation: Human Rights Adjudication and Prisoners' Rights to Vote' (2013) *PL* 292.

[11] *Hirst v. the United Kingdom (no. 2)* [GC], no. 74025/01, ECHR 2005-IX.

judgment, the following judgment on the same issue in the case of *Greens and M.T.* v. *the United Kingdom* was. In the latter case the Court stated:

> It is ... clear that legislative amendment is required in order to render the electoral law compatible with the requirements of the. In light of the lengthy delay which has already occurred and the results of the delay in terms of follow-up applications, the Court, like the Committee of Ministers, is anxious to encourage the speediest and most effective resolution of the situation in a manner which complies with the Convention's guarantees. The question therefore arises whether it is now appropriate for the Court to provide the respondent Government with some guidance as to what is required for the proper execution of the present judgment.[12]

The Court did not specify what legal regime the UK government needs to adopt, but it was clear that legislative amendments are necessary to eliminate blanket disenfranchisement of prisoners. The UK government had to amend section 3 of the Representation of the People Act 1983 which prohibits prisoners from voting. Although these legislative changes were proposed to the Parliament, they were voted down and section 3 remains unamended. That means that the government failed to achieve what it was asked to do by the Court. Despite this, the Committee of Ministers closed the supervision of the judgments of the *Hirst No. 2* group, stating:

> After having examined all options through parliamentary and other procedures, and in light of the impossibility of passing legislation through Parliament, the authorities decided that a range of administrative measures were the best approach credibly, effectively and swiftly to address the issue. They therefore made changes to the policy and guidance to the prison service to make it clear that two categories of previously effectively disenfranchised convicted prisoners – those on temporary licence and on home detention curfew – are now able to vote.[13]

One can argue that the Committee of Ministers closed its supervision of this case because it was costing too much to the reputation of the Strasbourg system rather than because the UK genuinely complied with the ECtHR judgments in *Hirst No. 2* and *Greens and M.T.*[14] Effectively, prisoners are still disenfranchised in the UK, section 3 of

[12] *Greens and M.T.* v. *the United Kingdom*, nos. 60041/08 and 60054/08, ECHR 2010, para. 112.

[13] State of Execution of *Hirst No. 2* available at http://hudoc.exec.coe.int/eng?i=004-2204.

[14] Ergul Celiksoy, 'Execution of the Judgments of the European Court of Human Rights in Prisoners' Right to Vote Cases' (2020) 20 *HRL Rev* 555.

the Representation of the People Act 1983 remains in force and the Court's efforts to change European public order in this area are far from being effective. Although the Court tried to establish a new standard in Europe regarding prisoner voting, the effort met with some very noticeable resistance in a few European countries. Arguably, the judgment in *Hirst No. 2* aimed to amend European public order because the rule developed in this case was of general character[15] and it is applicable to similar situations that existed not only in the UK in the material time.[16] This judgment can be considered as a revolutionary change in European public order for at least two reasons, as follows.[17]

First, the Court extended the scope of the ECHR; arguably, Article 3 of Protocol 1 does not contain an enforceable individual right. Although in *Mathieu-Mohin and Clerfayt* v. *Belgium* the Court rejected such interpretation, it is not totally implausible. In *Mathieu-Mohin* the Court relied on the Preamble to the Convention and Protocol 1. The Court also considered the intention of the drafters of the Protocol as reflected in the *travaux préparatoires*. The Court then stated:

> [T]he inter-State colouring of the wording of Article 3 does not reflect any difference of substance from the other substantive clauses in the Convention and Protocols. The reason for it would seem to lie rather in the desire to give greater solemnity to the commitment undertaken and in the fact that the primary obligation in the field concerned is not one of abstention or non-interference, as with the majority of the civil and political rights, but one of adoption by the State of positive measures to 'hold' democratic elections.[18]

In this case the Court approved the evolutive interpretation of Article 3 of Protocol 1 by stating that this right has developed from the idea of ensuring that free elections are held regularly to the concept of universal suffrage.[19] Having said that, the contracting parties still enjoy a wide margin of appreciation in selecting an appropriate model of elections.[20] In its very first judgment relevant to Article 3 of Protocol 1 the Court reconceptualised the legal meaning of Article 3 and applied an evolutive

15 The rule is that 'blanket disenfranchisement of prisoners should be prohibited'.
16 See Celiksoy (n. 14) 556.
17 The subsequent discussion draws upon arguments that have been presented in Kanstantsin Dzehtsiarou, 'Prisoner Voting Saga: Reasons for Challenges' in Helen Hardman and Brice Dickson (eds.), *Electoral Rights in Europe: Advances and Challenges* (Routledge 2017).
18 *Mathieu-Mohin and Clerfayt* v. *Belgium*, 2 March 1987, App. No. 9267/81, Judgment of 2 March 1987, para. 50.
19 Ibid., para. 51.
20 Ibid., para. 52.

interpretation to it. In other words, the Court effectively re-drafted the Article in order to insert a voting rights protection clause into the Convention. The Court pointed out that Article 3 of Protocol 1 implies rather than establishes individual rights to vote and to stand for elections.[21] This is shaky legal ground for a far-reaching evolutive interpretation in this area. It clearly differentiates Article 3 of Protocol 1 from qualified rights enshrined in the Convention, such as, for example, the right to privacy (Article 8 ECHR), which at least creates an individual right. The right implied in Article 3 of Protocol 1 is 'super-qualified' and therefore should be granted subject to a wide margin of appreciation for the states concerned. Despite this, the ECtHR set a new standard in *Hirst No. 2* which affected a significant number of the contracting parties to the Convention.

The second reason is that there was no clear consensus at the time of adoption of *Hirst No. 2*. The Court emphasised that a blanket ban on prisoner voting exists in a minority of the contracting parties and 'even if no common European approach to the problem can be discerned, this cannot in itself be determinative of the issue'.[22] The ECtHR failed to explain why it was not determinative, especially since a lack of consensus usually means a wide margin of appreciation.[23] This point was also emphasised by the dissenting judges in this case. They maintained that the Court's conclusion that states enjoy a broad margin of appreciation is hard to reconcile with the Court's statement that a prisoner voting ban clearly falls outside 'any acceptable margin'.[24] The dissenting judges claimed that the Court should intervene only if the restriction at issue goes to the core of the right provided and it is arbitrary.

The Court then tried to add some appeal to this problematic rule established in *Hirst No. 2* by resorting to the pilot judgment procedure; perhaps the judges of the Court hoped that this would push the UK to adopt the requested changes. Arguably, the Court used the pilot judgment procedure to legitimise the rule of general application; at the same time the Court used this pilot procedure to get rid of a high number of clone applications similar to the one dealt with in *Hirst No. 2*.[25] The questionable execution of

[21] *Ahmed and Others* v. *United Kingdom*, 2 September 1998, Reports of Judgments and Decisions 1998-VI, para. 75.

[22] *Hirst No. 2* (n. 11) para. 81.

[23] See, for example, *Evans* v. *the United Kingdom* [GC], no. 6339/05, ECHR 2007-I, para. 94.

[24] Joint Dissenting Opinion of Judges Wildhaber, Costa, Lorenzen, Kovler and Jebens. *Hirst No. 2* (n. 11) para. 5.

[25] *Greens and M.T.* v. *the United Kingdom* (n. 12) paras. 116–22.

this set of judgments shows that this strategy might not necessarily work, but it is quite clear that, by means of the pilot procedure, the Court is trying to set a rule of general application. The Court did the same, implicitly, long before the pilot judgment procedure was introduced, but stating it explicitly reveals the Court's ambition to shape European public order.

Another noticeable feature of the pilot judgment procedure is that it tries to address the weakness of the enforcement mechanism of the Court's judgments. I have argued already that one of the challenges to the Court's attempts to shape European public order is the fact that the Court cannot effectively impose its vision of European public order. Moreover, the contracting parties have broad discretion as to how to implement the Court's judgments, which might distort the standards envisaged by the ECtHR.[26] In the mid-1990s the Court shifted from purely declaratory judgments to much clearer and unambiguous remedies; this shift has arguably peaked in the pilot judgment procedure. Here, the Court usually spells out what general measures[27] should be adopted by the contracting parties.

> At the start of its operation, the ECtHR issued only declaratory judgments, meaning that if the Court had found a violation of the Convention it would not prescribe the exact measures that the Contracting Parties should undertake in order to ensure compliance with the Convention. Although the judgments of the Court are binding on the Contracting Parties under Article 46, this approach meant that the Court would avoid interfering with (or being accused of interfering with) the sovereignty of the Contracting Parties by dictating the mode of execution of a particular judgment.[28]

This approach does not always work as planned. As the prisoner voting pilot procedure showed, the UK did not actually implement the substance of the remedies listed in the pilot judgment and got away with that. Another example of the Court's pilot judgment backfiring is the

[26] See Chapter 3 for more detail.

[27] 'Execution of judgments ... requires general measures to prevent violations similar to those found by the Court (whether through changes of legislation, case law or through other kinds of measures). Ensuring the effectiveness of domestic remedies is an important concern', available at www.coe.int/en/web/execution/the-supervision-process#{%2214997692%22:[0]}. See also Fiona de Londras and Kanstantsin Dzehtsiarou, 'Mission Impossible? Addressing Non-execution through Infringement Proceedings in the European Court of Human Rights' (2017) 66 *Int'l & Comp LQ* 467.

[28] Fiona de Londras and Kanstantsin Dzehtsiarou, *Great Debates on the European Convention on Human Rights* (Palgrave 2018) 168.

group of cases that followed the pilot judgment in *Ivanov* v. *Ukraine*. In this case the Court ruled that non-execution of the final national judgments is a violation of Article 6 of the ECHR and that the delay in execution should be covered by an appropriate compensation.[29] This is a rule of general application. Comparable judgments were delivered in cases against Russia[30] and Moldova.[31]

In *Ivanov* v. *Ukraine*, the Court stated:

> [T]he respondent State must grant adequate and sufficient redress, within one year from the date on which the present judgment becomes final … In the Court's view, such redress may be achieved through implementation proprio motu by the authorities of an effective domestic remedy in those cases or through ad hoc solutions such as friendly settlements with the applicants or unilateral remedial offers in line with the Convention requirements. If, however, the respondent State fails to adopt such measures following a pilot judgment and continues to violate the Convention, the Court will have no choice but to resume the examination of all similar applications pending before it and to take them to judgment so as to ensure effective observance of the Convention.[32]

The Court, however, failed to fulfil its promise. Arguably, the ECtHR could not ensure that the standard applicable in cases of the *Ivanov* type is effectuated on the national level. Moreover, it failed to provide individual redress and fulfil its technical adjudicatory function in similar cases pending before the Court after *Ivanov* was delivered. In 2017 the Court pronounced a judgment in *Burmych and others* v. *Ukraine*, in which it stated that 'despite the significant lapse of time since the delivery of the Ivanov pilot judgment on 15 October 2009, the Ukrainian Government have so far failed to implement the requisite general measures capable of addressing the root causes of the systemic problem identified by the Court and to provide an effective remedy securing redress to all victims at national level'.[33] After stating that, the Court explained that it

> is faced with a serious problem of case overload which originates in structural or systemic situations in different contracting States. This phenomenon carries the risk of preventing the Court from being able to focus on cases raising new and serious issues of Convention compliance in the States concerned and from

29 *Yuriy Nikolayevich Ivanov* v. *Ukraine*, no. 40450/04, 15 October 2009.

30 *Burdov* v. *Russia (no. 2)*, no. 33509/04, ECHR 2009.

31 *Olaru and Others* v. *Moldova*, nos. 476/07 and three others, 28 July 2009.

32 *Yuriy Nikolayevich Ivanov* v. *Ukraine* (n. 29) para. 99.

33 *Burmych and Others* v. *Ukraine* (striking out) [GC], nos. 46852/13 and others, 12 October 2017, para. 146.

dealing with such cases in good time. The pilot-judgment procedure, the essence of which is to transfer back to the domestic system responsibility for affording redress once the problem has been identified by the Court in a pilot judgment, was developed as a response to this threat.[34]

The Court has effectively identified that it sets the standard in its judgment and it is the state's obligation to apply this standard, making sure that the ECtHR is not flooded by repetitive applications. So, the meta-function of the Court is to set generally applicable standards. If the respondent state fails to apply this standard, then the Court is not effective in fulfilling its meta-function because the new standard is not effectuated by the contracting party. As a result, the Court faces a huge number of individual cases in which the Court is expected to fulfil its technical function and put an end to the conflict between the applicant and the respondent state. However, the case of *Burmych* shows that the Court also fails to fulfil its technical function in these cases. Here, the Court simply transferred around 12,000 clone cases to the Committee of Ministers without any decision.[35]

Every time the Court delivers a pilot judgment, it tests its own reputation and legitimacy. Non-execution of any judgment of the Court brings some damage to the Court's legitimacy, but non-execution of a pilot judgment is much more damaging. The Court gives clear instructions and sets time limits – this is much more intrusive in the respondent state's sovereignty than a non-pilot judgment, and non-execution of a pilot judgment is much more 'visible'. Since cases of non-execution happen, the Court cannot act as if it is the only authority in Europe; it needs to bear in mind what is possible and realistic. Demanding unrealistic standards undermines the authority of the Court. It does not mean that the pilot judgment procedure is a failure, however, far from it. Some of the pilot judgments were implemented. However, the Court should be very careful about setting general rules by means of pilot judgments; the ECtHR needs to engage in dialogue with the contracting parties in such cases.

The pilot judgment procedure shows that the Court is trying to increase its impact on European public order through explicitly listing the changes that the respondent governments are expected to undergo as a result of the judgment. By designing the pilot judgment procedure, it has institutionalised delivering of rules of general character which are

[34] Ibid., para. 210.
[35] Ibid., para. 221.

applicable to multiple situations in the respondent state as well as in other contracting parties to the Convention in which the same human rights problem might exist. Simultaneously, the Court is trying to overcome the weakness and vagueness of its remedies by stating the Court's demands and indicating the timescale for compliance. However, this institutionalised impact on European public order can backfire either by principled disobedience, evident in the prisoner voting cases, or by dilatoriness and limited financial resources, evident in *Ivanov* type cases.[36]

5.2.2 *Interim Measures*

Perhaps one of the clearest examples of extending the institutionalised impact of the ECtHR on European public order is its approach to interim measures. I argued that European public order can be approached as an analytical as well as a legal concept. Although this chapter mostly treats European public order as an analytical concept, the Court explicitly referred to European public order in the context of interim measures.[37] The ECtHR claimed that if the respondent state fails to comply with interim measures, this undermines the 'effectiveness of the Convention as a constitutional instrument of European Public Order'.[38] The Court has not explained what aspect of European public order is affected or why a violation of interim measures is a more significant interference with European public order than any other violation of the Convention or failure to comply with the judgments of the ECtHR. Yet again, the legal value of the reference to European public order is problematic, but it might be useful to consider whether the Court's attempts to influence European public order as an analytical concept through interim measures are justifiable.

As I have argued before, European public order understood analytically is a set of fundamental standards shared by the contracting parties to the Convention.[39] In order to establish a relationship between European public order and interim measures, one needs to find a connection between the seemingly technical tool of interim measures and European public order. Perhaps one such connection is the fact that interim measures are requested when the situation is still ongoing and a human rights violation can be prevented rather than remedied *post*

[36] See de Londras and Dzehtsiarou (n. 27).
[37] See Chapter 2.
[38] *Savriddin Dzhurayev* v. *Russia*, no. 71386/10, ECHR 2013, para. 77.
[39] See Chapter 1.

factum. This makes interim measures more impactful, but this impact is nevertheless predominantly individual; in other words, this impact can help a particular applicant rather than develop a broader standard of human rights protection. I have already pointed out that European public order can be shaped by general non-individualised rules adopted by the Court. To the contrary, effective interim measures are purely individual and they do not attempt to shape European public order. When the Court starts applying interim measures more generally, their impact and legitimacy might fade away.[40] In this section, I will first explain what makes interim measures effective, then I will show that the Court has clearly widened the scope of application of interim measures in the last few decades and argue that broadening their scope or aiming to impact European public order through interim measures might undermine their value as a preventive measure.

5.2.2.1 The Effectiveness of Interim Measures

The key purpose of interim measures is to ensure the effectiveness of human rights adjudication.[41] Interim measures should be used to prevent clearly defined irreparable harm,[42] and to maintain human rights practical and effective.[43] Such interim measures guarantee that human rights adjudication remains meaningful and saves the option for the parties to resort to *restitutio in integrum* if acts of one of the parties are found to be in breach of the rights enshrined in the Convention.[44] The vast majority of interim measures are of negative character; they oblige the addressee not to worsen the situation.[45] More rarely, the contracting parties are asked to fulfil certain duties.[46] Simple negative obligations are usually prescribed to the contracting parties as requirements

[40] This section is based on the argument earlier published in Kanstantsin Dzehtsiarou, 'Can the European Court of Human Rights Prevent War? Interim Measures in Inter-State Cases' (2016) *PL* 254.

[41] In this case, the Court had to decide whether Turkey violated the Convention by extraditing the applicants against the Court's interim measures. *Mamatkulov and Askarov* v. *Turkey*, App. Nos. 46827/99 and 46951/99, Judgment of 4 February 2005, para. 102. See also Henrik Jorem, 'Protecting Human Rights in Cases of Urgency: Interim Measures and the Right of Individual Application under Article 34 ECHR' (2012) 30 *Nordic J Hum Rights* 404, 413.

[42] *Mamatkulov and Askarov* v. *Turkey* (n. 41) para. 104.

[43] Ibid., para. 108.

[44] George Letsas, 'International Human Rights and the Binding Force of Interim Measures' (2003) *EHRLR* 527, 530.

[45] Extradition or deportation.

[46] Transfer a prisoner to a civil hospital.

of the interim measures of the ECtHR because such obligations are easier to formulate and it is easier to assess compliance.

Interim measures can achieve their purpose of ensuring the effectiveness of human rights adjudication only if they are considered to be legally binding and are routinely followed by the contracting parties to the Convention. The Court's interim measures enjoy a high level of compliance. The compliance rate with interim measures has been more than 99 per cent, while each instance of non-compliance triggered an immediate negative reaction from the Court.[47] This section will now consider possible reasons why interim measures have been so successful in the past.

5.2.2.1.1 Low Cost

Interim measures are designed to prevent imminent and irreparable damage to the applicant which would render human rights adjudication useless. Blatant disregard of the Court's decisions is rare and it is arguably justified for the contracting parties only if non-compliance will bring more benefits than the reputational damage that may be caused.[48] It seems rather uncontroversial to suggest that more costly and demanding decisions of the Court are less likely to be complied with by contracting parties. In the majority of cases, compliance with interim measures does not cost much and therefore the compliance rate is fairly high.[49] This can explain why some contracting parties fail to honour interim measures in cases considered sensitive; the perceived cost of compliance is prohibitively high for them. For instance, Turkey resisted complying with interim measures in the highly politicised *Öcalan* case. This case was concerned with criminal proceedings against

[47] While prima facie the compliance rate seems extremely high (99%), about 70% of the incompliances have been committed over the past 12 years (1999–2010), which is rather awkward in the light of the fact that although it has been established (since 2003) that non-compliance can generate the violation of Article 34 ECHR, the tendency not to follow the orders of provisional measures continues to increase. (Yves Haeck, Clara Burbano Herrera and Leo Zwaak, 'Strasbourg's Interim Measures under Fire: Does the Rising Number of State Incompliances with Interim Measures Pose a Threat to the European Court of Human Rights?' (2011) *European Yearbook of Human Rights* 375, 380)

[48] Dothan argues that '[w]hen making the decision whether to comply or not to comply, the executive considers whether the material cost of compliance is greater than the sum of the reputational benefit it will gain if it complies and the reputational sanction for noncompliance ("the reputational payoff")'. Shai Dothan, *Reputation and Judicial Tactics* (Cambridge University Press 2014) 71.

[49] See Nico Krisch, *Beyond Constitutionalism. The Pluralist Structure of Postnational Law* (Oxford University Press 2010) 144–5.

the leader of the Kurdish Workers' Party, a paramilitary organisation fighting for the independence of Kurdistan.[50] Haeck, Burbano Herrera and Zwaak argued that contracting parties are reluctant to execute interim measures in cases which relate to national or international conflicts. They pointed out: '[T]he special feature of … "conflict-related" incompliances is undoubtedly … that such cases are very sensitive (and exceptionally also high-profile …) … at the domestic political level … [G]overnments do not wish [the] public … to think that they are harbouring alleged or proven terrorists or people recruiting terrorists on their territory.'[51] These exceptional scenarios are rare and therefore they do not affect the overall statistics of the effectiveness of interim measures in individual cases. However, this does not mean that the situation will not change if the Court increases the number of interim measures, which can be excessively demanding for the contracting parties.

5.2.2.1.2 *Clarity, Preciseness and Unambiguity*

It is argued that the success of interim measures, at least to some extent, is due to their precise and unambiguous formulation that specifies the conduct required from the states addressed. For instance, it is hard to misinterpret the Court's order not to deport a particular individual. Having said that, when it comes to positive actions demanded by the Court, some disagreements in interpretation are still possible, even if the measure is quite precise. For example, in the case of *Paladi* v. *Moldova*, the Court instructed the government with seemingly unambiguous measures: '[T]he applicant should not be transferred from the RNC [Republican Neurological Centre] until the Court has had the opportunity to examine the case.'[52] The Court ruled that, if transferred back to prison, the applicant, who was seriously ill, would not receive adequate medical treatment. Nevertheless, the applicant was transferred,[53] but he was returned to the RNC three days later.[54] The applicant and the government disagreed about whether the latter had complied properly with the interim measures indicated by the Court. The government argued that 'all reasonable steps had been taken to

[50] *Öcalan* v. *Turkey*, App. No. 46221/99, Judgment of 12 May 2005, para. 5. See also Eva Rieter, *Preventing Irreparable Harm: Provisional Measures in International Human Rights Adjudication* (Intersentia 2010) 980.

[51] Haeck et al. (n. 76) 399.

[52] *Paladi* v. *Moldova*, App. No. 39806/05, Judgment of 10 March 2009, para. 45.

[53] Ibid., para. 46.

[54] Ibid., para. 94.

comply with the interim measures'.[55] The Court disagreed with the government and found a violation of Article 34 ECHR.[56] This shows that, even in a case of relatively straightforward measures, some degree of misinterpretation is possible; this degree will substantially increase in relation to vague and broad-brush interim measures.

If the Court uses broad and vague measures, states become more reluctant to comply with them, even in the context of individual applications. For example, in *Aleksanyan* v. *Russia* the ECtHR ordered the national authorities 'to secure immediately, by appropriate means, the in-patient treatment of the applicant in a hospital specialised in the treatment of Aids and concomitant diseases'.[57] In *Öcalan* v. *Turkey* the Court also used a broad definition of interim measures, namely, 'the Court requested that the Government take interim measures within the meaning of Rule 39, notably to ensure that the requirements of Article 6 were complied with in proceedings which had been instituted against the applicant in the National Security Court'.[58] In both cases, execution of broad interim measures was problematic as the contracting parties questioned the legitimacy of such measures[59] and challenged the fact that they failed to comply with them.[60]

On rare occasions in individual cases, the Court instructed the contracting parties to comply with abstract interim measures. As these examples show, the more ambiguous and abstract the formulation of interim measures, the more likely they will be problematic in terms of

55 Ibid., para. 95.

56 Ibid., para. 100.

57 *Aleksanyan* v. *Russia*, App. No. 46468/06, Judgment of 22 December 2008, para. 76.

58 *Öcalan* v. *Turkey* (n. 50) para. 5.

59 In *Öcalan* 'the legal adviser at the Turkish Permanent Delegation to the Council of Europe stated that the Government were not prepared to reply to the Court's questions, as they went far beyond the scope of interim measures within the meaning of Rule 39'. Ibid.

60 In *Aleksanyan* the Russian authorities argued that they were taking all necessary steps in order to examine the applicant's medical condition, establish the diagnosis and provide him with adequate medical aid. Furthermore, such measures had been taken even before the applicant's complaint had been communicated to the Russian Government. The quality of medical services in the prison hospital was not only equal to but in some respect better than in many civilian hospitals. Thus, the applicant's transfer to a civilian hospital was not necessary from a medical point of view. Nevertheless ... pursuant to the recommendation of the medical team which had examined the applicant ... he was transferred to city hospital no. 60. The delay in the implementation of this measure was fully imputable to the applicant himself, who refused to be subjected to specific analysis and treatment. (*Aleksanyan v. Russia* (n. 57) para. 223)

execution. In turn, this challenged execution poses threats to the legitimacy of interim measures.

The Court itself has highlighted that it issues very precise interim measures and only in situations where immediate harm to the applicant is possible. Since these measures are clear and used rarely, the ECtHR expects the contracting parties to comply. The Court has emphasised

> the special importance attached to interim measures in the Convention system. Their purpose is not only to carry out an effective examination of the application but also to ensure that the protection afforded to the applicant by the Convention is effective; such indications subsequently allow the Committee of Ministers to supervise execution of the final judgment. Such measures thus enable the State concerned to discharge its obligation to comply with the final judgment of the Court, which is legally binding by virtue of Article 46 of the Convention. The crucial significance of interim measures is further highlighted by the fact that the Court issues them, as a matter of principle, in truly exceptional cases on the basis of a rigorous examination of all the relevant circumstances. In most of these, the applicants face a genuine threat to life and limb, with the ensuing real risk of grave, irreversible harm in breach of the core provisions of the Convention. This vital role played by interim measures in the Convention system not only underpins their binding legal effect on the States concerned, as upheld by the established case-law, but also commands the utmost importance to be attached to the question of the States Parties' compliance with the Court's indications in that respect.[61]

The quote highlights that, according to the Court, precision and deployment in very specific, clearly defined situations should predetermine high effectiveness and the good compliance record with interim measures.

5.2.2.1.3 *Ultimate Control of Contracting Parties over the Execution of Interim Measures*

The significance of this reason for the success of interim measures in individual cases becomes more apparent if considered in comparison with interim measures in inter-state cases where their execution can depend on external factors: namely, the behaviour of other states, non-state actors like para-military groups, and other situations that cannot be controlled by the contracting party. In individual cases, compliance with interim measures is normally under the full control of the contracting party. For instance, deportation or extradition of an individual can be stayed by issuing a relevant order by the state authorities; the prison governor can authorise the transfer of a prisoner to a civil hospital and this authorisation will be honoured. The possibility of

[61] *Savriddin Dzhurayev* v. *Russia*, no. 71386/10, ECHR 2013, paras. 212–13.

executing interim measures does not and should not depend on external circumstances. The ECtHR would find no violation of the ECHR if the contracting party had no real possibility of following the interim measures. In *Muminov* v. *Russia* the Court agreed with the Russian authorities that it was impossible for the respondent state to prevent a deportation following the Court's interim measures because the applicant had already been deported.[62] The Court should aim to instruct the contracting parties with interim measures that can be executed; otherwise, it hampers their effectiveness. It is logical to suggest that general interim measures would have more impact on European public order than more precise individual ones, but the effect of the former will depend on the co-ordinated actions of more than one contracting party to the Convention, which might be challenging.

If there is a slight possibility of arguing that non-compliance was due to certain external circumstances, the authorities would surely use this opportunity to shift the blame for the violation of human rights. In *Savriddin Dzhurayev* v. *Russia* the applicant was transferred to Tajikistan despite the Court's interim measures. The Russian authorities argued that the applicant voluntarily crossed the Russian border and surrendered to the Tajik authorities. The Court found a violation in this case, claiming that the factual account submitted by the Russian authorities was implausible and that forcible removal could not have happened without the involvement of the Russian secret services.[63] This case, however, shows that states are ready to use external factors as a justification for non-compliance with interim measures instructed by the ECtHR. Therefore, if there is a chance of blaming external factors for non-compliance, the contracting parties involved might be more inclined to disregard interim measures.

A high success rate of interim measures in individual cases is due to their precise meaning, the low cost of compliance and the fact that their execution does not depend on external factors. They are also deployed on very rare occasions to prevent harm to particular known individuals; such measures provide clear instructions of what has to be done by the state.

5.2.2.2 Extending the Scope of Interim Measures

The ECtHR has clearly and consistently extended the scope of interim measures. This tactic is threefold: first, the Court applies interim measures

[62] *Muminov* v. *Russia*, App. No. 42502/06, Judgment of 4 November 2010, paras. 136–7.
[63] *Savriddin Dzhurayev* v. *Russia* (n. 61).

in relation to the Articles of the Convention which previously were not considered suitable for interim measures. Second, by means of interim measures the Court is requesting the contracting parties to undertake a broad spectrum of obligations which previously would not fall within the scope of interim measures. Third, the Court started using interim measures of general application in relation to an indeterminate number of people, usually in the context of military confrontation within inter-state cases.

Traditionally, the ECtHR has requested interim measures in cases in which the applicant was in immediate danger of torture or death and mostly in the context of expulsion.[64] Such measures were also given in inter-state cases, but they still comply with the named conditions. An example of such interim measures can be found in the case of *Greece* v. *the United Kingdom*.[65] Despite the fact that this was an inter-state application, the interim measures concerned a particular individual who was sentenced to death in Cyprus. In response to the request sent by Greece, the Commission stated:

> [I]n order to avoid any irreparable act, to address an urgent request to the Government of the United Kingdom asking that the abovementioned sentence on Nicolas Sampson should not be carried out until the Sub-commission has been fully informed as to the facts of this case and has had the opportunity to present to the Government of the United Kingdom such observations as it may think right to make in this matter.[66]

The death sentence was not carried out; the United Kingdom complied with the interim measures. Despite its having been issued in an inter-state case, this measure is very precise (preventing the state from execution of a convicted individual) and directed towards a particular known individual (Nicolas Sampson). For these reasons, such a measure cannot be categorised as a measure of general character.

Traditionally, interim measures were used if the applicant's rights under Articles 2 and 3 were at risk. Later, the Court started using interim measures in cases concerning Article 8 when, for example, deportation would destroy the applicant's family life[67] and Article 6 when the

64 See, *Cruz Varas and Others* v. *Sweden*, 20 March 1991, Series A no. 201, para. 55.

65 *Greece* v. *the United Kingdom*, App. No. 176/56, Decision of 26 September 1958.

66 Ibid., 34.

67 See *Othman (Abu Qatada)* v. *the United Kingdom*, no. 8139/09, ECHR 2012; *X* v. *Croatia*, no. 11223/04, 17 July 2008.

actions of the respondent state would lead to a flagrant denial of justice.[68] Later still, the Court extended the scope of interim measures even further. In at least two cases, the Court granted interim measures in protecting freedom of expression under Article 10 ECHR.

In *Rustavi 2 Broadcasting Company LTD and others* v. *Georgia* the Court issued interim measures preventing the authorities from closing down one of the TV stations in Georgia.[69] In the pending case of *Sedletska* v. *Ukraine*[70] the Court prevented the authorities of Ukraine from accessing the journalistic sources of an applicant. This case also concerned Article 10 of the Convention. It is open for discussion whether violations of freedom of expression can lead to immediate, serious and irreparable harm, but what is quite evident is that the ECtHR is trying to broaden the application of interim measures. While interim measures started as a very narrow and clearly defined tool usually dealing with cases of extradition or deportation, they have grown into a mechanism that can be applied to a broad range of serious cases.

The second pattern of extension of interim measures is related to a broader 'list of demands' that the state authorities are expected to comply with as a result of interim measures. While initially the Court would simply demand that states prevented the extradition of the applicant,[71] in more recent cases the Court has requested the contracting parties, for example, to move the applicant from prison to a civilian hospital[72] or to provide legal aid.[73] The ECtHR has recently granted interim measures following a request of the representatives of Aleksey Navalnyy, the opposition leader from Russia. Navalnyy was poisoned in Russia and the Court requested the Russian authorities

- to ensure that the applicant's family (wife) has access to his medical file from Omsk hospital;
- to ensure that the medical practitioners appointed by the applicant's family have access to him in order to examine him and conclude if the applicant is fit for transfer for further treatment in Germany;

[68] *Amrollahi* v. *Denmark*, no. 56811/00, 11 July 2002; *Eskinazi and Chelouche* v. *Turkey* (dec.), no. 14600/05, ECHR 2005-XIII.

[69] *Rustavi 2 Broadcasting Company Ltd and Others* v. *Georgia*, no. 16812/17, 18 July 2019.

[70] *Sedletska* v. *Ukraine*, no. 42634/18, available at http://hudoc.echr.coe.int/eng?i=001-188248.

[71] See *Soering* v. *the United Kingdom*, 7 July 1989, Series A no. 161.

[72] *Kondrulin* v. *Russia*, no. 12987/15, 20 September 2016.

[73] *X* v. *Croatia* (n. 67).

- to inform the Court of the medical treatment the applicant receives, if any, and his current condition.[74]

The Court's request to transfer the applicant to a foreign country for treatment is a clear extension of the usual scope of interim measures. This case is clearly exceptional and, while it seems that the ECtHR is not going to demand that other patients be transferred to different countries for treatment, it shows that the Court does not see itself as being restricted by a narrow interpretation of interim measures. By demanding immediate actions,[75] the Court is trying to influence ongoing crises. In turn, this means that the Court is increasing its authority and immediate impact on European public order.

Finally, seemingly the most significant development in relation to the Court's ability to influence a situation beyond a particular individual application is the Court's recent practice of issuing general measures vis-à-vis an indeterminate number of potential applicants. These measures are usually granted in the framework of inter-state applications. There are a few cases in which the Court deployed this type of interim measures: *Georgia* v. *Russia (II)*,[76] *Ukraine* v. *Russia*,[77] *Armenia* v. *Azerbaijan*[78] and *Armenia* v. *Turkey*.[79]

The applicant government in *Georgia* v. *Russia (II)* complained that Russia had committed multiple violations of the ECHR in the context of the armed conflict that occurred between Russia and Georgia in August 2008. The government of Georgia requested interim measures from the Court, which were granted. The Court stated:

> On 12 August 2008 the President of the Court … decided to apply Rule 39 of the Rules, calling upon both the High Contracting Parties concerned to honour their commitments under the Convention, particularly in respect of Articles 2 and 3 of the Convention. In accordance with Rule 39 § 3, he further requested both Governments concerned to inform the Court of the measures taken to ensure that the Convention was fully complied with.[80]

[74] Press release of the ECtHR. The Court grants an interim measure in favour of Aleksey Navalnyy, 21 August 2020.
[75] In the Navalnyy case the request was granted on 21 August and the measures had to be complied with by the noon of 22 August.
[76] *Georgia* v. *Russia (II)* (2012) 54 EHRR SE10.
[77] *Ukraine* v. *Russia (I)* (20958/14).
[78] *Armenia* v. *Azerbaijan* (42521/20).
[79] *Azerbaijan* v. *Armenia* (43517/20).
[80] *Georgia* v. *Russia (II)* (n. 76) para. 5.

These measures were extended by the Court and new information was requested on 26 August, 16 September, 6 October and 25 November 2008. Moreover, the Georgian government informed the Court that, despite the indication of interim measures, the Russian government continued violating the Convention while the measures were in force.

In *Ukraine* v. *Russia*, the Court adopted interim measures following a request submitted by Ukraine in relation to human rights violations committed by Russia during its occupation of part of the Ukrainian territory – the Crimean Peninsula. The Court held:

> Considering that the current situation gives rise to a continuing risk of serious violations of the European Convention, the President of the Third Section has decided to apply Rule 39 of the Rules of Court. With a view to preventing such violations and pursuant to Rule 39, the President calls upon both Contracting Parties concerned to refrain from taking any measures, in particular military actions, which might entail breaches of the Convention rights of the civilian population, including putting their life and health at risk, and to comply with their engagements under the Convention, notably in respect of Articles 2 (right to life) and 3 (prohibition of inhuman or degrading treatment).[81]

More recently, the Court has given interim measures in two inter-state cases concerning the military escalation in the Nagorno-Karabakh region. In the case of *Armenia* v. *Azerbaijan*, the Court requested both parties 'to refrain from taking any measures, in particular military action, which might entail breaches of the Convention rights of the civilian population, including putting their life and health at risk, and to comply with their engagements under the Convention, notably in respect of Article 2 (right to life) and Article 3 (prohibition of torture and inhuman or degrading treatment or punishment) of the Convention'.[82] The Court extended these measures in the case of *Armenia* v. *Turkey* by addressing them to 'all States directly or indirectly involved in the conflict'.[83]

The interim measures in these cases have clear similarities: both the applicant and the respondent states are instructed to comply with the Convention, in particular with the most crucial Articles 2 (right to life)

[81] ECtHR press release: Interim measure granted in inter-state case brought by Ukraine against Russia.

[82] Request for Interim Measures Lodged by Armenia against Azerbaijan, available at https://hudoc.echr.coe.int/eng-press#{%22itemid%22:[%22003-6807941-9105368%22]}.

[83] The Court's Decision on the Request for an Interim Measure Lodged by Armenia against Turkey, available at https://t.co/GLsUe6kQUT?amp=1&fbclid=IwAR3TgkNqr-_oqm20xjQ0CX1rjrdRK3244knuBOwznkjlZKMXYgyHBiCsgoA.

and 3 (prohibition of torture). It is worth mentioning that the contracting parties should comply with these Articles simply by virtue of their signing and ratifying the ECHR.[84]

Interim measures in all cases are vague and open to many possible interpretations. These measures are not directed to protect some particular known individuals but, rather, cover an indefinite number of events and beneficiaries which are often extremely hard to identify.[85] The Court will have to engage with intensive fact-finding missions to be able to conclusively and convincingly decide that the contracting parties have or have not put the 'life and health [of the civilian population] at risk'.[86] Moreover, in *Armenia* v. *Turkey*, the Court also directed these measures to an indefinite number of potential respondent states.

In the past, the effectiveness of interim measures rested on their rare application and only in cases with clearly identifiable immediate risk to the life and health of the applicant. This instrument was created by the Court, but it was purely individual and very narrowly targeted. The Court's desire to influence ongoing events and by doing that to influence European public order necessitated a broader approach to interim measures. The Court consistently increases the use and the scope of interim measures. The same was concluded in relation to the pilot judgment proceedings. The Court's own institutional developments consistently increase the Court's potential impact on European public order. Section 5.3 will show that the contracting parties to the ECtHR are much less consistent and send mixed signals as to the role of the ECtHR vis-à-vis European public order.

The evolution of interim measures illustrates the dangers of shifting from individual adjudication to more general regulations. The effectiveness of interim measures rests on their precise meaning, rare application and low costs. These features disappear when the Court applies interim measures in inter-state cases. They become generic, vague and difficult to implement. This underpins the claim of 'minimalist effectiveness' put forward in this monograph. Having said that, perhaps these broader interim measures have a better chance of impacting European public order if they are executed. The major challenge is whether they would in fact be properly executed.

84 Article 1 ECHR.

85 Brian Griffey, 'Irreparable Harm in the Ukraine Conflict: Protection Gaps and Interim Measures' in Eva Rieter and Karin Zwaan (eds.), *Urgency and Human Rights* (Asser Press 2021) 183–4.

86 Ibid.

The final point that should be made in this regard is relevant to the argument that I made in Chapter 3 that the ECtHR cannot be considered a strategic body. One can argue that the tendency to extend its authority beyond individual cases discussed in this chapter is quite a strategy. However, building European public order requires a more all-encompassing strategy in substantive questions of human rights protection. The Court has extended its institutional and decision-making capacity in pilot judgments and interim measures, but building European public order also suggests a strategic development of the Court's approach to controversial human rights issues. Here, the Court's case law is less consistent and often points in different directions.

5.3 Mixed Signals from the Contracting Parties

In Section 5.2, I showed that the Court has consistently tried to institutionalise its attempts to influence European public order. The reform efforts of the contracting parties are a mixed bag of messages. Some of the statements and reform activities seemingly show that the contracting parties are in favour of more general rulings emanating from the Court and its wider engagement in enforcement of its judgments. For instance, the Court's involvement in infringement procedures[87] and extension of the advisory competences of the ECtHR[88] arguably enhance the Court's ability to influence European public order. Some other reforms show that the contracting parties would prefer the Court to stick to its narrowly defined role of a decision-maker in individual cases. For example, inclusion of references to 'subsidiarity' and 'margin of appreciation' seemingly points in that direction.[89] This section analyses the official statements and reform efforts of the contracting parties in order to show that they do not have a consistent purpose when assessed from the point of view of enhancing the ability of the Court to impact European public order.

[87] Article 46 of the Convention was amended by Protocol 14 which entered into force in 2010.

[88] Protocol 16 to the Convention broadens the Court's ability to deliver advisory opinions.

[89] Protocol 15 to the Convention will amend the text of the Preamble to the Convention: 'Affirming that the High Contracting Parties, in accordance with the principle of subsidiarity, have the primary responsibility to secure the rights and freedoms defined in this Convention and the Protocols thereto, and that in doing so they enjoy a margin of appreciation, subject to the supervisory jurisdiction of the European Court of Human Rights established by this Convention.'

5.3.1 *The Contracting Parties' Views on the Role of the Court*

In this section, I will examine the contracting parties' views on the institutional design of the ECtHR. I will use only the official sources of these views, namely the final declarations of the high-level conferences dedicated to the reform and functioning of the ECtHR, starting from the Interlaken Conference in 2010.[90] I am using these declarations because they represent a view on the Court which is commonly accepted by all contracting parties. Of course, the political leaders of the contracting parties may well express a much more uncensored opinion on the ECtHR,[91] but this view might not be shared by the majority of the contracting parties. Therefore, although the declarations are limited, they are useful in establishing an average approach of the state representatives to what the core aim of the Court should be.

I will briefly outline the core messages of each declaration and then highlight the key aspects that might enhance or reduce the ability of the Court to influence European public order. The first conference on the future of the ECtHR took place in the Swiss Alps in Interlaken. In 2010, the Court was in the midst of its backlog crisis. The number of pending applications was reaching 150,000 and the entering into force of Protocol 14, which would enhance the Court's ability to process these applications, was blocked by Russia. Shortly before the start of the conference, Russia ratified Protocol 14 and, soon after, it came into force.[92] This context is important for understanding the substance of the Interlaken Declaration and the subsequent developments of the so-called Interlaken Process.

The main intention of the Interlaken Declaration was to solve the backlog crisis.[93] However, it also makes a few statements as to the role of the Court. The message of the Interlaken Declaration seems incoherent. Although the state parties confirm their strong commitment to

[90] The Interlaken, Izmir, Brighton, Brussels and Copenhagen Declarations were considered for this subsection.

[91] Former prime minister of the UK David Cameron famously called the ECtHR a small claims court, emphasising that the Court spends too many resources on cases that are not important. Nicholas Watt, 'David Cameron Calls for Reform of European Court of Human Rights', *The Guardian* (25 January 2012) available at www.theguardian.com/law/2012/jan/25/david-cameron-reform-european-court.

[92] See Alastair Mowbray, 'The Interlaken Declaration – The Beginning of a New Era for the European Court of Human Rights?' (2010) 10 *HRL Rev* 519,525.

[93] Lize R. Glas, 'From Interlaken to Copenhagen: What Has Become of the Proposals Aiming to Reform the Functioning of the European Court of Human Rights?' (2020) 20 *HRL Rev* 121, 127.

human rights, the Preamble to the Interlaken Declaration also stresses 'the subsidiary nature of the supervisory mechanism established by the Convention and notably the fundamental role which national authorities, i.e. governments, courts and parliaments, must play in guaranteeing and protecting human rights at the national level'.[94] This statement seems to represent a pushback against the Court's attempts to create its own vision of European public order.[95] The main part of the Declaration also repeats this claim, stating that the principle of subsidiarity 'implies a shared responsibility between the State Parties and the Court'.[96]

The Declaration also calls for 'clarity and consistency of the Court's case-law'; this claim is an indication of the challenge that ECtHR case law is facing. Although the Declaration does not explicitly say so, one can plausibly suggest that deployment of vague and unclear terms such as European public order in its legal sense would go contrary to this demand of the Declaration. Generally speaking, although the Declaration expresses the member states' support for the Court, this support is subject to a number of subtle conditions, one such perhaps being that the Court leaves the development of European public order to the reserved domain of the member states.

A year later, another high-level conference was organised in Izmir, Turkey. The context in which the conference was organised had not changed much in comparison to Interlaken.[97] However, the tone of the Izmir Declaration is changed slightly.[98] The principle of subsidiarity is called 'fundamental and transversal' and both the contracting parties and the Court are requested to take it into account.[99] Curiously, the Declaration mentions interim measures, discussed in Section 5.2.2 of this chapter. The state parties express their concern that the number of interim measures had increased.[100] The states maintain that the Court's creativity as to its approach to interim measures has not gone unnoticed. It seems that the Izmir Declaration envisages a more restrictive role for the Court than that described in the Interlaken Declaration. However, at the same time, the Izmir Declaration envisages a new mechanism that could potentially enhance the role of the ECtHR in shaping European public order. The

94 The Interlaken Declaration, 6.
95 The role of subsidiarity is discussed in Section 5.3.2.
96 The Interlaken Declaration, 3.
97 Glas (n. 93) 127.
98 See Angela Patrick, 'Building on Brighton: A Foundation for the Future of the European Court of Human Rights?' (2012) *Justice J* 32, 35.
99 Izmir Declaration, para. 5.
100 Ibid., para. 12.

Izmir Declaration pronounces that 'some States Parties have expressed interest in a procedure allowing the highest national courts to request advisory opinions from the Court concerning the interpretation and application of the Convention'.[101] Such advisory opinions could potentially be used to express a general rule in a particular area of European human rights law.

The Brighton conference was designed to put the ECtHR in its (proper) place.[102] Helfer pointed out that 'the delegates in Brighton gathered under a cloud of vociferous protests against the Court by the public and government officials in the United Kingdom'.[103] Although the final Brighton Declaration was much less negative than the draft version prepared by the UK authorities,[104] it still showed dissatisfaction with the intrusive nature of the Court's case law in some areas. Although the Declaration still contains some mixed messages about the role of the Court in shaping European public order, the principle of subsidiarity has become the leitmotiv of this Declaration. Madsen pointed out: 'Although the Declaration at times seems to look in several directions at once, its main message is that national institutions, ranging from courts and human rights institutes to parliaments, should play a more substantial role in interpreting and developing the European Convention of Human Rights.'[105] Section B of the Declaration is dedicated mainly to emphasising the subsidiarity of the Convention system and the margin of appreciation that the contracting parties enjoy in effectuating the rights enshrined in the Convention.[106]

The Brighton Declaration was significant in curtailing the Court's attempts to shape the scope of European public order. The Brighton Conference

> [w]elcomes the steps that the Court is taking to maintain and enhance the high quality of its judgments and in particular to ensure that the clarity and consistency of judgments are increased even further; welcomes the Court's longstanding recognition that it is in the interests of legal certainty, foreseeability

[101] Ibid., para. 13.

[102] Sarah Lambrecht, 'Reforms to Lessen the Influence of the European Court of Human Rights: A Successful Strategy?' (2015) 21 *EPL* 257, 271.

[103] Laurence Helfer, 'The Burdens and Benefits of Brighton' (2012) 1 *ESIL Reflections* 1.

[104] Antoine Buyse, 'Brighton Outcomes' *ECHR Blog*, 23 April 2012, available at http://echrblog.blogspot.com/2012/04/brighton-outcomes.html; see Lambrecht (n. 102) 272–5.

[105] Mikael Rask Madsen, 'Rebalancing European Human Rights: Has the Brighton Declaration Engendered a New Deal on Human Rights in Europe?' (2017) 9 *J Int'l Disp Settlement* 199, 200.

[106] Interlaken Declaration, section B.

and equality before the law that it should not depart without cogent reason from precedents laid down in previous cases; and in particular, invites the Court to have regard to the importance of consistency where judgments relate to aspects of the same issue, so as to ensure their cumulative effect continues to afford States Parties an appropriate margin of appreciation.[107]

This seems to be a subtle attack on how the Court applies evolutive interpretation. The Court can shape European public order through the means of evolutive interpretation. If, however, the Court is reminded about its subsidiary role and its ability to evolve is curtailed, then it shows that the state parties do not see the ECtHR as a driving force behind European public order.

The Brighton Declaration makes a couple of attempts to strengthen the Court's rule-making capacity and its ability to act strategically. The idea that was first mentioned in the Izmir Declaration about the enhanced advisory jurisdiction of the Court is repeated in the Brighton Declaration and then transformed into Protocol 16, which recently entered into force.[108] Although, on the face of it, the enhanced advisory jurisdiction might improve the Court's ability to influence European public order, in fact, as Section 5.3.4 of this chapter argues, it might allow the national courts to pre-empt some changes that they consider overly far-reaching.

Another proposal that is enshrined in the Brighton Declaration relates to the composition of the Grand Chamber of the Court. The Declaration invites the Court to consider 'whether the composition of the Grand Chamber would be enhanced by the ex officio inclusion of the Vice Presidents of each Section'.[109] This suggestion would slightly stabilise the composition of the Grand Chamber. Effectively, of the seventeen members of the Grand Chamber, only six would be selected by a coin toss if this suggestion were adopted.[110] Even if this proposal were accepted, it would not undermine my argument that the Court cannot act strategically.[111] Although the composition of the Grand Chamber would be more predictable, this would not allow the Court to frame any substantive long-term strategy of human rights protection. The presidents and vice-presidents of the Court sections change

[107] Brighton Declaration, para. 25(c).
[108] Protocol 16 entered into force after ten ratifications on 1 August 2018, www.coe.int/en/web/conventions/full-list/-/conventions/treaty/214.
[109] Brighton Declaration, para. 25(e).
[110] The president of the Court, five section presidents and five section vice presidents would account for eleven members of the Grand Chamber.
[111] See Chapter 4 for more detail.

regularly and it is very likely that among the eleven 'fixed' members of the Grand Chamber would be judges with significantly diverging views on substantive questions of human rights protection as provided by the Court. However, this proposal was not supported by the ECtHR and it has never been implemented. The reasons for the lack of support included the difficulty of ensuring fair geographical representation on the bench, and recognition that the rotation of judges is a valuable asset for the Grand Chamber.[112]

The final two Declarations – from the conferences in Brussels and Copenhagen – had arguably much less impact on the reform process, but also require some attention. The Brussels Declaration focuses on implementation of the Court's judgments. I have argued that this is an area where the Court's view on European public order can become diluted and the end result of its rule-making might be different from what the Court anticipated. The Brussels Declaration again reiterates the primary obligation of the contracting parties as being to 'fully secure [... Convention rights] at national level, in accordance with the principle of subsidiarity'.[113] The general gist of this Declaration is that the states must implement judgments of the Court comprehensively and in a timely manner while clearly stating that the Court has to act having the principle of subsidiarity in mind.

Finally, the Copenhagen Declaration was adopted in 2018. According to some commentators, it does not contain 'really new or exciting solutions and ideas'.[114] As with the Brighton Declaration, the draft Copenhagen Declaration was much more critical about the Court but it was watered down in the final version.[115] The Declaration again emphasises 'the concept of shared responsibility, which aims at achieving a balance between the national and European levels of the Convention system, and an improved protection of rights, with better prevention and effective remedies available at national level'.[116] Importantly for this monograph, the Copenhagen Declaration more clearly than before states what is actually meant by subsidiarity and focuses on the national procedures. The Declaration states:

[112] Glas (n. 93) 144.
[113] Brussels Declaration, para. 2.
[114] Janneke Gerards and Sarah Lambrecht, 'The Final Copenhagen Declaration: Fundamentally Improved with a Few Remaining Caveats', *Strasbourg Observers* (18 April 2018) available at https://strasbourgobservers.com/2018/04/18/the-final-copenhagen-declaration-fundamentally-improved-with-a-few-remaining-caveats/.
[115] Glas (n. 93) 128.
[116] Copenhagen Declaration, para. 9.

> [S]trengthening the principle of subsidiarity is not intended to limit or weaken human rights protection, but to underline the responsibility of national authorities to guarantee the rights and freedoms set out in the Convention. Notes, in this regard, that the most effective means of dealing with human rights violations is at the national level, and that encouraging rights-holders and decision-makers at national level to take the lead in upholding Convention standards will increase ownership of and support for human rights.[117]

It might mean that the contracting parties see themselves as being responsible for shaping common European public order and the Court needs to react to the developments that have already taken place on the ground rather than go ahead of these developments. At the same time, the Copenhagen Declaration reiterates that the enhanced advisory opinion procedure is a mechanism of dialogue and welcomes the entering of Protocol 16 into force.

Some preliminary conclusions should be articulated here. First, the states have significantly diverging attitudes towards the Court. Some states are much more critical than others and when their reform proposals are discussed, the final accepted common statements become much more favourable to the Court. The drafts proposed by the UK and Danish governments of the Brighton and Copenhagen Declarations respectfully show this tendency. This might mean that different contracting parties might react differently to the Court's attempts to build European public order, with some states perhaps eagerly accepting these attempts,[118] but that common public order can function when it is accepted by everyone. Another conclusion is that, through these Declarations, the states are sending mixed signals to the Court. On the one hand, each of the Declarations makes a clear connection to the principle of subsidiarity and the margin of appreciation, which suggests a limited impact of the Court on European public order and reaffirms the primacy of the contracting parties in this respect. At the same time, the Declarations increase the Court's decision-making capacity through infringement procedures and enhanced advisory jurisdiction. The following subsections will closely look into the key reform efforts which have happened during the last decade.

[117] Ibid., para. 10.

[118] In the prisoner voting saga discussed earlier in this chapter, there was an episode when the Austrian authorities accepted a much more far-reaching standard of prisoner voting than requested from the UK. See *Frodl* v. *Austria*, no. 20201/04, 8 April 2010. However, it does not mean that other contracting parties affected by this standard were happy to accept it.

5.3.2 *Subsidiarity and Margin of Appreciation in the Preamble to the Convention (Protocol 15)*

Every one of the declarations on the future of the ECtHR discussed in Section 5.3.1 includes references to subsidiarity and the margin of appreciation. Robert Spano, the current president of the ECtHR, has famously argued that the Court is entering the age of subsidiarity.[119] The doctrine of the margin of appreciation is perhaps the most discussed method of interpretation of the ECHR.[120] The Court has been using both of them for many years and I will argue here that, legally speaking, their addition to the Preamble of the Convention will not have a significant impact on the case law of the ECtHR. At the same time, it seems that the contracting parties are sending a clear political message that the ECtHR should take a 'passenger seat' in shaping European public order.

According to Article 1 of Protocol 15, the following statement should be added to the Preamble of the Convention: 'Affirming that the High Contracting Parties, in accordance with the principle of subsidiarity, have the primary responsibility to secure the rights and freedoms defined in this Convention and the Protocols thereto, and in doing so enjoy a margin of appreciation, subject to the supervisory jurisdiction of the European Court of Human Rights established by this Convention.' This amendment is a direct consequence of the Brighton Declaration, according to which, 'for reasons of transparency and accessibility, a reference to the principle of subsidiarity and the doctrine of the margin of appreciation as developed in the Court's case law should be included in the Preamble to the Convention . . .'.[121]

If there is any legal impact at all of the inclusion of the margin of appreciation and subsidiarity into the Convention, this impact will be

[119] Robert Spano, 'Universality or Diversity of Human Rights?: Strasbourg in the Age of Subsidiarity' (2014) 14 *HRL Rev* 487.

[120] See, for example, Eyal Benvenisti, 'Margin of Appreciation, Consensus, and Universal Standards' (1999) 31 *NYU J Int'l L & Pol* 84; Steven Greer, *The Margin of Appreciation: Interpretation and Discretion under the European Convention on Human Rights* (Council of Europe 2000); Yutaka Arai-Takahashi, *The Margin of Appreciation Doctrine and the Principle of Proportionality in the Jurisprudence of the ECHR* (Intersentia 2001); Michael R. Hutchinson, 'The Margin of Appreciation Doctrine in the European Court of Human Rights' (1999) 48 *Int'l & Comp LQ* 638; Janneke Gerards, 'Pluralism, Deference and the Margin of Appreciation Doctrine' (2011) 17 *ELJ* 80; George Letsas, 'Two Concepts of the Margin of Appreciation' (2006) 26 *OJLS* 705; Oddný Mjöll Arnardóttir, 'Rethinking the Two Margins of Appreciation' (2016) 12 *EuConst* 27.

[121] Brighton Declaration, para. 12(b).

very limited. The doctrine of the margin of appreciation was developed by the ECtHR itself, without it being mentioned in the Convention. The Court has been applying this doctrine since the *Handyside* case in the 1970s[122] and it has mentioned it in thousands of cases since then.[123] The margin of appreciation is among the most well-established doctrines of interpretation of the Convention. Every book that discusses the Court's case law mentions the margin of appreciation plenty of times. It is unclear, however, how the reference to the margin of appreciation in the Preamble to the Convention influences interpretation of the Convention by the Court. The Court rarely mentions the Preamble in its reasoning; one can argue that it has a predominantly rhetorical value rather than a legal one. Although the exact scope of the margin of appreciation depends on the particularities of each given case, it is unlikely that the fact that the margin is included in the Preamble will significantly broaden its scope. It is extremely likely that the Court's methodology of assessment of the scope of the margin[124] will not change after Protocol 15 enters into force.

The argument that the amendments to the Preamble will not have much direct legal effect is even more evident when one considers how the principle of subsidiarity is used by the Court. It seems that the Court has this principle in mind but it does not play a decisive role in the specific circumstances of the case. The ECtHR has emphasised that it 'exerts its supervisory role subject to the principle of subsidiarity',[125] but the exact meaning of subsidiarity depends on the particularities of the case rather than the fact that subsidiarity is enshrined in the Preamble to the Convention.

The amendments to the Preamble of the Convention enshrined in Protocol 15 are not significant from a legal standpoint because the Court has already been using subsidiarity and the margin of appreciation in its reasoning and their impact on the outcome of the case depends on the particularities of the facts of the case rather than on whether they are mentioned in the Convention. These two arguments are quite obvious and one can plausibly suggest that the drafters of

122 *Handyside* v. *the United Kingdom*, 7 December 1976, Series A no. 24.

123 A rough HUDOC search shows that the term 'margin of appreciation' was mentioned in 2,412 judgments as of 22 October 2020.

124 The factors that the ECtHR considers when assessing the scope of the margin are listed in *S. and Marper* v. *the United Kingdom* [GC], nos. 30562/04 and 30566/04, ECHR 2008, para. 102.

125 *Vilho Eskelinen and Others* v. *Finland* [GC], no. 63235/00, ECHR 2007-II, para. 61.

Protocol 15 were aware of them. This begs the logical question of why it nevertheless was decided to amend the Convention in a way that would have no tangible legal impact. It seems that the message of Protocol 15 is largely political. In individual cases, the scope of the margin is unlikely to change, but when the Court decides to go beyond the confines of a particular case, the message about the principle of subsidiarity and the margin of appreciation might have more appeal.

The recent case of *Perovy* v. *Russia* can be used as an illustration of the point I am trying to make here.[126] In this case the applicants are two parents with a child living in Russia. One day an Orthodox priest performed a rite of blessing of the classroom in the presence of the applicants' child and other pupils. The applicants complained that their freedom and religion and right to education were violated. The Chamber of the Court did not find a violation of the Convention, pointing out that the state has a broad margin of appreciation in reconciling 'exercise of the functions [that states] assume in relation to education and teaching with respect for the right of parents to ensure [that] such education and teaching [are] in conformity with their own religious and philosophical convictions'.[127] On this level, the declared scope of the margin of appreciation is wide. It is wide now and it will still be wide after Protocol 15 enters into force. After declaring that the margin of appreciation is wide, the Court then applied this wide margin to the case and decided whether the state's actions were within the margin. Here, the Court considered the nature of the interference, the behaviour of the state and other relevant factors. In the case of *Perovy* v. *Russia*, the Court focused on whether the blessing rite had a significant impact on the child[128] and how the authorities handled the complaints by the applicants.[129] It is unlikely that Protocol 15 would have a major impact on this part of the Court's reasoning.

The inclusion of subsidiarity and the margin of appreciation might have an impact if the Court decides to change its general strategic approach to these tools of interpretation. Using the same case as an example, the Court would perhaps overstep its subsidiary role if it ruled that any religious rituals in public schools fall outside the margin of appreciation. Although such a ruling would have a significant impact on European public order, it goes against the spirit of the amendments

[126] *Petrovy* v. *Russia*, no. 47429/09, 20 October 2020.
[127] Ibid., para. 63.
[128] Ibid., para. 66.
[129] Ibid., para. 68.

introduced by Protocol 15. It seems that these amendments are designed to curtail the Court's strategic rule-making capacity by reminding the Court that it has to act in accordance with the principle of subsidiarity. It might impact the meta-function of the Court while the technical function remains intact. Although this development aims to curtail the Court's ability to produce general rules capable of shaping European public order, other recent institutional innovations are much less straightforward in this sense.

5.3.3 *Infringement Proceedings (Protocol 14)*

I have already pointed out that the system of implementation of the Court's judgments is relatively weak.[130] The Court cannot forcibly impose execution of its judgments on respondent states. This is especially so in relation to cases that aim to impact European public order because the contracting parties might have principled disagreement with such judgments.[131] This disagreement might destabilise the whole inter-state system of human rights protection. Moreover, another body is responsible for implementation of the Court's judgments, namely the Committee of Ministers of the Council of Europe, which acts through persuasive powers and reputational threats rather than direct enforcement through military or economic coercion. The nuclear option of suspension of membership of the Council of Europe for the state that persists in non-execution of the Court's judgments is available to the Committee of Ministers, but it has never been fully implemented and currently exists only as a theoretical threat.[132] Historically, the Court's role in prescribing certain remedies and directing implementation was very limited. Recently, the Court has become much more involved in the process of execution of its judgments. Broadening the Court's role in this process is perhaps an attempt to make its influence on European public order more direct and predictable. It seems that the contracting parties support the Court's initiative to be more engaged in

[130] This section uses and elaborates on ideas from chapter 8 of Fiona de Londras and Kanstantsin Dzehtsiarou, *Great Debates on the European Convention on Human Rights* (Palgrave 2018).

[131] See Marten Breuer (ed.), *Principled Resistance to ECtHR Judgments – A New Paradigm?* (Springer 2019); de Londras and Dzehtsiarou (n. 27); Mikael Rask Madsen, Pola Cebulak and Micha Wiebusch, 'Backlash against International Courts: Explaining the Forms and Patterns of Resistance to International Courts' (2018) *Int'l JLC* 197.

[132] See Kanstantsin Dzehtsiarou and Donal K. Coffey, 'Suspension and Expulsion of Members of the Council of Europe: Difficult Decisions in Troubled Times' (2019) 68 *Int'l & Comp LQ* 443.

the implementation of its judgments: Protocol 14 has amended Article 46 of the Convention by adding new powers of the Court in this area.

At the start of its operation, the ECtHR issued only declaratory judgments, meaning that the Court would pronounce a violation of the Convention but it would not prescribe any measures that the contracting parties should undertake in order to ensure compliance with the ECHR. Although judgments of the Court are binding on the contracting parties under Article 46, this approach meant that the Court avoided interfering with (or being accused of interfering with) the sovereignty of the contracting parties by dictating the mode of execution of a particular judgment. In recent years, the Court has become more prescriptive in respect of the measures that a respondent state needs to undertake to comply with the Convention; moreover, the ECtHR can get involved in the execution of its judgment.[133] I have already briefly discussed the role of the Court in formulating more precise remedies through its pilot judgments procedure. As I explained earlier in this chapter, the pilot judgment procedure was developed by the Court itself and its legal foundation is enshrined in the Rules of Court.[134] However, an even more active role for the Court on the stage of implementation was granted to the Court by the contracting parties and enshrined in the Convention. This seems to suggest that the contracting parties do not object to the extended involvement of the Court in the process of implementation and, as a result, in potentially shaping European public order. Two new competences in the area of implementation of the Convention were added by Protocol 14 in 2010.

[133] A growing body of literature looks into the Court's role in execution of its own judgments. See, for example, Helen Keller and Cedric Marti, 'Reconceptualizing Implementation: The Judicialization of the Execution of the European Court of Human Rights' Judgments' (2016) 25 *EJIL* 829; Lucius Caflisch, 'New Practice Regarding the Implementation of the Judgments of the Strasbourg Court' (2006) 16 *Italian Yearbook Int'l L* 3; Valerio Colandrea, 'On the Power of the European Court of Human Rights to Order Specific Non-monetary Measures: Some Remarks in Light of the Assanidze, Broniowski and Sejdovic Cases' (2007) 7 *HRL Rev* 396; Linos-Alexander Sicilianos, 'The Involvement of the European Court of Human Rights in the Implementation of Its Judgments: Recent Developments under Article 46 ECHR' (2014) 32 *NQHR* 234; Linos-Alexander Sicilianos, 'The Role of the European Court of Human Rights in the Execution of Its Own Judgments: Reflections on Article 46 ECHR' in Anja Seibert-Fohr and Mark E. Villiger (eds.), *Judgments of the European Court of Human Rights – Effects and Implementation* (Routledge 2014); Alice Donald and Anne-Katrin Speck, 'The European Court of Human Rights' Remedial Practice and Its Impact on the Execution of Judgments' (2019) 19 *HRL Rev* 83; Lize R. Glas, 'The European Court of Human Rights Supervising the Execution of Its Judgments' (2019) 37 *NQHR* 228.

[134] Rule 61 of the Rules of Court.

The first of these two competences is enshrined in Article 46(3); pursuant to it, the Committee of Ministers can send a judgment back to the Court if its interpretation is unclear.[135] This request should be triggered by a majority of two-thirds of the members of the Committee of Ministers; at the time of writing, it has never been used.[136] It is unlikely that this tool could be used effectively for a number of technical reasons. First, it would not be easy to make sure that two-thirds of the Committee of Ministers voted in favour of sending the case back to the Court for interpretation. To justify the effort, there would have to be a significant disagreement about interpretation of the judgment that could not be resolved by the Committee itself. Second, it would be reputationally damaging for the Court because it would show that its judgment is not clear enough. Third, it might be reputationally damaging for the Committee of Ministers too as it would confirm that it had failed to interpret the meaning of the Court's judgment. It is unlikely that the Committee of Ministers would willingly undermine its reputation. Finally, this process of going back and forth between the Committee and the Court would delay the execution of the initial judgment.

Another innovation introduced by Protocol 14 was the infringement procedure. The Committee of Ministers obtained the legal power to initiate proceedings before the Court under Article 46(4). It provides:

> If the Committee of Ministers considers that a High Contracting Party refuses to abide by a final judgment in a case to which it is a party, it may, after serving formal notice on that Party and by decision adopted by a majority vote of two-thirds of the representatives entitled to sit on the committee, refer to the Court the question whether that Party has failed to fulfil its obligation under [Article 46(1)].[137]

Two key challenges associated with infringement proceedings are relevant to this monograph. First, their effectiveness is questionable. Although the Court is provided with an opportunity to influence the execution, its real impact is problematic. Second, although this mechanism can be used to ensure that changes to European public order initiated by the Court are properly implemented, it is quite unlikely that it will be used in practice to effectuate implementation of general abstract standards developed by the Court. These two challenges I will now consider in turn.

Whether the infringement proceeding under Article 46(4) is likely to be useful is the subject of ongoing debate. On the one hand, the

[135] Article 46(3) ECHR.
[136] October 2020.
[137] Article 46(4) ECHR.

Parliamentary Assembly of the Council of Europe, human rights activists and some commentators encourage the Committee of Ministers to use infringement proceedings against states on which other forms of pressure have been ineffective.[138] On the other side of this debate are those who think that its utilisation will have limited practical effect while placing a significant burden on the Court's legitimacy.[139]

The idea behind Article 46(4) was to give the Committee of Ministers an enforcement tool that would be more effective than mere diplomatic actions such as resolutions and expressions of concern but less detrimental to the Council of Europe than suspension and expulsion of member states. In principle, this might be a very appealing idea because the toolkit of the Committee of Ministers is indeed limited. However, the utility of this tool is questionable. First, it is not clear whether the basic requirements for triggering Article 46(4) could be met in practice in relation to cases which are not exceptional. In other words, achieving the required two-thirds of votes in the Committee of Ministers would be extremely challenging.

> For an infringement procedure to be initiated it would have to be supported by at least 31 Contracting Parties, which might themselves face similar infringement procedures in the future, potentially dissuading its use in practice. Relatedly, political complications are likely to arise in respect of which country is . . . to have infringement proceedings taken against it. Such a State may well consider the initiation of infringement proceedings to be illegitimate on the basis that it is being unfairly targeted by the Committee of Ministers; 'why us, when so many others also fail to execute?'.[140]

The second practical challenge is that by using this procedure the Committee of Ministers would implicitly be accepting that it has failed in supervising the execution of a particular judgment. Lambert-Abdelgawad has well observed that international institutions do not readily make manifest their failures in such a way,[141] which may

[138] Klaas de Vries, 'Implementation of Judgments of the European Court of Human Rights' (PACE, Report, 9 September 2015, Doc. 13864) available at www.assembly.coe.int/nw/xml/XRef/X2H-Xref-ViewPDF.asp?FileID=22005&lang=en; Alice Donald, 'Tackling Non-implementation in the Strasbourg System: The Art of the Possible?', *EJIL:Talk* available at www.ejiltalk.org/tackling-non-implementation-in-the-strasbourg-system-the-art-of-the-possible/.

[139] de Londras and Dzehtsiarou (n. 27).

[140] Ibid., 483.

[141] Elisabeth Lambert-Abdelgawad, 'The Court as a Part of the Council of Europe: the Parliamentary Assembly and the Committee of Ministers' in Andreas Føllesdal, Birgit Peters and Geir Ulfstein (eds.), *Constituting Europe: The European Court of Human Rights in a National, European and Global Context* (Cambridge University Press 2013) 280.

suggest simply that attempts to trigger Article 46(4) would not normally be successful owing to the lack of political willingness within the Committee of Ministers itself.

Perhaps the greatest contestation on the question of infringement proceedings relates to what, if anything, they would achieve if the practical challenges of triggering Article 46(4) were overcome. The only example of triggering infringement proceedings at the moment of writing is *Mammadov* v. *Azerbaijan*.[142] The applicant in this case is a political activist in Azerbaijan who was arrested in 2013 for allegedly breaching public order and for resistance to, or violence against, public officials. Even before the final national judgment in his criminal case, the ECtHR declared that these charges were politically motivated and that the true purpose of his arrest was to remove him from the political life of Azerbaijan, contrary to Articles 18 and 5(1)(c) ECHR.[143] Despite multiple requests from the Committee of Ministers to release the applicant, the Azerbaijani authorities failed to do so. The Committee of Ministers managed to initiate infringement proceedings in this case and one can argue that they were successful in putting pressure on the respondent state because the applicant was released even before the ECtHR had a chance to pronounce its judgment. It is, however, difficult to draw far-reaching conclusions from this isolated case. Some commentators argue that '[t]he mechanism appears to have been used effectively, but we would also acknowledge that there was significant contributory pressure being exerted on the Azerbaijani authorities from a range of Council of Europe institutions, including the Secretary General who had instigated an Article 52 inquiry into the case'.[144] Moreover, the nature of the right involved, the personality of the applicant and the fact that Azerbaijan became among the clear outcasts[145] in the Council of Europe created conditions for this infringement procedure to be effective. That said, more general challenges related to the effectiveness of this procedure persist. For instance, it is not clear whether a finding of further infringement under Article 46(4) would

[142] *Ilgar Mammadov* v. *Azerbaijan*, no. 15172/13, 22 May 2014.

[143] See Kanstantsin Dzehtsiarou, 'Introductory Note to Mammadov v Azerbaijan' (2020) 59 *Int'l Legal Material* 35, 35.

[144] Clara Sandoval, Philip Leach and Rachel Murray, 'Monitoring, Cajoling and Promoting Dialogue: What Role for Supranational Human Rights Bodies in the Implementation of Individual Decisions?' (2020) 12 *J Hum Rights Prac* 71, 84.

[145] The Azerbaijani authorities were implicated in the corruption scandal. See Report of the Independent Investigation Body on the allegations of corruption within the Parliamentary Assembly, available at http://assembly.coe.int/Communication/IBAC/IBAC-GIAC-Report-EN.pdf.

really achieve anything from a practical perspective in other cases if they ever ended up in the Court under infringement proceedings. The reality is that an Article 46(4) ECHR procedure effectively tells us what we already know: that the respondent state has failed to respect a judgment of the Court. One might argue that if a state cared enough about its international reputation, it would already have executed the judgment in question. If not, it is difficult to tell what difference a further judgment from the Court would make to the willingness to execute. Certainly, an adverse finding in an Article 46(4) proceeding may create greater and refreshed international pressure for execution of the original judgment, but the impact of that pressure cannot be easily foreseen. Much is likely to depend on how other political powers – neighbours, allies and fellow Council of Europe members – use that pressure created by the international court, and how domestic courts and domestic political structures respond to it in the 'fresh' domestic litigation that might be taken at the national level. The potential usefulness of Article 46(4) may, then, lie in reigniting the effective political pressure on the respondent state to execute the original judgment against it. This, however, calls into question why such effective pressure was not imposed on that state in the first place.

With this questionable effectiveness, the second challenge to the Court's ability to influence European public order on the stage of execution becomes even more pressing. Although the *Mammadov* case shows that the Court can influence the execution of individual measures stemming from the judgment, when it comes to general measures, the Court's ability to change state policies through infringement proceedings is limited. Relevant general measures were discussed by the ECtHR in the *Mammadov* case: 'The ... elements of just satisfaction and general measures relating to the execution of the first *Mammadov* judgment fall within the scope of the infringement proceedings given the wording of Article 46 § 4.'[146] Although the Court left open an opportunity to apply infringement proceedings to general measures, it decided not to do this in the current case. The Court restrained itself to mentioning that the Committee of Ministers continues supervision of general measures in cases similar to *Mammadov*.[147]

In *Mammadov*, the Court exercised deference and did not interfere with the execution of the general measures. One can suggest that the

[146] *Ilgar Mammadov* v. *Azerbaijan* (infringement proceedings) [GC], no. 15172/13, 29 May 2019, para. 177.

[147] Ibid., para. 179. See also Başak Çalı, 'No Going Nuclear in Strasbourg', *Verfassungsblog* (30 May 2019) available at https://verfassungsblog.de/no-going-nuclear-in-strasbourg/.

Court left the general measures outside the scope of the proceedings in *Mammadov* in order to keep the chance alive that infringement proceedings will be initiated again in other cases against other member states. While individual measures are relevant only to the respondent state, the Court's ruling on general measures might impact many contracting parties, which would make the agreement of the Committee of Ministers to send future cases back to the ECtHR even less likely. Here, the Court could have been more forthcoming with its treatment of the general measures and it would perhaps have a more significant impact on European public order, but at the same time it would perhaps trigger a negative reaction from the states that face issues with the execution of judgments somewhat similar to *Mammadov*, for example, judgments where the Court found a violation of Article 18 ECHR.

The amendments that were included in Article 46 through Protocol 14 seem to send mixed messages about the Court's ability to shape European public order. On the one hand, the described amendments clearly enhance the Court's competences in execution of its own judgments. Moreover, the Explanatory Report to Protocol 14 pointed out that '[r]apid and full execution of the Court's judgments is vital. It is even more important in cases concerning structural problems'.[148] It means that the aim of these amendments was to assist effective implementations of general measures stemming from the case law. General measures have more impact on European public order and Articles 46(3) and 46(4) could be utilised by the Court to impose its vision of European public order on the contracting parties. At the same time, the difficult process of bringing infringement procedures to the Court, their exceptional nature[149] and the evidently individual character of the submitted requests[150] make the utility of such measures in effectively shaping European public order limited. Moreover, the ECtHR itself exercised self-restraint in the only case brought to it for infringement proceedings.

5.3.4 *Advisory Opinions (Protocol 16)*

Another recent innovation in the design of the ECtHR is the extended competence of the Court to deliver advisory opinions. This innovation

148 Explanatory Report to Protocol No. 14 to the Convention for the Protection of Human Rights and Fundamental Freedoms, amending the control system of the Convention, para. 98. See also para. 16.

149 Ibid., para. 100.

150 The only Article 46(4) request was submitted in the case where the applicant was detained despite multiple requests of the Committee of Ministers to release him.

has already generated a significant body of academic commentaries.[151] Pursuant to Article 1 of Protocol 16, the highest courts and tribunals of a contracting party to the Convention may request the Court to give advisory opinions on questions of principle relating to the interpretation or application of the rights and freedoms defined in the Convention. Before Protocol 16 entered into force, the ECtHR could deliver advisory opinions but a much more curtailed version of them. According to Article 47 ECHR, the Court could give advisory opinions at the request of the Committee of Ministers on questions of interpretation of the Convention. However, these questions count not be connected to the content and scope of the Convention rights and freedoms. The rationale for this restrictive regime was to avoid duplication of the Court's competencies in contentious cases and advisory opinions. As a result, under the old regime there were only three requests for advisory opinions and only two opinions were actually delivered by the ECtHR.[152] Both of them concerned issues of election of ECtHR judges. The regulations under Protocol 16 are different in two key areas: the requesting agents are the national courts as opposed to the Committee of Ministers and the ECtHR is now allowed to give advisory opinions on substantive questions of interpretation of the Convention rights. The

[151] See, for example, Thomas Voland and Britta Schiebel, 'Advisory Opinions of the European Court of Human Rights: Unbalancing the System of Human Rights Protection in Europe?' (2016) 17 *HRL Rev* 73; Christos Giannopoulos, 'Considerations on Protocol N°16: Can the New Advisory Competence of the European Court of Human Rights Breathe New Life into the European Convention on Human Rights?' (2015) 16 *German LJ* 337; Ada Paprocka and Michal Ziolkowski, 'Advisory Opinions under Protocol No. 16 to the European Convention on Human Rights' (2015) 11 *EuConst* 27; Janneke Gerards, 'Advisory Opinions, Preliminary Rulings and the New Protocol No. 16 to the European Convention of Human Rights: A Comparative and Critical Appraisal' (2014) 21 *Maastricht J Eur & Comp L* 630; Kanstantsin Dzehtsiarou, 'Interaction between the European Court of Human Rights and Member States: European Consensus, Advisory Opinions and the Question of Legitimacy' in Spyridon Flogaitis, Tom Zwart and Julie Fraser (eds.), *The European Court of Human Rights and Its Discontents* (Edward Elgar 2013); Alice Margaria, 'Parenthood and Cross-Border Surrogacy: What Is "New"? The ECtHR's First Advisory Opinion' (2020) 28 *Med L Rev* 412; Kanstantsin Dzehtsiarou and Noreen O'Meara, 'Advisory Jurisdiction and the European Court of Human Rights: A Magic Bullet for Dialogue and Docket-Control?' (2014) 34 *LS* 444.

[152] The Court declared inadmissible the request to give an advisory opinion: *Decision on the competence of the Court*, 2 June 2004, available at http://hudoc.echr.coe.int/eng?i=003-1339293-1397515. The Court delivered two advisory opinions: *Advisory opinion on certain legal questions concerning the lists of candidates submitted with a view to the election of judges to the European Court of Human Rights* [GC], 12 February 2008; *Advisory opinion on certain legal questions concerning the lists of candidates submitted with a view to the election of judges to the European Court of Human Rights (no. 2) [GC]*, 22 January 2010.

'old' advisory jurisdiction of the ECtHR had almost no impact on European public order understood analytically because the Court could only deal with certain technical issues of interpretation of the Convention. The 'new' advisory opinion mechanism seems to be a tool that allows the Court to interpret the Convention and formulate rules of general application. So, from the outset, this innovation seems to strengthen the role of the Court in shaping European public order. However, the advisory opinions can act as an invitation to consider a particular standard set by the ECtHR rather than an ultimate solution to a particular legal problem. Moreover, as I pointed out earlier, national courts can use advisory opinions to pre-empt the ECtHR imposing its solution; in their requests for an advisory opinion, national courts can suggest solutions to be accepted by the ECtHR.

Protocol 16 was called a 'protocol of dialogue'.[153] The idea was to establish an institutionalised means of co-operation between the ECtHR and national courts.[154] However, some aspects of the legal design of the advisory opinion procedure call into question whether such dialogue can be achieved in practice. Moreover, the ability of the highest courts to disagree with the Court's opinion, which should not be automatically executable,[155] emphasises the subsidiary role of the Court and arguably limits the role of the Convention as the 'constitutional instrument of European Public Order'.[156]

Together with Noreen O'Meara, I argued that the legal regulation of advisory opinions might 'create more obstacles to dialogue than it removes'.[157] All advisory opinions have to be adopted by the Grand Chamber of the ECtHR. Given that the Grand Chamber has a very limited capacity[158] and that advisory opinions have to be delivered promptly,[159] one of two solutions will have to be adopted here: either the Grand Chamber will have to prioritise advisory opinions and put its decision-making aside in contentious cases or the Court will have to

153 Dean Spielmann, 'Opening Speech' in *Dialogue between Judges* (Strasbourg 2014) 31; see also 'Noreen O'Meara Reforming the European Court of Human Rights through Dialogue? Progress on Protocols 15 and 16 ECHR' available at https://ukconstitutionallaw.org/2013/05/31/noreen-omeara-reforming-the-european-court-of-human-rights-through-dialogue-progress-on-protocols-15-and-16-echr/.

154 Voland and Schiebel (n. 151) 74.

155 Giannopoulos (n. 151) 349.

156 *Loizidou* v. *Turkey* (preliminary objections), 23 March 1995, Series A no. 310, para. 93.

157 Dzehtsiarou and O'Meara (n. 151) 462.

158 It consists of seventeen judges and delivers up to about thirty judgments per year.

159 Advisory opinions should be given in cases pending before the national courts and perhaps have to be adjourned while the cases are pending in Strasbourg.

start rejecting many requests to give advisory opinions. Of course, one could suggest that a special sub-division of the Court to deal with advisory opinions could be created, but this would demand that the Court devise new working methods and make significant budgetary investments, which is unlikely to happen in the current climate. The abovementioned two solutions do not significantly change the infrastructure or the budget requirements of the ECtHR; yet both are suboptimal.

Limiting the decision-making capacity of the Grand Chamber would reduce the influence of the most authoritative formation of the Court in delivering legally binding judgments in contentious cases.[160] Even now, it takes years for a case to reach the Grand Chamber and then more years for it to deliver a judgment. If there are only a few slots left for contentious cases, many important issues will not be considered by the Grand Chamber in a timely manner or at all. This means that, although in principle Protocol 16 has given the Grand Chamber another opportunity to formulate general rules in advisory opinions, in fact it might reduce its ability to formulate legally binding rules in contentious cases. Another solution to the challenge of excessive case load would be a wider use of the Court's competence to reject requests for advisory opinions. At the moment of writing, the Court has delivered only two advisory opinions and has not yet rejected any requests.[161] However, only fifteen contracting parties have ratified Protocol 16 thus far,[162] so, the backlog is unlikely to be substantive; if this mechanism were to gain some popularity, the Court would have to start rejecting requests. Such rejections might be challenging. The Court would arguably have to provide reasons for rejections[163] and even this would have some resource implications. But, more importantly, it is difficult to see how

[160] Advisory opinions are not legally binding but persuasive.

[161] *Advisory opinion concerning the recognition in domestic law of a legal parent-child relationship between a child born through a gestational surrogacy arrangement abroad and the intended mother* [GC], request no. P16-2018-001, French Court of Cassation, 10 April 2019; *Advisory opinion concerning the use of the 'blanket reference' or 'legislation by reference' technique in the definition of an offence and the standards of comparison between the criminal law in force at the time of the commission of the offence and the amended criminal law* [GC], request no. P16-2019-001, Armenian Constitutional Court, 29 May 2020. Although the Court has not yet rejected the request in full, it has rejected responding to some of the questions listed in the requests.

[162] Chart of signatures and ratifications of Treaty 214: Protocol No. 16 to the Convention for the Protection of Human Rights and Fundamental Freedoms, available at www.coe.int/en/web/conventions/full-list/-/conventions/treaty/214/signatures?p_auth=y5fbqnSF.

[163] Dzehtsiarou and O'Meara (n. 151) 466–7.

such rejections would enhance the dialogue between the ECtHR and the contracting parties.

It is assumed that in order to be able to impact European public order effectively, the ECtHR needs to have means of persuading or coercing contracting parties into accepting a particular standard. For this to happen, the advisory opinions need to have some legal significance and their substance needs to be specific enough to be applicable. I will deal with these two issues now in turn.

What is the legal value of advisory opinions? Even from the name of this mechanism, it is clear that these opinions are not binding but merely 'advisory'. Arguably, they cannot be used in national law as a legally binding source even when this is possible for ECtHR judgments. It was argued that advisory opinions 'have mainly political significance and oblige their addressees only to consider the Court's position'.[164] Gerards argued that the success of advisory opinions is 'rooted in the legal or precedential force' of the case law of the ECtHR.[165] In other words, irrespective of the formal declared legal value of advisory opinions, their inherent connection to the Court's case law makes it difficult for national courts to disregard them. Although this argument might work in relation to some countries, in others the formal lack of binding legal force might create a perception that advisory opinions are just a way to receive legal advice from the ECtHR on the issue of Convention law with the reserved right to disagree with the advice. Some national courts might also use this tool as a way to rubberstamp their vision of how a particular issue is to be decided. While this tool might be useful as it would create a feedback loop between the Court and the contracting parties in relation to certain aspects of interpretation of the Convention, it would reduce the Court's role as a single-handed author of European public order, especially since Protocol 16 itself underlines the principle of subsidiarity in its Preamble.[166]

Even for this feedback loop to operate effectively, at least three conditions need to coincide: the request must be submitted in relation to a truly novel issue where evolutive interpretation of the Convention is possible; second, the Court's opinion must be precise enough for the national court to be able to follow it if it wishes to do so; third, the

[164] Paprocka and Ziolkowski (n. 151) 290.

[165] Gerards (n. 151) 644.

[166] Preamble of Protocol 16.

national court must explicitly discuss the implications of the advisory opinion for the pending case in relation to which the opinion was requested and propose a solution. If the same question returns to the ECtHR as a contentious case, the feedback loop will be complete and the Court will be able to agree or disagree with how the national court applied its advisory opinion. I will now briefly consider whether the two advisory opinions that have been delivered so far are capable of creating an effective feedback loop.

The first request came from the French Court of Cassation and concerned the legal regulations of surrogacy.[167] It was argued that this very first advisory opinion did not live up to expectations as the Court's guidance was vague and open to interpretation.[168] Moreover, the Court did not elaborate on its approach to surrogacy and did not really create a rule of general application but limited its discussion to the facts of the case at hand.[169] Effectively, the ECtHR mostly stated what was already known from its previous case law, namely that 'the general and absolute impossibility of obtaining recognition of the relationship between a child born through a surrogacy arrangement entered into abroad and the intended mother is incompatible with the child's best interests, which require at a minimum that each situation be examined in the light of the particular circumstances of the case'.[170] This advisory opinion is paradoxical in some sense because, although the ECtHR is sometimes eager to formulate general rulings in individual cases which are arguably less suitable for this sort of pronouncement, when it was given a legitimate opportunity to come up with a generalised rule, it decided to exercise self-restraint and dramatically limited the scope of the advisory opinion.

The second request was submitted by the Armenian Constitutional Court. Here, the ECtHR was asked to consider whether 'criminal legislation by reference' as such violates the ECHR and whether the retrospective application of such legislation breaches Article 7 ECHR. This

[167] *Advisory opinion concerning the recognition in domestic law of a legal parent-child relationship between a child born through a gestational surrogacy arrangement abroad and the intended mother* (n. 161).

[168] See Laurens Lavrysen, 'The Mountain Gave Birth to a Mouse: The First Advisory Opinion under Protocol No. 16', *Strasbourg Observers* (24 April 2019) available at https://strasbourgobservers.com/2019/04/24/the-mountain-gave-birth-to-a-mouse-the-first-advisory-opinion-under-protocol-no-16/.

[169] See Margaria (n. 151) 421.

[170] *Advisory opinion concerning the recognition in domestic law of a legal parent-child relationship between a child born through a gestational surrogacy arrangement abroad and the intended mother* (n. 161) para. 42.

advisory opinion is different from the perspective of European public order. Unlike the first advisory opinion, this one is quite generic in scope, although the general rule, again, is fairly straightforward. So, this type of advisory opinion is unlikely to change European public order. Criminal legislation by reference to other laws and regulations is very widespread so the Court would be unlikely to declare the whole legislative technique to be in violation of the ECHR. Thus, the Court stated:

> Using the 'blanket reference' or 'legislation by reference' technique in criminalising acts or omissions is not in itself incompatible with the requirements of Article 7 of the Convention. The referencing provision and the referenced provision, read together, must enable the individual concerned to foresee, if need be with the help of appropriate legal advice, what conduct would make him or her criminally liable.[171]

At the same time, the Court left a wide area of discretion to the national court in how this interpretation is applied to the given case. So, it is quite likely that the same case will come back to the ECtHR in its contentious form.

This discussion shows that the advisory opinions send mixed messages vis-à-vis the ECtHR's ability to shape European public order. On the one hand, the Court is given a legitimate opportunity to come up with general Convention standards which are linked to a particular case but can provide guidance for deciding comparable cases in future. This idea clearly enhances the Court's ability to shape European public order. However, at the same time, Protocol 16 emphasises the subsidiarity principle in relation to advisory opinions and emphasises the non-binding character of these opinions. This crucially limits the Court's authority to change the fundamental standards of European public order. Moreover, the case law of the ECtHR under Protocol 16 shows that the Court itself is very cautious as to how advisory opinions are drafted; it tries not to overstep its perceived limits.

5.4 Conclusion

This chapter showed that the ECtHR is consistently increasing its institutional capacity to influence European public order. Two major recent

[171] *Advisory opinion concerning the use of the 'blanket reference' or 'legislation by reference' technique in the definition of an offence and the standards of comparison between the criminal law in force at the time of the commission of the offence and the amended criminal law* (n. 161) para. 92.

innovations give the Court the ability to formulate rules of general application, to engage in the process of implementation and to impact ongoing events. The pilot judgment procedure and increased deployment of interim measures, especially in inter-state cases, illustrate this point well. Although the Court is consistent in the direction of its innovations, they are not always successful and it is possible that the Court's attempts to produce general rules can backfire. The contracting parties might not be overly excited about the Court assuming the role of a body capable of creating and imposing rules of general application.

The contracting parties are much less consistent in their approach to the institutional reform of the Court from the perspective of its ability to shape European public order. On the one hand, they make sure that the Court is acting within some sort of reserve domain taking subsidiarity and the margin of appreciation into account. This perhaps means that the Court should not even attempt to engage in significant restructuring of European public order. Having said that, the contracting parties extended the advisory opinions and added new infringement proceedings to the ECtHR's toolkit. Both of these mechanisms seemingly increase the Court's impact on European public order. However, the details of their design might curtail the Court's role as a creator of European public order.

6 Views of the ECtHR Judges on Their Role in Shaping European Public Order

6.1 Introduction

The views of the ECtHR judges influence the interpretation of the European Convention on Human Rights (ECHR) and are also crucial for resolving the existential questions of the Court's functionality and development. The practice of the ECtHR is such that the individual views of the judges are rarely explicitly expressed in the judgments. The voices of individual judges can be identified from their dissenting and concurring opinions but, even then, their views are often expressed in relation to particular cases and rarely cover broad theoretical questions. This chapter predominantly listens to the voices of the ECtHR judges; it is based on a set of interviews with the sitting judges. The preliminary observation is that these voices are not singing in 'unison'; they are quite 'polyphonic', competing with and contradicting each other. However, this is not surprising and does not make discovering and analysing the views from the bench any less interesting or useful.

The main purpose of this chapter is to check whether the core arguments of this monograph resonate with the judges of the ECtHR. It will consider whether European public order can be defined and, if so, how it is perceived by the judges of the Court. This monograph argues that reference to European public order makes the case law of the Court vague, abstract and unclear. This suggestion would have been rebutted if the judges had a clear and common approach to European public order. However, this chapter shows that this is not the case and judges' understanding of European public order varies considerably. This monograph also looks at the meta-function of the ECtHR. It examines whether the Court can be a strategic constitutional actor entrusted with the task of shaping the components of European public order. This monograph argues that the ECtHR cannot strategically define and shape European public order and should concentrate on the task of gradual change of precise human rights standards, rather than engaging in abstract review of a vaguely defined order. Many judges seem to agree with the latter statement, but there are noticeable disagreements on the bench as to the extent to which the engagement of the Court in the strategic development of human rights standards is justified.

This chapter is divided into three sections. Section 6.2 explains the empirical research methodology used for this chapter. In the subsequent sections, I will present the most illustrative ideas that the judges expressed during the interviews. The interviews were analysed, and the quotations were systematised, but the interview data itself is the main asset and resource of this chapter. Sections 6.3 and 6.4 examine the views of the judges on the substantive and procedural aspects of European public order. The substantive aspect means the definition of European public order, its components and the Court's role in defining and establishing it. Section 6.3 summarises the judges' views on this complex and multi-layered issue. Section 6.4 assesses the procedural aspects of the role of European public order in the case law of the ECtHR. Here, I consider how European public order is used in the text of the ECtHR judgments and whether European public order influences the outcome of any particular case. Finally, the section examines the role of European public order during the deliberations.

6.2 Methodology

This chapter is based on twenty-four semi-structured interviews with the judges of the ECtHR.[1] The interviews took place in 2018 and 2019. To

[1] For a description of semi-structured interviews, see Tom Wengraf, *Qualitative Research Interviewing: Biographic Narrative and Semi-structured Methods* (Sage 2001) 5; Steinar Kvale, *Interviews: An Introduction to Qualitative Research Interviewing* (Sage 1996); Ian Dobinson and Francis Johns, 'Qualitative Legal Research' in Mike McConville and Wing Hong Chui (eds.), *Research Methods for Law* (Edinburgh University Press 2007). Wengraf points out:

> Semi-structured interviews are designed to have a number of interviewer questions prepared in advance but such prepared questions are designed to be sufficiently open that the subsequent questions of the interviewer cannot be planned in advance but must be improvised in a careful and theorized way. As regards such semi-structured interviews, they are ones where research and planning produce a session in which most of the informant's responses cannot be predicted in advance and where you as interviewer therefore have to improvise probably half and maybe 80 per cent or more of your responses to what they say in response to your initial prepared question or questions.

avoid selection bias, I contacted almost all of the sitting judges of the ECtHR, directly via their court emails. The emails consisted of an invitation to participate in the study as well as a short explanatory note. The majority of the judges replied, although not everyone could meet with me.[2] Some of them refused to be interviewed; the most common reasons were that they do not give research interviews as a matter of principle or that there were problems with scheduling these interviews. However, other judges gave more curious excuses. For instance, one of the judges explained: 'I do not know how I [could] be useful for you. It would be better if you talk[ed] to other judges who are more experienced in these questions.' This was not a newly elected judge but apparently s/he had had very little experience in dealing with European public order during her/his time in Strasbourg. Another judge informed me that s/he is 'not a specialist in public order'.

Twenty-four judges[3] cleared about an hour of their time to discuss the issue of European public order with me and I am immensely grateful for this. All interviews took place at the Human Rights building, which is the home of the ECtHR in Strasbourg. All of the interviews were digitally recorded, then transcribed. The transcripts were sent back to the judges to check and verify. Then the transcripts were anonymised and I carefully reviewed them; the most representative citations were used for this chapter and elsewhere in this monograph. The draft of this chapter was sent back to the sitting judges to check that their citations fairly represented their ideas. Their feedback was implemented in the final draft of this chapter.

The main aim of this chapter is to shed more light on how the judges interpret the Convention and how they perceive their own role. Interpretation is not an exact science; by studying the Court's reasoning, one can come closer to understanding how the Court sees its own role and function. This monograph has an ambition to go beyond what can be taken from the case law of the ECtHR or the official speeches of the judges. I wanted to know what individual judges think about the role of the Court within the delicate architecture of the national and international system of human rights protection and whether they think that the Court has an ambition to shape European public order.

(Tom Wengraf, *Qualitative Research Interviewing: Biographic Narrative and Semi-structured Methods* (Sage 2001) 5).

2 See Appendix.

3 The Registrar of the Court, Roderick Liddle, was among these twenty-four judges, but he is labelled as a judge for the purposes of this chapter.

Of course, one of the key challenges of interviews as a method of research is to ensure that the interviewees reveal their honest motivation.[4] Judges could both conscientiously and subconsciously hide their motivation for various reasons such as loyalty to the Court or to fellow judges, limited experience, or restrictions concerned with general limited public engagement of judges. A number of techniques were used to minimise this challenge. First, the interviewed judges were informed that all interview data would be anonymised, and all quotations attributed to a code such as 'Judge 1', 'Judge 2', etc. Second, most of the judges did not know the questions in advance of the interview. Spontaneous answers offer more truthful motivation than prepared ones. Finally, none of the questions concerned pending cases to avoid any potential conflict of interest. On occasion, judges referred to ECtHR judgments, but they were not prompted to do so.

So, what is the added value of the interviews? There are at least three reasons why interviews are helpful in unpacking the role of the ECtHR in shaping European public order. First, these interviews with the key decision-makers in Strasbourg provide original data on what European public order means and why it is deployed by the Court. Second, the interviews help one to understand how the jurisprudence of the Court will develop in the near future because the judges were discussing the case law trends and tendencies. Finally, the interviews explore the mission of the Court beyond the officially accepted position of the ECtHR.

Interviews were deliberately chosen for this project. I could have submitted questionnaires to the judges, as an alternative method of data collection. However, interviews are generally seen as a more satisfactory tool of research despite the fact that they are more time- and resource-consuming.[5] Interviews were chosen to ensure that the judges themselves responded to the questions rather than delegating the task to someone else. Moreover, it is impossible to get spontaneity of answers when someone is filling out a written questionnaire.

In the following sections I will analyse the most illustrative answers that the judges offered during the interviews and compare them with the main arguments of the book.

[4] This issue is discussed here: Lee Epstein and Gary King, 'The Rules of Inference' (2002) 69 *U Chi L Rev* 1, 93. See also Brian Flanagan and Sinéad Ahern, 'Judicial Decision-Making and Transnational Law: A Survey of Common Law Supreme Court Judges' (2011) 60 *Int'l & Comp LQ* 1, 7; Jeffrey Segal and Harold Spaeth, 'The Authors Respond' (1994) *Law and Courts* 3, 16.

[5] See Kenneth D. Bailey, *Methods of Social Research* (Free Press 1994) 174.

6.3 The Substantive Aspects of European Public Order

This section looks into the substance and the content of European public order as they are seen by the judges of the ECtHR. It also touches upon a more fundamental but related question of what the meta-function of the Court is and whether the Court can or should shape European public order in its judgments.

6.3.1 *The Definition of European Public Order*

This monograph argues that it is almost impossible to define European public order. It can mean mutually exclusive phenomena in different contexts. Moreover, its role in the case law of the ECtHR is not always clear; it is too vague and flexible. In this respect, the analysis of the interviews demonstrates the following preliminary conclusions. First, there are multiple different views of what the Court means when it talks about European public order and there is no clarity as to what it is used for. Second, the majority of judges agreed that it is difficult to define European public order in abstract. Third, there was a disagreement as to whether this challenge of an absence of a definition is fatal for the utility of this concept. I will try to illustrate these three points in the following section.

As I argued in Chapter 4, public order is used in law in various different senses. The judges also emphasised different aspects of public order in their answers. Some of them pointed out that European public order can mean the most fundamental rights. For example, Judge 13 explained:

> It [European public order] has been used for many years by the Court on different occasions and in different contexts to mean either the basic fundamental values of the system or the democratic principles or different components of the rule of law or what is referred to in the Preamble to the Convention, namely, common ideas, values, ideologies. So, by looking into the cases in which the Court has used the concept, you can build up a theory using the collective wisdom of the Court. My inclination would be to say that this notion reflects common values, common history and common ideology. It reflects basic democratic principles, it reflects values and rules pertaining to the rule of law, separation of powers, underogable rights, for instance Article 3 which reflects the most basic value. It is European public order in that sense.[6]

Although it is unlikely that by looking at the case law of the ECtHR one can build a clear theory of what European public order really means, many judges agreed with Judge 13 and made a reference to the fundamental

6 Interview with Judge 13.

rights. Judge 12, for instance, emphasised the nature of the Convention as a guardian of the core rights: 'There is a public guarantee of a list of rights, whose enforcement is not limited in the bilateral relationships between the Contracting States; it is considered as a common interest, a collective interest of all the states.'[7] Although this definition is plausible on this level of abstraction, it is difficult to use it as such a definition requires at least some mechanism for identifying what these core rights are. Some judges explicitly acknowledged that challenge. Judge 7 pointed out: 'From a legal point of view, for me European public order does not mean that much. In the domestic legal order, public order has a meaning and consequences. The Convention, by contrast, does not make a distinction between what belongs to public order and what does not belong to public order.'[8] Judge 12 also argued that European public order is a core of human rights and contrasted this core with the margin of appreciation. S/he pointed out:

> It is impossible to define the notion exactly because it depends on the functioning of the famous doctrine of the margin of appreciation. The margin of appreciation doctrine tolerates that there is not only one way to protect human rights in Europe. There are differences. Differences are normally allowed but there is a core part – a hard core – in which the differences are not possible and this is European public order. It is the hard core which means that the way in which the Convention applies cannot vary among member states.[9]

This statement suggests that everything that does not fall under the margin of appreciation is European public order. This means that the scope of European public order is quite broad. From this definition, it seems that the scope of almost all rights consists of two areas: the margin of appreciation and European public order. This effectively means that every violation of the Convention is by the same logic a violation of European public order.

In contrast, some judges saw European public order as not completely synonymous to the rights protected by the Convention, although they were not entirely sure how to draw the line between European public

[7] Interview with Judge 12. Judge 7 made a similar point:

> For me the European public order started as an idea of common public order, but meaning that the Convention is a treaty that has to be respected irrespectively of reciprocity. It imposes obligations on the states that by ratification of the Convention they need to abide by. And now I think that when we speak of European public order, and you see it in a few more recent cases, it refers to a set of fundamental values. It is of course difficult to identify European values, but together they are the basis of European public order.

[8] Interview with Judge 7.

[9] Interview with Judge 12.

order and rights that would fall outside of its scope. One of the judges jokingly pointed out that if I succeed in defining European public order, I deserve a Nobel prize.[10] Unfortunately, I will not get a Nobel prize just yet because I argue in this monograph that European public order is hardly possible to define.

The key challenge of defining European public order was highlighted by a few judges. Judge 13 mentioned that European public order is extremely flexible:

> European public order is everything and nothing. It is everything because you can include democratic principles, you can include rule of law, different aspects of rule of law which is also a very rich concept, you can include non-derogable rights. And at the same time, it is a symbol. So, it can be a very rich concept, if you want to make it a rich concept. This is an empty shell if someone does not want to give this notion its real content and its concrete content.[11]

It was also argued that European public order 'is not a well-defined concept'.[12] Judge 5 called it an 'essentially contested concept'.[13] Judge 16 was even more critical of the possibility of identifying European public order:

> When it comes to European public order, in my view, it is a beautiful linguistic construction which is empty and we can put inside whatever we want. In my view, European public order is a set of values, the values that, according to our perceptions, create the human rights world, a human rights–friendly world. It is a regional set of values and nothing more; it is an empty construction, a lip service.[14]

Judge 17 emphasised that it would not be possible to agree on what a definition of European public order should include:

> It is difficult. I would find it very hard to define that concept even if I should be the only judge. You can imagine seventeen judges in the Grand Chamber. It would be very difficult to agree and, to a certain extent, it would not be compatible with the idea of that concept coming within the case law. Because it is and it should be a concept that in and of itself is dynamic and open-ended.[15]

Some of the judges tried to identify European public order by listing the components that can be included in its definition. Section 6.3.2 will look into the constituent parts of European public order. It is enough

[10] Interview with Judge 6.
[11] Interview with Judge 13.
[12] Interview with Judge 9.
[13] Interview with Judge 5.
[14] Interview with Judge 16.
[15] Interview with Judge 17.

just to give a couple of examples here. Judge 1 pointed out that 'European public order is those basic elements that turn Europe into a society which one can recognise nowadays as a society subscribing to the rule of law, fundamental human rights.'[16] Judge 18 included the vague notion of 'cultural and ideological environment which is based on the superiority of human rights and dignity' in the content of European public order.[17] Judge 20 pointed out:

> The Court has never defined the concept of European public order. I understand it as a set of values, principles and rules perceived to be fundamental for today's European society. Democracy and rule of law are fundamental components of the European public order – the Court has stressed this repeatedly. Principles and rules constituting the European public order have clear priority over domestic laws and practices.[18]

Despite the fact that it is very difficult to even approximately define the scope of European public order, some judges were in favour of the Court's continued utilisation of this concept. For example, Judge 10 pointed out that European public order 'is really the core of the values that this Court stands for. And that is why it is relatively rare in the case law but when it is used, it is indeed used in very important cases'.[19] S/he added: 'This concept of public order is very similar to the eternal clause of the constitutional law. These are the basic non-negotiable values of the Convention law that really are beyond and above all political majorities; they cannot be put at risk even by democratically elected majorities.'[20] Other judges placed much less importance on European public order, calling it just a 'nice phrase'.[21]

Irrespective of the views of the judges as to the role of European public order in the case law of the Court, one of the key challenges remains: it is unclear what is included in the non-negotiable values expressed through the medium of European public order. The following section examines what the judges consider to be the core components of European public order.

6.3.2 *The Components of European Public Order*

This section shows that it is unclear what European public order consists of. Some judges were of the opinion that it is the role of the ECtHR

[16] Interview with Judge 1.
[17] Interview with Judge 18.
[18] Interview with Judge 20.
[19] Interview with Judge 10.
[20] Ibid.
[21] Interview with Judge 4.

to identify the components of European public order. For instance, Judge 1 pointed out that 'the Convention states set up a Court precisely to ensure the proper enforcement of Article 1 of the Convention and within the context of that function – why not? – to identify the constituent elements of what goes into European public order'.[22] It seems that in more than sixty years of its existence, the Court did not add much clarity to this area. While it might be a task of the Court to elaborate on the components of European public order, it seems that there is no unanimity in terms of what exactly these components should or might be. Most judges agreed that some core values that can only be defined at a high level of abstraction can be included in European public order. However, it seems that the Court itself does not shape these values; it takes them either from the Convention itself or from the law and practice of the contracting parties.

The majority of the judges were able to identify the most general and abstract components of European public order which also require narrowing down and defining. Among the most commonly mentioned components were core European values, the rule of law and democracy. Judge 1, for example, mentioned that European public order includes 'fundamental human rights, respect for human dignity, rule of law and absence of arbitrariness'.[23] All of them require a good deal of specification to be useful in human rights adjudication. In a similar vein, Judge 14 stated:

> The rule of law, the principles of constitutional democracy which are in the Preamble to the Convention, they are the themes and principles with normative force which run through the fabric of the Convention system. Whether you then decide that these principles are part of European public order is probably okay; it is probably one way of semantically conceptualising these principles.[24]

Judge 9 opined:

> What is part of European public order? Basically, the Convention values but, of course, some are more important than others. Some of them are not necessarily included when you allow for a margin. But there are core elements. Instinctively, I would say that we use European public order when we speak about our core values which are not only linked to human rights but when human rights have a spill-over effect on democracy and rule of law.[25]

[22] Interview with Judge 1.
[23] Interview with Judge 1.
[24] Interview with Judge 14.
[25] Interview with Judge 9.

Judge 11 went even further and argued that 'European public order is the core of the Constitution of Europe. These are the values and principles which are of so high-ranking status in the legal order of Europe that they prevail over everything.'[26] Having said that, the core challenge here still remains the same – how can one identify what is within this core and translate the abstract core values into legal rules and regulations? Taking the level of abstractness and the vagueness of the key components into consideration, one can assume that the Court arbitrarily defines the core. Judge 12 disagreed with this assumption. S/he pointed out that 'the Court does not invent it [European public order]. The Court finds it in the Convention'.[27]

Two judges offered insights into how these core and fundamental values can be identified. For both of them, the European consensus argument[28] is the way to identify those core values. For instance, Judge 16 pointed out:

> European consensus helps us to understand our current European values because values are changing. So, today's values are like this and they create European public order, as we perceive it as judges. We look around and we see what values are, and therefore we understand what European public order is. But we do not teach and we do not promote certain values and we do not explain.[29]

It is curious that Judge 16 felt that the Court does not promote certain values. It seems that if the Court confirms that a particular value is part of European public order, it perhaps aims to promote the said value. Judge 6 stated:

> If we want to know whether what we understand under European public order has some roots in the member states, we turn to these research activities: on our own and from this superior courts network.[30] I think that this gives us more legitimacy. We can say that we did research and this is something of concern, of importance also for the member states. Then we can conclude that it can be a cornerstone of European public order.[31]

[26] Interview with Judge 11.
[27] Interview with Judge 12.
[28] For a more detailed account, see Kanstantsin Dzehtsiarou, *European Consensus and the Legitimacy of the European Court of Human Rights* (Cambridge University Press 2015).
[29] Interview with Judge 16.
[30] In order to enrich dialogue and implementation of the Convention, the Court launched the Superior Courts Network in 2015. It facilitates the exchange of information between the highest national courts and the ECtHR. More information available at www.echr.coe.int/Pages/home.aspx?p=court/dialoguecourts/network&c=.
[31] Interview with Judge 6.

This short section showed that it is difficult to identify what is included in European public order. These quotes support three partially contradicting statements: (1) European public order is a set of values that are abstract and fundamental and require some specialisation; (2) the Court does not discover it but takes it from the Convention, although, in this case, it is unclear what the rationale is for mentioning European public order if it is tantamount to the Convention rights; and (3) some judges think that these values are discoverable through analysis of the laws and practices of the contracting parties to the Convention. However, if one assumes that a particular value is fundamental and crucial, there should be no disagreement as to its at least abstract definition. That said, the disagreements are common. Section 6.3.3 looks into what can happen if European and national public orders collide.

6.3.3 *European Public Order v. National Public Order*

I argued in the previous chapters that the Court should not protect European public order against interference from the contracting parties;[32] European public order and national public orders develop simultaneously through a complex multi-directional network of incremental changes. This section will consider whether the judges see the interaction between European public order and national public orders differently. Judge 3 described this process of interaction between national systems of human rights protection and the Strasbourg system as follows:

> Very often the Court would look into the domestic systems of different countries and will copy from those countries: legal constructions, the way issues have been defined and handled. And then because of its position as a pan-European court it would make the standard for everyone. It is both copying and standard setting. The Court often is seen in a rather hierarchal perspective. It is not – it is one player among others in the field. The Court has more influence, however, as it has jurisdiction with respect to many countries. More than any other court in Europe. But this is also a restraint. Every time it does set a new standard, it has to consider it from the perspective of all other countries that would be affected.[33]

The question about the clash between European and national public orders brought a variety of opinions. These opinions ranged from existential denial that such clashes can happen to diverging opinions as to what should happen if and when such clashes actually take place.

[32] See Chapters 3 and 4.
[33] Interview with Judge 3.

Judge 9 opined that if there is a clash between European public order and the public order of a particular state then one of two things is possible: either the state does not really belong to the group of states sharing common values or the notion of European public order is so stretched that it does not reflect the reality:

> If you have taken in an element that is not generally accepted – let's say openness for refugees is considered to form part of European public order whereas some countries say 'no, this is definitely against our national public order', then either the European public order idea has been stretched too far and does not reflect European reality or the state with such a national order should no longer be allowed to form part of the Convention system.[34]

These two options are the extreme examples; in this case, either the Court needs to significantly reshape its case law or the contracting party needs to be expelled. There is a vast area between these two extremes where the fine-tuning of the standards happens.

Judge 18 stated that a clash between European public order and national public order cannot happen. S/he pointed out:

> There is no legal basis behind the argument that there is a contradiction between the Convention and the domestic legal system. Because there is such a procedure in the countries before joining the European Convention, they are verifying whether their Constitutions (written and codified, written but not codified, mixed ones) align with the European Convention on Human Rights. They are organising a special group consisting of local experts and international experts. If it is necessary, they make amendments in the Constitution. Only after that can they join the European Convention on Human Rights. From this point of view, it is difficult to understand in which way there is a contradiction between the European Convention on Human Rights and these Constitutions. By the way, all forty-seven states did it voluntarily.[35]

This statement was not shared by the majority of judges, but this is not due to the fact that Judge 18 was wrong in his/her statement; rather, it is because there is a wide array of meanings of European public order and European public order changes over time. Judge 18 used a very abstract view that the ECHR itself is synonymous to European public order and on that level of abstraction these contradictions are rarely possible. Surely, none of the constitutions of any of the member states of the Council of Europe allows torture or fails to secure the right to property. In these general terms, the contradictions between European public

[34] Interview with Judge 9.
[35] Interview with Judge 18.

order and national public orders are unlikely. However, the Court has to narrow down the broad provisions of the Convention to concrete cases. Then, when one moves to a more precise level of definition, the contradictions between the ECHR and national laws and practice are much more common. Judge 10 pointed that out by stating:

It is often very difficult to understand each other. We are dealing with cases in which we do not understand the language, the traditions, the law. And certain clashes or at least divisions between different traditions are evident: north/east, Nordic/southern, Caucasian, former Soviet states. This is surprisingly rich, to put it in a positive sense, or incredibly divergent, speaking less positively.[36]

Here, the question of what order should have priority remains: should the Court always ensure that European public order prevails? Many judges said that they look carefully into the development at the national level, in fact confirming the argument developed in Chapter 4 that the Court reflects the incremental development of public orders of the contracting parties rather than prioritising European public order over national orders.

Judge 14 pointed out that it is first and foremost for the national states to develop human rights standards. S/he said:

Yesterday we had judges of the Supreme Court [of one of the member states of the Council of Europe] here and one of them asked what role is there for the national judge in developing the Convention rights and Convention principles when there is no clear Strasbourg case law? For me the answer is clear – you should definitely do it. You should conceptualise your own public order concept domestically infusing the Convention case law. But it is the grassroots level where real public order becomes effectuated.[37]

Some judges opined that there is some clear core of the Convention that cannot be interfered with, but, beyond this core, the Court needs to take into account the developments within the contracting parties. Judge 17 made the following argument:

What I try to achieve as a judge through every particular case is to see to it as far as possible that we open up for the domestic approach but on the same footing [so] that there should [be] no doubt that when it comes to the core values, when it comes to what is actually the Convention rights, there could be no discussion as to the domestic practices and the member states need to comply with the Court's case law. This is a dynamic process; it has been going on from the very start.[38]

[36] Interview with Judge 10.
[37] Interview with Judge 14.
[38] Interview with Judge 17.

S/he continued:

> I think that the main approach in this Court should be to accommodate, to find what could be labelled as the common European ground. Part of that would be what I have already explained – the development within the domestic systems – and part of it would be also the international development and particularly on the European level.[39]

Judge 17 also emphasised that the Court needs to be pragmatic and consider natural developments in the contracting parties to the Convention:

> My personal perception is that it is necessary to be pragmatic. Although you might have a strong wish personally to push the development in a certain direction – and most of us at the Court would have a strong interest in a specific development – you need to be careful and pragmatic in order to achieve that in the longer run. If you act too rapidly, you would run the risk of destroying the project as such. That is the fine balance of the Court. Being a Court, it is expected that we do not act too rapidly or too far, taking too big steps at a time. This Court is supposed to take small steps.[40]

Although many judges focused on national developments as the key driving force behind the Court's case law, some were of the opinion that European public order should normally prevail. Judge 12 pointed out that 'national public order can never be an absolute value in the framework of the Convention, in any event under the control of the Court'.[41] Judge 23 argued that 'some of my colleagues referred to this notion of European public order or some called it multi-tier constitutionalism – to try to reinforce and restate the primacy of the Convention and the duty of the states to comply with Article 1 of the Convention'.[42] Judge 7 maintained that European public order and national orders collide only when important and fundamental questions are discussed in the judgment and then European public order should prevail. S/he observed:

> There are a lot of violations that the ECtHR finds, which means that things go wrong. Some of them are incidents and there we do not need to speak about values. If there are structural violations based on deeply rooted sentiments in the country, then the issue of European public order becomes important. One case that comes to my mind is *Bayev and Others* v. *Russia*.[43] In this case I see a clash

[39] Ibid.

[40] Ibid.

[41] Interview with Judge 12.

[42] Interview with Judge 23.

[43] *Bayev and Others* v. *Russia*, nos. 67667/09 and two others, 20 June 2017. In this case the ECtHR found a violation of the Convention in relation to Russia's ban on 'homosexual propaganda'.

between national values and European public order. A given value is important in Russia: many Russians believe in that value, but the Court holds that it is against European public order.[44]

It seems that discussion of the primacy of the Convention vis-à-vis national law is problematic: this relation is much more complex than stating that one is more important than the other. Their dynamic is not linear but multi-layered and co-dependent. Although the states are obliged to comply with the judgments of the ECtHR, they can send clear signals of dissatisfaction through political rhetoric and national judicial reasoning. If this dissatisfaction is well-founded, the Court has to take that into account. Of course, this is not a legal duty but a duty that flows from the institutional position of the ECtHR. This discussion is closely connected to how the Court's function is seen by the judges. If the meta-function of the Court is to single-handedly build European public order then it does not need any feedback or dialogue and should impose the standards that it sees fit. However, if the meta-function of the Court is less clear then the Court needs to consider a complex network of relationships with the contracting parties when framing human rights standards.

6.3.4 *The Meta-function of the European Court of Human Rights*

One can suggest that the Court's meta-function is to build European public order and to become a constitutional court of Europe; some judges might see it as a grand aim of the Court. In the words of Judge 12, 'in *Loizidou*[45] the Court did not say that but implicitly the Court meant by that statement[46] that it has the ambition to be the constitutional court of Europe. Of course, this is something that the Court will never say in a judgment.'[47] This section will look into whether the judges think that it is the role of the Court to build European public order. At the outset, I have to observe that the judges expressed a wide range of ideas about the nature of the meta-function of the ECtHR and they did not show any commonly accepted view on this issue.

In Chapter 4, I argued that it is not particularly helpful to discuss the constitutional nature of the ECtHR because the term 'constitution'

[44] Interview with Judge 7. It needs to be noted that Judge 7 was not the judge elected in respect of Russia sitting on that case.

[45] *Loizidou* v. *Turkey* (preliminary objections), 23 March 1995, Series A no. 310.

[46] In *Loizidou* the Court stated that 'the Convention ... [is] a constitutional instrument of European public order (ordre public)'. Ibid., para. 75.

[47] Interview with Judge 12.

brings unnecessary connotations, misunderstandings and complications. A few judges also opined that the ECtHR can be called a constitutional court, but it very much depends on what that term means. Judge 3 pointed out:

> A constitutional court obviously has powers in other fields such as the interplay between the different institutions, like executive and legislature. We do not have such powers. But a constitutional court has also another component in its work, namely, the protection of basic rights. And from that perspective it is identical, so you can say that we are a constitutional court in that limited sense.[48]

The same idea was expressed by Judge 9, who pointed out that 'a constitutional court is a court that does not only adjudicate human rights but also questions of constitutional order, like formation of government, who has to take some political decisions . . .'.[49] Since the ECtHR does not normally engage with these questions, it cannot be called constitutional. Judge 12 stated:

> What does 'constitutional court' mean? In vague terms, not strictly legal terms, we can refer to this court as a constitutional court in the sense that, like most national constitutional courts, this Court is called upon to put different interests in balance, so in this sense our work is similar to the work of a constitutional court. Of course, there is also another meaning – if there are core values and [a core] essence of the rights, which is European public order, then this Court defends this core and in doing so it acts as a constitutional court. It is a form of embryonic constitution of forty-seven participating states and we have an international guardian of this embryonic constitution.[50]

Judge 14 emphasised the negative connotations that come with the term 'constitutional court'. In other words, the term 'constitutional' creates an impression that the ECtHR can and should do more than it actually does. It looks like the ECtHR interferes with the very core of the national social structure. S/he pointed out:

> I would say that I do not like the word constitutional; I do not like using the word constitutional court for an international court. I know that there are strands of scholarship, especially political science scholarship, using constitutionalism in the international sphere. I think it is not useful – because it creates a reaction which is not helpful. The member states do not like the Court being viewed as a constitutional court. But if the question is framed differently – does the Court

[48] Interview with Judge 3.
[49] Interview with Judge 9.
[50] Interview with Judge 12.

in fact shape European public order within the concept that we are talking about now? My answer is definitely yes. I think that it is simply something that flows from the system itself.[51]

A connected question is whether the ECHR can then be called a constitution of Europe. This question has divided the judges. Many of them argued that the ECHR is not a constitution. For instance, Judge 5 stated that 'a constitution does not have gaps; the Convention has a lot of gaps. In borderline cases we always examine if some measures fall under the Convention or not'.[52] To the contrary, when I asked Judge 11 whether s/he thinks that the ECHR is a constitution, s/he answered:

Of course. It is not me, it is *Baka*,[53] it is *Sejdić and Finci*,[54] it is all of these cases where we say that this Convention is the criterion to check whether constitutional provisions of the member states are compatible with European Convention standards. We take the Convention as something beyond and above the national constitutions.[55]

When it comes to the normative question of whether the Court should act as a constitutional court loosely defined, the views of the judges were again polarised. Judge 24 explained this polarisation and the dynamic of the Court's internal attitudes, ranging from more to less 'activist' approaches to the function of the Court. S/he pointed out:

You have the judges in the Court who consider and see the Court as a constitutional instrument. Then you have other judges who believe that the Court should not be so. I think at this moment you would even have the majority of the judges believing that it should not be understood in this way and should not act as such. It depends to whom of the judges you are talking. I think it is very much related to subsidiarity. The notion of subsidiarity is considered as a key element of the functioning of the Court. You can feel that. You can see it in earlier judgments, but I think [that] if you look at the Court's judgments, it is already visible now, even looking at that from the outside.[56]

One can place all judges into four overlapping groups according to their views: those who are in favour of the ECtHR being viewed as

[51] Interview with Judge 14.

[52] Interview with Judge 5.

[53] *Baka* v. *Hungary* [GC], no. 20261/12, 23 June 2016.

[54] *Sejdić and Finci* v. *Bosnia and Herzegovina* [GC], nos. 27996/06 and 34836/06, ECHR 2009.

[55] Interview with Judge 11.

[56] Interview with Judge 24. Judge 2 also identified the same tendency, pointing out: 'Before 2017 the Court was much more activist. Now it is much more conservative. We find fewer and fewer violations of the Convention. Since 2017 barely any violations.' Interview with Judge 2.

a constitutional court, those who are against it and two groups which either do not see the value in labelling the ECtHR as a constitutional court at all or feel that the Court is forced to act as a constitutional court on occasion. I will illustrate these four groups in turn.

First, some judges were very much against considering the ECtHR as a constitutional court for a multiplicity of reasons. One such reason is that the Court is not designed to initiate societal changes. Judge 17 pointed out:

> I do not think it is the task of a court to be the driving force; we are not supposed to, that is my view, initiate big societal changes. This is a matter for the political institutions; this is a matter for the society as such. We are a court, a very particular court. The judges are elected based on our background, our competence; it is not particularly aimed to really develop the society by taking initiatives to changes. The Court should not be a driving force in order to develop the European society in a particular direction which is not already, so to say, underway.[57]

Judge 17 also expressed another reason why the ECtHR cannot be considered a constitutional court. For her/him, the differences among the forty-seven member states of the Council of Europe are still too significant to have a federal-type constitutional court. In her/his words:

> I think at some point there was a dream that the Court should be such a constitutional court. I do not perceive it as such now. I feel the differences between the member states are still too big. There is too much going on. For now, we do not have the legitimacy to act as such. If we perceived ourselves as that, it would pose a big danger to the institution as such.[58]

For Judge 1, the Court is not a constitutional court of Europe because it is not explicitly provided in the Convention. S/he suggested:

> The Court is not really a constitutional instrument because after all there is nothing in the Convention that says that it is a constitutional instrument. And we take great pains and we go to great lengths to impress in our judgments that the Convention and the Court have a subsidiary role. Indeed, the primary responsibility for enforcing the Convention rests squarely on the states.[59]

Judge 3 argued that the ECtHR should not be a constitutional court because this will naturally mean taking more power than it can hold. Judge 3 opined that the Court should

[57] Interview with Judge 17.
[58] Ibid.
[59] Interview with Judge 1.

take it case by case, and not try to legislate from the bench. This is a natural limitation of the power of courts. Being abusive and taking too much power will necessarily backfire and it does not matter in which direction. Logically, it could support different causes, but you are undermining the whole institution and that is why courts do act on individual cases and there should be a clear and consistent logic in every case.[60]

Irrespective of the reasons that this group of judges expressed, their overarching idea was that the ECtHR should not revolutionise human rights standards; it does not have the institutional and normative legitimacy to do so. They did not see the meta-function of the Court as significantly reshaping European public order but, rather, as protecting the core values and making incremental changes in the human rights standards.

Judges from the second group argued that the Court is forced to act as a constitutional court but in fact is an inevitable by-product of its core activities. For instance, Judge 16 made the following statement:

You know that after almost each and every judgment we have these general measures, meaning that the state should change something. Whenever the state changes either legislation or administrative practice, the whole construction changes. Of course, the values are changeable as well. Even though it is not our primary goal, and often we do not realise that exactly, . . . we are changing values step by step by pushing states to change relevant legislation and practice whenever we find violations. Again, for me it is not a clear distinction between the Court as a constitutional court and purely an adjudicator of minor things. Sometimes, rather quite often, they really clash.[61]

Judge 2 argued that the Court 'is forced to go into analysis of national provisions if these provisions concern . . . fundamental rights'.[62] Similarly, Judge 4 pointed out that 'the Court is very well aware that we should not play the role of a constitutional court, and we do that in very exceptional cases in which we need to set a minimal standard. But apart from that, the Court does not play a role similar to a national constitutional court.'[63] Judge 4 also explained why the ECtHR should not act as a constitutional court. Her/his main reason is that the Court can only supervise human rights while national constitutions cover much more ground. Therefore, for Judge 4, 'it might be a little dangerous to put this Court in the role of a constitutional court when you have only a limited picture'.[64]

[60] Interview with Judge 3.
[61] Interview with Judge 16.
[62] Interview with Judge 2.
[63] Interview with Judge 4.
[64] Ibid.

The judges placed in this group argued for a court which does not have a constitutional role and acts as a constitutional court temporarily only when the circumstances force it to do so. For these judges, the Court's meta-function is a by-product of the adjudicatory role of the Court.

Third, some judges were in favour of the Court taking the role of a constitutional court, although they understood this role differently and deployed different reasons to justify it. For Judge 20, a constitutional court means a court that promotes certain values and principles and in this sense the ECtHR is certainly a constitutional court. In her/his own words, 'if it is to serve as a constitutional tribunal/Court, then it is the role of the Court to promote European values and principles'.[65] Judge 24 pointed out:

> I think I belong to the minority. I think that the Court to a certain extent should act as a constitutional court. I would be somebody who would say that the living instrument is alive. Of course, that does not mean that the Court can go wherever it would like to go. There are certain limits. But the function of the Court is to interpret the Convention and to overview whether this Convention is applied at the domestic level in the right way. These are the two main functions of the Court. To what extent does it give the foundation for the constitutional and public order? Of course, it does. If you go to each state that has a constitution, you can see that the great part of the constitution is human rights. So, if we are the institution which is on the top to say what human rights and how they should be interpreted, then in these terms 'yes'. We are a constitutional institution to that extent and we are somebody who is determining what European public order is. We are shaping that.[66]

Judge 5 argued that the Court can be constitutional only if it is generally accepted as a constitutional court. S/he stated:

> If the label that the European Convention is a constitutional instrument of European public order is accepted by the general public, by researchers, by lawyers and so on, this definitely gives more authority and more legitimacy to the Convention. Otherwise, the Convention is just one of the treaties. And the purpose was to say that it is not just a treaty, it is *the* treaty. In a certain sense, it is *sui generis*. This Court is *sui generis*. It is not *sui generis* on the global scale, but it is very exceptional.[67]

Judge 8 understood the Court's constitutional role in a more technical procedural sense. For her/him, the Court needs to concentrate its sparse

[65] Interview with Judge 20.
[66] Interview with Judge 24.
[67] Interview with Judge 5.

resources on the most important cases, those cases that can influence the laws of many countries. Judge 8 pointed out:

> The thinking behind this proper constitutional role is that it should be concentrating on cases that really have an impact. It has always been my view and it is not so much about pick and choose,[68] but I want to see the Court being effective in respect of the cases which really drive forward human rights jurisprudence when it is necessary, which really ensures that the Convention system is effective and has an impact.[69]

Finally, some judges questioned the importance of labelling the Court's work as constitutional. In other words, it is less important how you label a court than what the court is in fact doing. For instance, Judge 7 pointed out: 'Whether it is "constitutional" or not: what is in the name? In many judgments the Court is not using the word constitutional. The Convention is an instrument of public order. That is the main message. Whether you call it a constitutional instrument or not is not so important.'[70]

What is fairly clear from this analysis is that the judges do not have a uniform view on two key issues discussed in this section. First, they define the meaning of the constitutional role of the Court differently. Its ambiguity makes a clear answer to the question of whether the ECtHR is a constitutional court hardly possible. The second question, which the judges could not agree upon, is whether the Court should aspire to be a constitutional court. If the judges of the Court do not have a clearly accepted strategic vision on what the meta-function of the Court is, it is difficult to at least start moving towards this abstract meta-function, as Chapter 4 of this monograph argued. In the words of Judge 3: 'I am not sure that the Court has a strategy to build upon this European public order. I think that it is a nice phrase.'[71]

6.4 Technical Aspects of European Public Order

While Section 6.3 examined the views of the judges of the ECtHR on the substance of European public order, this section is different as it considers whether the Court has a holistic approach to European public

[68] See Helen Keller, Andreas Fischer and Daniela Kühne, 'Debating the Future of the European Court of Human Rights after the Interlaken Conference: Two Innovative Proposals' (2010) 21 *EJIL* 1025, 1037.
[69] Interview with Judge 8.
[70] Interview with Judge 7.
[71] Interview with Judge 4.

order from a more technical point of view. By 'technical aspect' I mean whether the judges discuss the issues related to European public order explicitly in their judgments, how references to European public order impact the outcomes of particular cases and whether the judges have observed the phenomenon of the 'Brownian motion' of legal terms in the case law of the ECtHR. The preliminary conclusion is that many judges see European public order as a rhetorical tool that has little impact on the outcome of a particular judgment. It appears in the text of a judgment according to the preferences of the drafting lawyer and then the notion of European public order 'travels' through the case law by means of cross-referencing.

6.4.1 *The Role of European Public Order in the Case Law of the ECtHR*

The analysis of the interview data revealed a significant variety of views on the issue of what the role of European public order is in the judgments of the Court. It might seem surprising because, at the outset, European public order was often presented as a *fundamental* concept; thus, the way that such a fundamental concept is operationalised should be clear from within the Court. In fact, it is not; different judges see the utility of European public order quite differently.

Few judges insisted that the role of European public order is in the sense of 'public security' mentioned in the second paragraphs of Articles 9 to 11. Chapter 3 of this monograph discussed this meaning of public order too and concluded that this is not what the Court means when it talks about European public order. That said, Judge 2, for example, pointed out that 'the main aim of this concept is related to limiting human rights'.[72]

Other judges viewed the role of European public order as being similar to the one that public order plays in private international law with some *sui generis* differences relevant to international justice.[73] Judge 7 pointed out:

> What is against public order is illegal, at the domestic level. This means that a clause is null and void. We do not do that in the same way in Europe because we have the Convention and everything turns around the Convention. The only text that we apply is the Convention, but public order may come in to reinforce an argument.[74]

[72] Interview with Judge 2.
[73] See Chapter 3 for more details on this issue.
[74] Interview with Judge 7.

A few judges saw the role of European public order as a rhetorical anchor that emphasises the importance of a particular pronouncement. Judge 14, for example, suggested:

> The Court is giving messages and guidance to the member states on the framework in which the protection of human rights is taking place and also the limitations to possible exceptions to those rights. I would simply say that when the Court is engaged in this role, and in some very seminal cases, it uses this phrase to give an added impetus to the importance of its pronouncements. I would not go further than this. I am not one of those that is willing to give this language more meaning. From a purely legal point of view one can ask – is there some normative force, is there some normative content in this phrase? I am not sure about this. I think that this is to some extent a rhetorical device. It is a device that used to give added weight and symbolism to the Court's role, but I am not sure that I can identify the normative elements, the content.[75]

It is not entirely clear what is the purpose of such a rhetorical device. One can wonder who is the addressee of it and what this addressee is expected to do after getting the message emphasised by a reference to European public order. Judge 24 gave an example of the instrumentalising of European public order. S/he argued:

> All these are cases[76] where you have democracy and rule of law, the very basics, so you come and say European public order. This comes close to saying it is against the core human rights. So, we would not accept friendly settlement, for example. It has to be something really important because the general rule is to accept friendly settlements so when you introduce the possibility to get rid of the cases that are not of high importance, then if you emphasise and the party is asking that, then you really have to emphasise and demonstrate that this is of such importance that you cannot accept what they are asking. It is really the weapon of the European Court of Human Rights and it is meant for certain cases that have that importance. You are not trying to reaffirm that we are a constitutional instrument.[77]

Some judges also questioned the importance of this concept. Judge 23 pointed out that 'I do not see it as one of the primary major doctrines of the Court. I do not know whether this concept itself will have a much larger life than one can currently surmise.'[78]

Almost every judge saw the key aspect of the role of the European public order in the text of the judgments differently. This is problematic

[75] Interview with Judge 14.
[76] Cases where European public order was used.
[77] Interview with Judge 24.
[78] Interview with Judge 23.

from the perspective of process legitimacy.[79] The Court's judgments need to be clear to instigate compliance. When a judgment is ambiguous or open to interpretation and full of rhetorical devices of unclear meaning, its utility and effectiveness might diminish.[80] Particularly, the Court should not allow the Brownian motion of unclear concepts, as Section 6.4.2 demonstrates.

6.4.2 *The 'Brownian Motion' of Legal Terms*

In Chapter 2, I argued that some terms deployed by the ECtHR 'travel' through its case law in a trajectory that is something akin to 'Brownian motion'. This term is used in physics and chemistry to describe 'the erratic random movement of microscopic particles'.[81] I use this term metaphorically to show that some concepts adopted by the ECtHR can move erratically between different judgments. They are cross-referenced, but the context in which they have been used initially is not always considered. This is especially possible in relation to vague and unclear concepts. Judge 22 pointed out that the Court recycles fundamental concepts that appear in its previous judgments. S/he mentioned:

> If you look at how this concept [European public order] is used in the judgments, you will discover that it is used with a reference to another judgment and not on its own. That is how the Court works. It builds on its own case law. If the Court wants to say something very fundamental, it does so, but very often it refers to the sources where it has already done so.[82]

Often, fundamental concepts are abstract and vague. If the content of a concept is clear and well-established, it is less dependent on the context in which it is operating. If the content of a term is open-ended and ill-defined, then the context determines its meaning to a major extent. Some judges were openly sceptical about how certain terms are used in the Court's case law. The idea of the 'Brownian motion' of legal terms originates from my interviews and conversations with some of the judges, although it was not articulated explicitly.

[79] Dahl argues:

> [E]ven the best-designed judicial system can guarantee only procedural justice; it cannot guarantee substantive justice. A constitution can ensure a right to a fair trial; it cannot absolutely guarantee that a fair trial will always lead to the right verdict. But it is precisely because no such guarantee is possible that we place such a high value on a fair trial. (Robert A. Dahl, *Democracy and Its Critics* (Yale University Press 1989) 169)

[80] See Chapter 5 for more information about execution of the ECtHR judgments.

[81] *Oxford English Dictionary*, available at www.lexico.com/definition/brownian_motion.

[82] Interview with Judge 22.

It seems that a particular term needs to appear in the Court's jargon first in order to start its 'Brownian motion' across the case law. Judge 5 explained how that could have happened with European public order. S/he pointed out that 'the idea was proposed by some people who had their subjective vision of what the Convention was and what it had to become. And they had something on their minds which is not necessarily the same as collective judicial mind.'[83] This could have been a view of a drafting lawyer or a judge-rapporteur on the case and it stayed in the judgment for three possible reasons: (1) some judges from the majority acquiesced to this term because they did not think that it was particularly important; (2) other members of the majority actively agreed with the term; (3) other judges of the majority did not see it as a deal-breaker although they disagreed with it. Most likely, there were judges from all these categories in cases in which a particular concept was used for the first time. Moreover, sometimes it so happens that the judges do not pay enough attention to a particular formula deployed by the drafting lawyers, focusing only on the outcome of the specific case. Judge 5 explained:

> You just think okay, that is a good phrase, it is a coined phrase, stick it . . . where it belongs. Sometimes it serves the purpose; sometimes it is redundant. I was in one of the drafting committees in which I advocated that we do not use this phrase because I thought that it was simply not necessary. So, it was not used in that judgment, but it was used in the next judgment.[84]

Judge 17 explained the introduction of a new concept into the case law of the Court in the following words:

> Having been in the Court for a period, you begin to understand the drafting process. It starts with a drafting lawyer. He/she will try to develop the draft more or less as he/she would find in previous case law. So, if you find such an expression then it might pop up. Of course, you have the judge-rapporteur who also makes some decisions. Some judge-rapporteurs would say 'this is fine' and . . . others would go very deep into the drafting. Of course, the draft will be discussed in the Chamber,[85] if it is a Chamber case. However, I think [that] this kind of language – this is broad principled language – would normally be introduced for the first time in a Grand Chamber case.[86] I do not think that

[83] Interview with Judge 5.

[84] Ibid.

[85] The majority of difficult meritorious cases are dealt with by the Chambers consisting of seven judges.

[86] The Grand Chambers consist of seventeen judges and deal with the most complicated cases.

you would introduce it for the first time as a drafting lawyer or as a judge-rapporteur at the Chamber level, let alone at the Committee level,[87] because it really goes to the structures of the Convention, how we perceive the Convention. To develop that kind of concept is first and foremost a matter for the Grand Chamber.[88]

After initial introduction of the term, it can start its 'Brownian motion' into different and often quite unpredictable contexts. Some judges acknowledged this possibility. Judge 5 explained:

This is routinisation of a concept, but this routinisation is everywhere. Sometimes it is good because the Court finds good precedents or good formulas that can be used. But sometimes it is very mechanistic and artificial. In one of the drafts, certain formulas were quoted from other cases because it was very easy for a lawyer to find a formula but not to know the old case in which this formula was used. The facts of the latter case were very far from the case under examination – factually different situation, different legal reasoning and so on – but the phrase fits well and this seemed like a correct phrase.[89]

Judge 8 offered a similar explanation of how some terms appear and continue their life in the case law of the ECtHR. S/he pointed out:

Sometimes these concepts are just plucked out of thin air; thrown [in] because you do not know how to describe something. You can write a lot about margin of appreciation, but when you try to find where it originated from – this is a concept from French administrative law and then it was badly translated probably to a non-existent term in English. Then it took [on] a life of its own. And now, of course, it has come to mean something. European public order is used to mean completely different things in different contexts.[90]

However, unlike the margin of appreciation, the meaning of which, although far from being straightforward,[91] can at least be signposted,[92] the term European public order is so broad that it can mean almost

[87] Committees (three judges) deal only with meritorious cases that can be decided on the basis of the well-established case law.
[88] Interview with Judge 17.
[89] Interview with Judge 5.
[90] Interview with Judge 8.
[91] Fiona de Londras and Kanstantsin Dzehtsiarou, *Great Debate on the European Convention on Human Rights* (Palgrave 2018) 108–11; Anthony Lester, 'Universality versus Subsidiarity: A Reply' (1998) 1 *EHRLR* 73, 75–6; Janneke Gerards, 'Pluralism, Deference and the Margin of Appreciation Doctrine' (2011) 17 *ELJ* 80; Dominic McGoldrick, 'A Defence of the Margin of Appreciation and an Argument for its Application by the Human Rights Committee' (2016) 65 *Int'l & Comp LQ* 21.
[92] The Court itself defined the boundaries of margin of appreciation in the case of *S. and Marper v. the United Kingdom* [GC], nos. 30562/04 and 30566/04, ECHR 2008, para. 102.

everything in various contexts. Judge 17 agreed that the Court might be more rigorous in its treatment of the legal terminology:

> I think that it would be useful for us not to use it [the notion of 'European public order'] haphazardly. Everything we say should be very well thought through. And I think that this phrase, which came into the case law many, many years ago in *Loizidou*, which is a very seminal case, ... was talking about a situation that was new for the Court. You understand that the Registry lawyers in the old Commission and the old Court system wanted to give a rhetorical answer to the question [*sic*] of why is the Court dealing with these kinds of cases.[93]

It seems that deployment of abstract terms which lack definition is a challenging endeavour from the perspective of the process legitimacy of the judgments of the ECtHR. The judgments need to be persuasive, but persuasiveness can hardly be achieved if the Court uses terms that can mean different things but 'sound nice'. It seems that the 'Brownian motion' of legal terms is a concerning practice from the perspective of process legitimacy; if the Court often uses such reasoning then its reputation could be damaged.

6.4.3 *European Public Order in Deliberations*

In order to avoid the 'Brownian motion' of legal terms, these terms need to be discussed in deliberation. Of course, I realise that this takes time and that time is a sparse resource for the already overburdened Court.[94] That said, the terms of particular fundamental importance require some consideration; it seems that European public order is technically one of these terms. This section shows that European public order is almost never explicitly mentioned in deliberations. It will first enquire into the reasons for this lack of engagement. It shows that the judges see this concept as too abstract to be operational in individual cases most of the time. After that, this subsection considers whether the judges explore the impact of a particular judgment on European public order, without actually calling it European public order.

Many judges mentioned that they have never discussed European public order in deliberations in relation to a particular case. Judge 12,

[93] Interview with Judge 17.

[94] There are 59,900 pending applications before the Court. See Pending Applications Allocated to a Judicial Formation 2020, available at www.echr.coe.int/Documents/Stats_pending_month_2020_BIL.PDF. During the first 6 months of 2020, almost 20,000 applications were submitted to the Court. See European Court of Human Rights Statistics 1/1–30/6/2020, available at www.echr.coe.int/Documents/Stats_month_2020_ENG.PDF.

for example, stated: '[I]n my experience it has never been the core part of the debate.'[95] Judge 6 explained: 'I cannot remember any discussion of European public order as such. This notion is relevant in few cases.'[96] Judge 1 was more metaphorical in making this point: 'We are not playing God every other day. There are cases that call for this type of analysis and this is very much part of the individual thinking of all of us.'[97] Judge 9 pointed out that the nature and the quality of European public order do not call for a discussion during deliberations. S/he opined:

> I would not recall any discussions about European public order. To be honest, sometimes you might use it because you use a quotation of a case that fits in your case and this quotation includes also a reference to European public order and you get it in because you want such a citation. We discuss the margin [of appreciation] a lot, but we do not discuss European public order a lot. When you say that you have a margin that has direct consequences [for the outcome of the case at hand], that is why you have to discuss it in the deliberations.[98]

It seems that Judge 9 did not consider that European public order is a concept that might have a direct and clear impact on a particular case. Other judges were of the opinion that this concept is too abstract to be directly relevant. Judge 13 pointed out:

> The discussions are not necessarily on that theoretical level. Our discussions are more often about violation or not violation of the provisions of the Convention. When the rapporteur sees the whole draft of the judgment, in order to emphasise this or that aspect of the case, [it] may be that he or she will refer to European public order. I would say that the concept as such is not hotly debated at the Court. It arises only at the point of drafting the judgment between the rapporteur and the Drafting Committee: . . . they decide if they need to emphasise this or the other aspect then they refer to the concept. Of course, during the deliberations of the draft, I do not think that this concept would be a hotly debated one.[99]

Similarly, Judge 17 suggested that the Court 'normally works based on the case and on the details of the case rather technically. Normally

[95] Interview with Judge 12.

[96] Interview with Judge 6. Judge 22 also questioned the relevance of European public order in many cases: 'We discuss the concepts when there is a need to discuss the concepts. We do not discuss concepts on their own. I have not been in deliberations where this concept needed to be discussed.' Interview with Judge 22.

[97] Interview with Judge 1.

[98] Interview with Judge 9.

[99] Interview with Judge 13.

a judge and a court would not debate more theoretical issues like that.'[100] Despite the fact that these theoretical concepts are not debated, however, they appear sometimes in the text of the judgments and it seems that they are supposed to play at least some role in the Court's reasoning. So, the paradox here is the following: judges often do not see the relevance of abstract concepts like European public order, yet these concepts keep appearing in the judgments.

To explain this, one might hypothesise that the judges do not use the term European public order explicitly in their debates and deliberations but nevertheless consider the consequences of a particular judgment for the broader legal, political and social environment in Europe, which might be vaguely connected with European public order. Judge 18 pointed out:

> I do not remember during my being at the Court discussing European public order. During the deliberation of each case in the Grand Chamber and in the Chamber, we take into account what kind of consequences this case could have for other countries as well. We have never discussed the case only within the position of a given country, because we understand that case law is for all countries. Sometimes it takes quite a long time, because there are forty-seven very different countries with different traditions of judiciary, with different traditions of democracy – young democracies, old democracies – and with the differences in traditions of political and legal culture. That is why, in that sense, we are understanding that we are designing minimum standards for all forty-seven countries.[101]

Judge 16 advanced a similar argument: 'When we discuss, we do not use exactly this phrase European public order; rather, we discuss how our judgment will influence this or that legal situation or cultural situation in Europe. But, again, I do not remember that for us it is a stable concept and we always see how our judgments affect precisely European public order.'[102]

It seems that, at least for some judges, discussing a certain standard in relation to states other than the respondent state is to look into European public order. Shared values and shared standards often cropped up in the interviews. In order to influence shared values and standards, the Court needs to be effective in enforcing its judgments. Judge 3 directly linked European public order with implementation, explaining: 'I do not remember the term coming up in our deliberations, but we discuss the effects of our judgments. We discuss how they can be implemented. We are very

[100] Interview with Judge 17.
[101] Interview with Judge 18.
[102] Interview with Judge 16.

conscious of the fact that every judgment we make will have repercussions because it creates a precedent which is applicable to all countries in Europe.'[103]

The link between execution of a judgment and European public order can be explained as follows: a judgment of the Court aims to make a change in European public order, but this change can be effectuated only if the judgment is implemented and not only by the respondent state but by most (if not all) of the contracting parties. That said, considering the weakness of the enforcement mechanism of the Court's judgments, the ECtHR is unable to make revolutionary changes to human rights standards. The Court's incremental changes work in parallel with changes made on the national level. This view on the dynamic between national orders and European public order is discussed in more detail in Chapter 4. However, the fact that some judges mentioned the executability of their judgments makes a starting premise of this argument plausible.

Finally, Judge 24 pointed out that the concept of European public order is often discussed informally during meetings among judges: 'We discuss it in abstract in internal meetings, whether we have constitutional character, how … we feel about that, etc. We have our reflection meetings, but these are informal. They are not included in the case. They are not really related to the concrete case which is in front of the Court.'[104]

It seems that the rare presence of the issue of European public order in deliberations suggests the following three points. First, the 'Brownian motion' of the term European public order will continue if it is not clearly discussed and if its content is not at least signposted by the judges. Second, the doctrine is abstract and more useful for tea-break discussions among the judges rather than in the text of the judgments; if so, its utility in the text of the judgments is questionable. Third, the judges discuss the effects of judgments on human rights standards in general and do not 'play God' all the time.[105] Creation or development of European public order is a shared enterprise between the Court and the contracting parties.

6.5 Conclusion

This chapter attempted to present European public order as a vague and unclear concept that depends very much on the context in which it is

[103] Interview with Judge 3.
[104] Interview with Judge 24.
[105] In the words of Judge 1.

used. While this is not a ground-breaking discovery, this chapter revealed that the judges of the Court have different, often quite opposed, views on what European public order might mean and what the role of the ECtHR is in defining and shaping it. Although the differences in opinions are a sign of a healthy institution, they also show that there is no accepted or even predominant position as to what the Court has to achieve as a strategic actor in relation to European public order.

This chapter looked into both substantive and procedural aspects of European public order. Substantively, the judges' views on European public order range from its being an empty rhetorical device to the most fundamental core at the centre of the Convention, with plenty of half-tones in between. Likewise, the judges can be divided into those who consider the Court to be a strategic actor entrusted with shaping European public order and those who see the Court's role as preserving the core of the Convention and avoiding revolutionary changes. The quite opposite considerations make it difficult for the Court to act strategically. This conclusion is also supported by the fact that the Court is dealing with individual cases; the ECtHR consists of five rather separate sections and it is difficult for the Court to define coherent standards in all cases with the same level of precision.

Under the procedural aspect of European public order, I examined how references to European public order 'behave' in the Court's judgments and whether it is discussed in the deliberations. From the interview data, it became clear that the judges consider the concept of European public order very rarely. Some of them have even identified the 'Brownian motion' of this concept as it appears in a particular context and then gets cross-referenced in various judgments, often without particular attention to the original context. Such practice is concerning, especially since significant concepts like European public order are not often discussed in the deliberations and instead their deployment is left to the drafting lawyers.

This discussion illustrates the core ambition of this monograph well. First, European public order is a vague and unclear concept and, when deployed, it does not add much to the meaning of the Court's judgments. The concept of European public order might be useful in academic literature to explain the core European values on the highest level of abstraction, but its role in the case law is problematic. Second, it shows that the Court can hardly act as a strategic actor pushing for a clear and consistent human rights agenda.

7 Conclusion

In this monograph, I tried to answer the question of whether the European Court of Human Rights (ECtHR, Court) can shape European public order. My answer to this question is a qualified 'no'. The key reasons for that are twofold. The first reason is the unclear and illusive nature and definition of European public order. In other words, it is almost impossible to define this notion on a level that can be useful in adjudication. The second reason is that the Court was arguably not created to shape European public order. In any event, there is no agreement among the stakeholders as to what the meta-function of the ECtHR is. The whole monograph examined European public order from these two distinct but interrelated perspectives.

I argued throughout this monograph that European public order is a vague and unclear formula. This excessive vagueness is detrimental for European public order as a legal concept. The Court's references to it in its case law do not have a fixed meaning and they do not lead to a particular outcome in a given case. Deployment of the term like this undermines the legal certainty of the Court's judgments; it is problematic from the perspective of the process legitimacy of the ECtHR. This argument was substantiated by the detailed analysis of the case law of the ECtHR in Chapter 2. The Court uses references to European public order in various contexts and it is not always clear what role these references play in the reasoning of the judgment. Some common understanding of European public order can only be identified on a very high level of abstraction, which is not particularly helpful in practice. Moreover, the notions 'public order' and 'public policy' are used in various areas of national law, as Chapter 3 demonstrated, but the ambiguity of their content is a common feature everywhere. Further, these terms were traditionally used mostly to protect national order from interference from abroad. When this approach is elevated to the regional or international level, the meaning of public order turns out to be much diluted and the lack of clarity becomes critical. Therefore, this monograph argues that the Court should not use such vague formulas in its case law. As one of the judges interviewed for this monograph and quoted in Chapter 6 pointed out: 'I think that it would be useful for us not to use it ["European public order"] haphazardly. Everything we say should be very well thought through.'[1] It is fairly safe to conclude that the Court should either clarify what it means by European public order, which is extremely difficult, if not impossible, or stop using it altogether. Therefore, this monograph concludes that European public order as a legal doctrine only dilutes the reasoning of the ECtHR without adding much content to it.

European public order can also be perceived as an analytical concept. Here, I understand European public order as a set of standards of human rights protection applicable across the forty-seven member states of the Council of Europe. While European public order is still vague and ambiguous in this sense, its role is substantively different in comparison to the legal concept mentioned above. The role of European public order as an analytical concept is descriptive rather than normative. It does not pretend that it would lead to a particular outcome in a case in front of the ECtHR. It only reflects the Court's impact on the state of human rights law in Europe. In this sense, European public order is more helpful. The Court does have an impact on European public order because often the contracting parties to the European Convention on Human Rights (ECHR or Convention) change their laws and regulations as a result of the judgments of the ECtHR. However, the question remains as to how strategic these changes are. Does the ECtHR perceive itself as a sole herald of European public order?

When the ECtHR states that the Convention is an 'instrument of European Public Order',[2] the Court seems to declare an ambition to shape this order because the ECtHR is the only official interpreter of the Convention. Moreover, in Chapter 5, I argued that the reforms initiated by the ECtHR assist the Court in assuming the role of a rule-maker. Here, I pointed out that the Court can impact European public order most effectively when it can formulate rules of general application, participate in implementation of these rules and influence ongoing human

[1] Interview with Judge 17.

[2] *Loizidou* v. *Turkey* (preliminary objections), 23 March 1995, Series A no. 310, para. 93.

rights violations. Chapter 5 discussed two innovations that clearly demonstrate the ambition of the ECtHR to shape European public order, namely the pilot judgment procedure and its enhanced approach to interim measures. Although these innovations point to the conclusion that the Court is trying to act as a general rule-maker, the success rate of these innovations is not that straightforward. The Court's attempts to influence European public order can face fierce criticism from the contracting parties. Their unwillingness to play along with the Court can undermine these efforts. Having said that, the contracting parties have very diverging views on whether the Court should be in possession of legal instruments capable of impacting European public order. On the one hand, the contracting parties keep reminding the Court about its subsidiary role and the need to respect their margin of appreciation. Both of these concepts will appear in the text of the Preamble to the Convention when Protocol 15 enters into force. On the other hand, the contracting parties enhance the Court's competences in relation to execution of its judgments[3] and in relation to its ability to deliver more substantive advisory opinions than before.[4] Even if the Court's ability to impact European public order increases on paper as a result of the latter innovations, their design and application significantly undermine this potential impact. The contracting parties send a mixed bag of signals on whether the Court should indeed attempt to make strategic changes to European public order. This brings me to the question of whether it is indeed the function of the ECtHR to strategically shape European public order.

Chapter 4 of this monograph argued that the Court's function is twofold. First, the 'technical function' of adjudication suggests that the main aim of the Court is to find solutions to particular conflicts between the parties in each case. Second, the Court has a 'meta-function' which goes beyond the outcomes of particular cases; from this perspective, the key aim of the Court is to develop the standards of human rights protection in Europe. In other words, the Court's key purpose is to shape European public order. In this monograph I argued that the Court should not prioritise its meta-function, as the Court's impact on European public order understood analytically is the by-product of the Court's technical function of adjudication. Further, the

[3] Article 46 sections 3 and 4 were included by Protocol 14 which entered into force in 2010. This Article enhanced the role of the ECtHR in enforcement of its judgments.

[4] Protocol 16, which entered into force in 2018, provided the Court with a competence to deliver advisory opinions on substantive questions of interpretation of the Convention.

Court should not prioritise its meta-function because various stakeholders have critically different views on what this meta-function might entail. As Chapters 4 and 6 showed, even among the judges of the ECtHR there is no unanimity as to what the main function of the ECtHR is. If there is no agreement as to what the Court should do strategically, the prioritisation of a strategic meta-function does not seem particularly wise. The views of the ECtHR judges range from a very restrictive approach to the ECtHR's meta-function to a much broader conceptualisation of the ECtHR as a constitutional court of Europe. This range of opinions is not helping in choosing a particular strategy for influencing European public order.

Finally, the monograph argued that the ECtHR is not a strategic actor. It seems that it is unable to articulate long-term strategic changes to European public order understood analytically. The composition of the Court is not stable; it changes rapidly. The Court makes all important decisions collectively and all judges act in their individual capacity and cannot form alliances. Unlike, for example, parliaments, the Court has to connect any general rules it comes up with to the facts of the case at hand, which can curtail the outreach of such rules. However, it is not necessarily a negative feature of the Court's architecture that it cannot strategically change the content of European public order unilaterally. It forces the Court to focus on the individual cases and develop European public order in co-operation with the contracting parties as a by-product of its technical function. The Court and the contracting parties create a feedback loop: if all participants of this feedback loop are acting bona fide then the development of European public order happens naturally.

Appendix
List of Judges Approached to Be Interviewed for This Monograph

Judge	Country of origin	Contacted	Meeting date and time
Paulo Pinto de Albuquerque	Judge elected in respect of Portugal	9 August 2018	11 September 2018
Arnfinn Bardsen	Judge elected in respect of Norway	18 September 2019	24 September 2019
Marko Bošnjak	Judge elected in respect of Slovenia	18 September 2019	Agreed but could not be arranged
Lado Chanturia	Judge elected in respect of Georgia	13 September 2018	No response
Vincent A. De Gaetano	Judge elected in respect of Malta	8 August 2018	10 September 2018
Dmitry Dedov	Judge elected in respect of Russia	13 August 2018	10 September 2018
Tim Eicke	Judge elected in respect of the UK	9 August 2018 9 September 2019	Contacted twice but no response
María Elósegui	Judge elected in respect of Spain	13 August 2018 10 September 2019	Declined

(*cont.*)

Judge	Country of origin	Contacted	Meeting date and time
Felici Gilberto	Judge elected in respect of San Marino	18 September 2019	No response
Valeriu Griţco	Judge elected in respect of Moldova	13 August 2018	Declined
Yonko Grozev	Judge elected in respect of Bulgaria	30 November 2018	7 December 2018
Armen Harutyunyan	Judge elected in respect of Armenia	9 September 2019	26 September 2019
Lətif Hüseynov	Judge elected in respect of Azerbaijan	7 September 2018	25 September 2019
Jovan Ilievski	Judge elected in respect of Macedonia	9 September 2019	No response
Helena Jäderblom	Judge elected in respect of Sweden	13 August 2018	Declined
Ivana Jelić	Judge elected in respect of Montenegro	29 November 2018 9 September 2019	25 September 2019
Helen Keller	Judge elected in respect of Switzerland	8 August 2018	10 September 2018
Jon Fridrik Kjølbro	Judge elected in respect of Denmark	18 September 2019	Declined
Pauliine Koskelo	Judge elected in respect of Finland	3 September 2018 9 September 2019	Agreed but could not be arranged
Egidijus Kūris	Judge elected in respect of Lithuania	7 August 2018	13 September 2018

(*cont.*)

Judge	Country of origin	Contacted	Meeting date and time
Julia Laffranque	Judge elected in respect of Estonia	9 August 2018	13 September 2018
Paul Lemmens	Judge elected in respect of Belgium	9 August 2018	12 September 2018
Roderick Liddell	Registrar of the European Court of Human Rights	13 August 2018	11 September 2018
Branko Lubarda	Judge elected in respect of Serbia	9 September 2019	Declined
Mārtiņš Mits	Judge elected in respect of Latvia	9 September 2019	27 September 2019
Erik Møse	Judge elected in respect of Norway	9 August 2018	Declined
Iulia Motoc	Judge elected in respect of Romania	13 August 2018	12 September 2018
Angelika Nußberger	Judge elected in respect of Germany	3 September 2018	13 September 2018
Síofra O'Leary	Judge elected in respect of Ireland	13 August 2018 9 September 2019	Declined
Péter Paczolay	Judge elected in respect of Hungary	13 August 2018	10 September 2018
Darian Pavli	Judge elected in respect of Albania	9 September 2019	26 September 2019
Aleš Pejchal	Judge elected in respect of Czech Republic	13 August 2018 9 September 2019	Contacted twice but no response

(*cont.*)

Judge	Country of origin	Contacted	Meeting date and time
Alena Poláčková	Judge elected in respect of Slovak Republic	10 September 2019	No response
André Potocki	Judge elected in respect of France	13 August 2018 9 September 2019	Declined
Guido Raimondi	Judge elected in respect of Italy	7 August 2018	13 September 2018
Carlo Ranzoni	Judge elected in respect of Liechtenstein	9 September 2019	Declined
Georges Ravarani	Judge elected in respect of Luxembourg	10 September 2019	Declined
Raffaele Sabato	Judge elected in respect of Italy	18 September 2019	Agreed but could not be arranged
Jolien Schukking	Judge elected in respect of the Netherlands	3 September 2018 9 September 2019	Contacted twice but no response
Georgios Serghides	Judge elected in respect of Cyprus	9 August 2018	Declined
Linos-Alexandre Sicilianos	Judge elected in respect of Greece	3 September 2018	10 September 2018
Robert Spano	Judge elected in respect of Iceland	7 August 2018	7 September 2018
Ksenija Turković	Judge elected in respect of Croatia	9 September 2019	26 September 2019
Pastor Pere Vilanova	Judge elected in respect of Andorra	10 September 2019	Agreed but could not be arranged
Erik Wennerström	Judge elected in respect of Sweden	9 September 2019	No response

(*cont.*)

Judge	Country of origin	Contacted	Meeting date and time
Krzysztof Wojtyczek	Judge elected in respect of Poland	13 August 2018 9 September 2019	Contacted twice but no response
Ganna Yudkivska	Judge elected in respect of Ukraine	15 August 2018	11 September 2018
Saadet Yüksel	Judge elected in respect of Turkey	18 September 2019	No response

Index

For EU product safety concerns, contact us at Calle de José Abascal, 56–1°, 28003 Madrid, Spain or eugpsr@cambridge.org.

www.ingramcontent.com/pod-product-compliance
Lightning Source LLC
LaVergne TN
LVHW011812200926
848484LV00005B/1158
* 9 7 8 1 1 0 8 4 9 7 3 6 7 *